# The Country Gardener's Almanac

# The Country Gardener's Almanac

## THE COMPLETE MONTH-BY-MONTH, HOW-TO BOOK OF PRACTICAL ADVICE FOR GARDEN, FARM, AND HOUSEHOLD

by Martin Lawrence

The Main Street Press

Pittstown, New Jersey

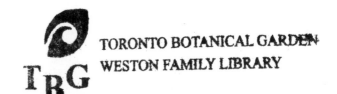

Copyright © 1979, 1984 by The Main Street Press

Published by
The Main Street Press, Inc.
William Case House
Pittstown, New Jersey 08867

Distributed in the United States by
Kampmann & Company, Inc.
9 East 40th Street
New York, New York 10016

Published simultaneously in Canada by
Methuen Publications
2330 Midland Avenue
Agincourt, Ontario M1S 1P7

Cover design by Frank Mahood

Printed in the United States of America

*Library of Congress Cataloging in Publication Data*

Lawrence, Martin.
 The country gardener's almanac.

 Includes index.
 1. Agriculture—Handbooks, manuals, etc.
2. Gardening—Handbooks, manuals, etc. 3. Home economics, Rural-Handbooks, manuals, etc. 4. Almanacs, American.  I. Title.
S501.2.L38  1984    635    84-902
ISBN 0-915590-42-5

# Contents

**Introduction**  8

**January**

Farm and Garden Work  12

Projects  19

*Root Grafting. Rotating Crops. Making
Permanent Hotbeds. Rabbit Hunting. Freezing Ice in
Blocks. A Fire Alarm. A Lamp for Cooking. A
Temporary Smoking Device. Use for a Tough
Log. Washing While Reading. Mending Glassware. Building
a Dog-Power Water Pump. Building Milking Stools.*

**February**

Farm and Garden Work  26

Projects  33

*Making Maple Sugar. Plans for a Cow
Barn. How to Set Up a Leach. To Sharpen Scissors.
Papering a Room. Removing Fence Posts. Homemade
Sleds. Propagating Plants from Cuttings.*

**March**

Farm and Garden Work  42

Projects  50

*Plain Directions for Grafting. Splitting
Firewood. Another Way to Split Wood. Laying Out a
Garden. Storing Water. A Barbed Wire Tightener. A Safe Way
to String Barbed Wire. How to Catch an Owl. Three Simple
Board Fences. Raising Evergreens from Seed.*

**April**

Farm and Garden Work  58

Projects  66

*Making Homemade Lime. Pulling Tree
Stumps. Four Ways to Make Hard Soap. How to Whitewash.
Cultivating Flax. Watering Livestock. Trapping
Moles. How a Stone Wall Should be Built. Helps in the
Garden*

## May

Farm and Garden Work   76

Projects   84

*How to Pitch Manure. Building Sod Walls.*
*Sowing Seed Evenly. Growing Mushrooms. How to Drop*
*Potatoes. Windmills for Farm Work. Building an Earth Closet.*
*Weeding and Trimming. Making and Maintaining*
*Tools. How to Stake Out Stock. Dog and*
*Sheep Power for Churning. Grapevines in the Garden.*
*Horseshoe Lever. An Elevated Clothesline. An*
*Easy Way to Pole Beans. Protecting Newly-Set Plants.*
*Moving a Large Tree.*

## June

Farm and Garden Work   94

Projects   102

*The Art of Making Good Butter. A Homemade*
*Beehive. Transplanting Trees. A Wire Fence Corncrib.*
*Hay Making. An Ingenious Hay Stacker. The Art of Shearing*
*Sheep. Breeding Work Horses. Farm Sleds for*
*Winter and Summer. Cheesemaking.*

## July

Farm and Garden Work   112

Projects   119

*Directions for Budding. Keeping Pastures in*
*Good Condition. Making a Handy Pig Catcher. A Bridge*
*for a Small Stream. Tying Useful Knots. Building*
*a Barn. Breaking and Training Colts. Building a Cistern and*
*Filter. A House for Drying Fruit. Hanging and*
*Curing Tobacco. Device for Extracting Beeswax.*

## August

Farm and Garden Work   128

Projects   136

*Rough Measurement of Land. Making Cheap Sheds*
*of Straw. Draining Land with a Plow.*
*Steaming Food for Cattle and Pigs. How to Build a*
*Rowboat. Keeping Food Cool in Summer. How to Build a Cheap*
*Greenhouse. A Homemade Water Cooler. Raising Huckle-*
*berries (Blueberries). How to Splice a Rope. Grow-*
*ing Currants.*

## September

Farm and Garden Work    146

Projects    154

*Digging, Stoning, and Curbing Wells. Propagating
Plants from Cuttings. Reclaiming Waste Land. Picking
Apples. Save the Leaves. A Homemade Cabbage Cutter.
Saving Seed Corn. Preventing Cows from Kicking.
Making Posts. How to Plow Wet Ground in Autumn.*

## October

Farm and Garden Work    166

Projects    174

*Sauerkraut. Breeding Trout and Other Fish. Making
Plank Drains. Cider Making. Cider Vinegar,
Quickly Made. Growing Spring Bulbs. Digging Potatoes.
Fattening Turkeys. Making a Good Barnyard. A Corn-
Husking Rack. A Homemade Feed Cutter. How to Make Concrete
Buildings.*

## November

Farm and Garden Work    186

Projects    193

*Building an Icehouse. Thatching Roofs.
A Farm Slaughterhouse. Protecting Trees in Winter.
About Cisterns. Covers for Wells. Repairing Split Trees.*

## December

Farm and Garden Work    200

Projects    207

*How to Make an Iceboat. Preparing Homemade
Kindling. Building a Simple Water Boiler. Building
Cold Frames. Felling Timber. Cutting Ice. Building a Smokehouse.
Hints on Hog Slaughtering, or, How to Use "Everything
but the Oink." Fences for Soil Likely to Heave.
A Snowplow. Two Jacks. Painting Tin Roofs.*

## Index    219

# Introduction

*And he gave it for his opinion . . . that whoever could make two ears of corn, or two blades of grass, to grow upon a spot of ground where only one grew before, would deserve better of mankind, and do more essential service to his country than the whole race of politicians put together.*

Jonathan Swift
GULLIVER'S TRAVELS

Not too long ago, in one of those contemporary country-living magazines for suburban gardeners and armchair farmers—you know, the kind that mingles ads for Mercedes-Benz with those for waterless toilets and woodburning stoves—an interesting article appeared in praise of steaming and cooking food for hungry pigs. Now, there probably weren't five dozen readers of that magazine who had ever come within a mile of a real live snorting hog, but the article itself made for highly entertaining and informative reading. It seems that cooking food for pigs not only cut down on waste and, hence, on the cost of feeding itself, but it led to the discovery that the refuse of nearby restaurants and markets could be gathered for the cost of carting alone and could be added with great economy to the steamer installed conveniently in the potting shed.

A novel idea born of contemporary Yankee ingenuity? Well, not exactly. The idea, although unmentioned in the article, was actually the prevailing practice among country gardeners in America a century and a quarter ago. "As to the profit of steaming," wrote one farmer in 1860, "one-third of the food is saved. Corn stalks that have moulded in the stack, musty oats which have been cut green and badly cured, and smoky hay—nearly the whole of which would be rejected if fed uncooked—are eaten with avidity and with evident benefit to the stock." And as to the novelty of sniffing around the refuse heap of the local Burger King, here is the editor of the *American Agriculturist* in 1870: "Every town and village allows valuable feed to go to waste, as does almost every farm. Have an eye to the various factories, breweries, and the like in the neighborhood, and see what their waste products are. It often happens that usable feed and good fertilizers may be had for the expense of carting."

Obviously, there's nothing new under the sun.

*The Country Gardener's Almanac* is a compilation of many of the very best and most practical agricultural ideas of the past. As its subtitle indicates, it is a "complete month-by-month, how-to book of practical advice for garden, farm, and household," a book filled with useful, relevant information culled from nineteenth-century farming magazines and handbooks. It is not only an informative guide to the best of country-style living, but a wonderfully entertaining picture book, crammed with hundreds of nostalgic engravings and hundreds of tried-and-true gardening practices that are as relevant for today's country gardeners as they were for those of grandma's day. Divided into twelve sections, one for each month of the year, *The Country Gardener's Almanac* provides general information about the garden work to be done throughout the year and features specific projects for each month, each described fully in step-by-step instructions.

Have you just spent twenty dollars for peat pots to get your spring planting off to an early start? Pocket the money next year and let *The Country Gardener's Almanac* show you how to fashion the same pots from the sod that's growing on your back lawn. That's how it was done in 1850, and the trick still works today. Are you thinking of buying new lilac shrubs or of putting in a hedge of forsythia? Why not learn to propagate your own, as most gardeners did a century ago, and cut down on your nursery expenses? And have you ever wondered how Tom Sawyer whitewashed Aunt Polly's picket fence? *The Country Gardener's Almanac* will show you how to mix up a batch of whitewash that's far less expensive than a can of paint, and it will teach you how to tint it various shades as well. Do you want to dig a well or raise evergreens from seed, build a windmill or an iceboat, a haystack or a corncrib, a smokehouse or a barn? Or would you rather grow fresh vegetables throughout the year, or even catch an owl or thatch a roof? Let *The Country Gardener's Almanac* show you how in articles and illustrations gleaned largely from *The American Agriculturist*, the most famous and dependable farm journal of the nineteenth century.

From making homemade cold frames and fertilizers, to planting hedges, raising bees, and shearing sheep; from propagating plants and laying out truck gardens, to making cider, curing pork, and planting trees; here are hundreds of wonderful ideas in a book that is as practical to use as it is entertaining to read.

# The Country Gardener's Almanac

FARM
AND GARDEN WORK FOR

# January

One year of work is done and another begins. Merchants and mechanics get rich and retire; professional men generally, like old soldiers, repose on their laurels when the hardest part of their life's warfare is over. But the farmers, as a class, work on, and die in the harness. We might learn many a lesson from commercial men, who, to be sure, labor too exclusively for wealth and think too little of health, intellectual enjoyment, and the comforts of life, and our lives would be much more comfortable if we were more thorough as business men. Not one farmer in five hundred knows *how* he makes his profits, or what they are. We know that we gain a fair living, that we get money from the sale of beef, or sheep, or corn; but what pays the best? On what do we expend labor to the greatest advantage? How is money invested in the farm or in its appointments made to pay the best interest? We ought to have *records* of cash and labor expended, of materials and time consumed, that we can refer to for a satisfactory solution of such problems. How many of us can do so? Few have even an accurate record of the days' work done, and we believe that in a majority of cases where a good account is kept the wife has a hand in it. All honor to such wives!

We stand at the beginning of a new year and look forward and backward, like Janus with two faces from whom this month is named. Our account books, journals, and memorandum books should be for us the retrospective face, and our course for the future should, as far as possible, be guided by experience — not that vague experience which is like a half-forgotten dream, and is well remem-

bered only when a blunder twice made wakes us up to the knowlege that it is too familiar; but an experience aided by a well-quickened memory, made clear and definite by memorandums, jotted down upon the spot. Such is a safe guide, and we may all have it for next year if we have it not now.

### Hints About Farm Work

**Building** — Timber may be gotten out and frames cut and fitted for new buildings, and alterations of houses or other structures may go on as well in winter as at any time since contractors are now desirous of having work for their men.

**Frost and Snow** — Look to the protection of water pipes, the root cellar, or roots wherever stored, against hard freezing. Never delay pathmaking after the storm is fairly over. In case of a very heavy fall of snow, endangering flat roofs, etc., clear it off immediately, lest, rain falling, the weight be greatly increased and serious damage occur.

**Icy Paths** are dangerous to both men and animals. Coal ashes are usually the most convenient article with which to cover icy spots, but they are dirty about the house. Sand is better, sawdust still more clean, and salt never advisable.

**Horses** — Look frequently to the caulks and never let them go smooth-shod, the strains and sprains occasioned by going over slippery ground being the frequent causes of spavins, splints, and other lamenesses. Horses not exposed to drafts of air do not need blanketing in the stable, except when they are warm from recent exercise. Unblanketed, they will eat a little more, but have better health.

**Cows**—Dry cows coming in the spring need just as good feed and care as if in full milk, but the food need not be so fattening. Roots are a very useful addition to their feed, and they should have the liberty of a sunny yard several hours a day.

**Milch cows** require, of course, food and treatment calculated to stimulate milk production.

**Young Cattle**—Spring calves are making their most rapid growth just when cold weather comes on. They should receive very much the treatment of older stock and not be wintered in the yards and open sheds. They will eat less and grow faster for warm stabling; besides, their manure will be worth more. Their growth will surprise one accustomed to wintering such stock in the old way.

**Beeves**—Oil cake can be extensively substituted for corn meal as feed for fattening stock this winter. Variety is to be desirable in feeding, salt is essential, regular watering indispensable, and the highest degree of comfort most profitable. Great quiet and warm stables, with good ventilation, and frequent and regular feeding, are the circumstances most favorable to rapid, healthy fattening.

**Sheep**—Stock sheep ought to have the range of good-sized yards and the shelter of warm sheds, to which they have free access during the day and in which they are confined at night. Ewes will do much better for a little grain daily, and their lambs will be stronger. Fatting sheep should be pushed forward during this month to be ready for a rise in

the market. Feed meal with care that all get their allowance; those that get too much may suffer for it.

**Swine**—Give brood sows good plain feed, not too fattening. If they have made their growth (and old sows are the best breeders), they will do best on really poor fare. They will even winter well on clover hay, with a few nubbins now and then, if they have good warm pens and plenty of litter.

**Fowls**—should receive special care towards the latter part of the month. With extra feeding, occasional feeds of chopped meat or scrap cake, they will soon lay freely; and if one has warm quarters for young chickens (a hotbed frame, with the sashes, of course, is excellent, and so is a cold grapery), it may be well to set hens as early as the last of this month. By employing cocks of the large breeds—Cochins, Bramahs, or Dorkings—large broilers may be ready for market by the time asparagus is fit to cut. It is not worthwhile, in raising chickens for stock or for autumn and winter marketing, to have them hatch before the middle of April.

**Manures**—Keep all the sources of supply—the yards, sties, and privies—well supplied with absorbents. The great error in all our farming is the neglect of the manure heap. Study constantly to increase this as the grand secret of success in farming. Keep your animals all stabled, or in close sheds, that all the manure may be daily thrown into heaps and mingled with muck and other absorbents. Keep the manure under cover, if possible, and if not, compost it in heaps. From the manure of fowls, and night soil, an excellent fertilizer may be prepared for hills and drills. Almost all crops are benefitted by these applications.

**Draining** can sometimes be attended to if the winter is open. Springy land seldom freezes so deep that drains may not easily be dug. No work is more satisfactory in its results.

**Fencing Materials**—Splitting rails and making posts is legitimate business for winter, and on most farms a few more are always wanted. Chestnut splits readily and endures exposure to the weather remarkably well. White cedar is still more durable, and the swamps are often accessible only in winter.

**Firewood**—"In peace prepare for war." Though the whole year is before us, trust that no future time will be better to cut firewood than the present—that is, the winter. Have cord wood piled to shed water to the east.

**Clearing Land**—This is a very good season in which to blast rocks, cut alders and willows, and often those tussocks of coarse grass called "bogs."

Ditches may be dug in swamps, and such work done.

**Thaws** — Those of the Northern states, where the land is often covered with great masses of snow, are liable to thaws, coming in consequence of heavy and warm rains. See that no damage occurs from a great rush of water over the frozen surface, or from its being dammed up behind drifts, and entering cellar walls; and stand ready to take advantage of even a temporary breaking up.

**Icehouses** — It rarely happens that ice does not form, during January, sufficiently to pack. Cut as soon as six inches of clear ice can be got. Icehouses fail to keep ice for one of three reasons: either there is not perfect drainage, in which case the ice goes very rapidly; or there is access of air to the ice through the foundation or under the sills; or the ice was not well packed. There should be a great abundance of straw or chaff on the floor, and the ice on all sides should be packed with sawdust, chaff, or straw, while plenty of straw should be used to cover the surface.

## HINTS ABOUT HORTICULTURAL WORK

The beginning of a new year is the proper time to lay work plans for the coming season, as without a plan of operation the gardener will never accomplish much. It is only by careful forethought, and working with a definite end in view, that men engaged in other branches of industry become successful, and our best horticulturists are those who plan for the future in a thorough, businesslike way. No other business requires a knowledge of a greater number of different subjects, and to master these a good library of standard works essential. A gardener should keep a journal in which the principal operations of each day are recorded, and he can afterwards examine the journal and learn where to avoid mistakes and where to do better. The directions given each month in this section contain much that will be useful to the commercial as well as to the amateur gardener.

### Orchard and Nursery

**Order Trees** early; if one lives near a nursery it will sometimes pay him to give an extra price for the privilege of digging his own trees.

**Rabbits** are troublesome, especially when the snow is on the ground. Among the various preventives, blood has been found the most easy of application and as efficacious as any. One sprinkling will last all winter. If blood cannot be obtained readily, rub the trunks of the trees with liver or bloody meat, but this is more troublesome.

**Mice** work under cover; keep all rubbish away from the trees, and tramp down light snow. When there are not many trees, it will pay to clasp the base of the trunks with a girdle of old tin or sheet iron.

**The Tent Caterpillar** is one of the most destructive insects in the orchard, and one of the most readily controlled. The eggs may now be seen glued on as a band around the twigs near their ends. Get them off at any expense of time and labor.

**Cions** — The sooner these are cut, the better, as experience has shown that a much larger proportion of early-cut grafts will live than of those taken after they have been exposed to the severity of the winter. This is especially the case when the autumn has been unfavorable to the ripening of the wood. Label correctly, and pack in boxes of fresh sawdust.

**Root Grafting** may be done; graft at the "collar" and never on tips of roots.

**Map the Orchard** — We cannot advise this too frequently! The best label will get lost or become obliterated in time, and memory is not to be trusted. If a homestead is to be sold, a *named* orchard will add much to its value.

**Nursery Stock** may be headed back and shaped any time during winter when the weather is mild.

## Fruit Garden

Whoever contents himself with a single variety of strawberry, currant, or other fruit, gets only half the satisfaction his garden is capable of affording, or, if he cultivates for market, only a portion of the profit he might otherwise receive.

With proper forethought in selecting early and late varieties to supplement the main crops of both ends, the season of most fruits may be much extended. Now is the time to think up such matters and to arrange for a succession of fresh fruit from the time the earliest strawberry ripens until the last winter pear and long-keeping grape is gone.

In the South, preparing the soil and even planting may go on, but in the colder climates but little can be done save preventing injury to trees by animals and horsemen, and in mild spells to:

**Prune** such grape vines and currant bushes as have been neglected until now.

**General Work**, such as protecting trees and removing the eggs of insects, is hinted at under "Orchard."

## Kitchen Garden

In the Southern states, whenever the condition of the soil will allow it, the hardy, early vegetables are sown in succession from January to April. The hardy vegetables include beet, carrot, parsnip, parsley, radish, turnip, onion, leek, lettuce, cress, cauliflower, cabbage, spinach, etc. Tender vegetables, such as cucumbers, melons, beans, tomatoes, etc., can only be sown with safety in the open ground at corn-planting time or when the peach is full bloom. These rules apply to any latitude.

**Seeds**—Their quality and integrity are of the greatest importance. It is better to be at any trouble and expense to get good seed, true to its kind, than to take that which is doubtful for nothing. Purchase early of reliable dealers only.

**The Vitality of Seeds** can only be positively ascertained by sowing a counted quantity in a box of earth in warm room. If three-fourths come up, the seeds may be considered of average good quality. Some seeds must be renewed each year, such as onions, parsnips, and leeks. The following should not be over two years old: beans, peas, peppers, carrot, eggplant, okra, salsify, sage, and other sweet herbs. Those considered safe for three years are asparagus, endive, lettuce, spinach, radish, and parsley. Those which are good at the end of four years are cabbage and its relatives (such as cauliflower, etc.), turnips, and celery. Those good from five to ten years are melons, cucumbers, and all of the squash family, beet, and tomato.

**Hotbeds** for raising seedlings are to be started about six weeks before the time at which it will be safe to set out the plants. Sashes should be got ready; paint, if need be, and replace broken panes. Make new sashes; the usual size is 6 x 3 feet.

**Straw Mats** are of great use in covering hotbeds and frames at night. There are several ways of making them, and one of the simplest is to stretch five cords of strong twine; lay on the straw evenly, with the butt ends towards the edges of the mat. Then put above the straw five other cords directly over the lower ones, and sew through the straw with a coarse needle and twine, catching both cords. The cords may be stretched on a frame made for the purpose. The mats should be a foot longer than the sash and of its width or a half wider, so that two mats may cover three sashes.

**Cold Frames**—Air in clear weather whenever

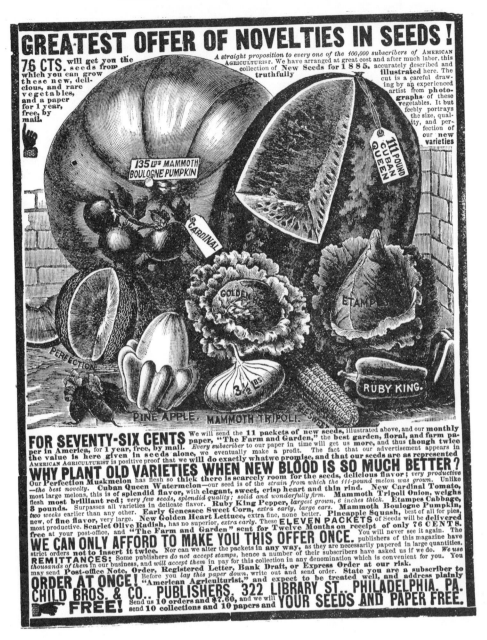

the temperature is not below 20° in the shade. If snow covers the glass after a mild spell, remove it, but if the plants are already frozen, let it remain.

**Manure** is a thing of which the gardener cannot have too much. Carting is better done now than later. Place the manure in good-sized heaps, and when it begins to "smoke" turn it over. The heaps should be large enough to prevent freezing.

**Tools** are to be overhauled and repaired, and those needed made or purchased. A homemade roller, marker, reel for a garden-line, and the like are great helps, even in a small garden.

*Flower Garden and Lawn*

But little can be done out of doors. Where improvements are contemplated, a plan should be drawn to a scale, and sufficiently large to serve as a guide in working. It will be found when the time comes to execute it that operations will be wonderfully facilitated by its use. Not only should walks, beds, etc. be properly laid down upon the plan, but the places for trees, shrubs, etc. should be indicated. Do all the thinking now and there will be no time lost in deciding where to place things at planting season.

Where much money is to be expended on a place, it will be cheaper in the end to employ a landscape gardener to make a plan.

**Cold Frames** or cellars in which plants are stored for the winter months must be aired when the weather is not too cold. Keep the temperature uniformly low and just above freezing.

**Trellises, Stakes,** and all the little appliances that will be needed in spring should be made and repaired while there is leisure.

**Snow** is apt to injure evergreens and dense shrubbery; shake off the accumulations before they become icy. Drifts around low-branching evergreens are apt to break off the lower branches as they settle and should be shoveled away.

*Greenhouse and Window Plants*

plants need a change of air and should have it whenever it can be given without chilling them.

**Insects** are easily kept under by fumigating.

**Dust**—Arrange some kind of shield of cloth or paper to put over the plants while sweeping.

**Water** is to be given only as the plants need it.

**Temperature** with house plants is less readily adapted to their wants than in the greenhouse. Very few plants will bloom below 60°, though they will keep healthy at a much lower degree.

**Air** is to be given in the greenhouse whenever the ventilators can be opened with safety. Window

# PROJECTS FOR
# JANUARY

## Root Grafting

Root grafting does not mean grafting into the roots, but taking up the roots of trees and grafting them indoors during cold weather. The essential points to be observed are noted below, and with a little practice will enable any man or boy who can whittle to become an expert. It is a good idea to make a few preliminary trials upon worthless twigs. This will soon give one the proper knack at cutting, and all the rest is very easy.

The stocks used for root grafting are one-year-old seedlings; these, if they have made good growth, will have a diameter of one-fourth to three-eights of an inch. The stocks are taken up in autumn and buried under a shed or in a cool cellar so that they will neither dry up nor be frozen. A sufficient quantity of cions are cut, carefully marked, and preserved in the same manner. The stocks and cions being on hand, the only additional materials required are a sharp knife and some waxed cloth. The best material for cloth is worn calico or muslin, no matter how thin and tender. This is torn into strips about 3 inches wide and made up into rolls or balls as large as one's fist, or larger. In making up the rolls, it is necessary to keep the strips flat, without any folds. These rolls are to be put into melted grafting wax and soaked until they are thoroughly penetrated by it. They are then laid out on a piece of board to drain and cool, when they are ready for use. Grafting wax is made by melting together over a slow fire 2 lbs. resin, 1¼ lbs. beeswax, and 3/4 lbs. tallow. The stocks are prepared by washing them and cutting

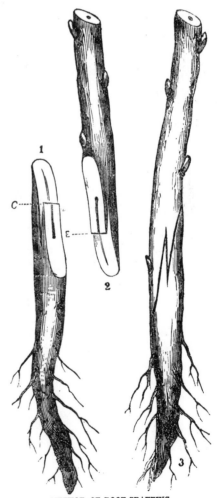

METHOD OF ROOT-GRAFTING.

off the long taproot. Make a cut sloping upward (like the mouthpiece of a whistle) from an inch to 1½ inches long. Then in the center of the slope, cut a tongue as shown at *C, fig. 1*. A cion about the same size as the stock, and 3 or 4 inches long, is cut in the same manner, except that the slope is downward: this, *E, fig. 2*, has also a tongue cut in it. The two are now fitted together as in *fig. 3*, pressing them together so that the inner bark of the stock and cion will exactly join, at least on one side. The union being satisfactorily made, the two are to be bound together. A portion of the waxed cloth is unrolled from the ball, and a piece large enough to cover the junction and go two or three times around the stem is torn off and applied by wrapping it around closely so as to exclude air and moisture. The grafted stocks are placed in boxes, with sand or sandy soil among their roots, and kept in a cool cellar or other place, neither too dry nor too cold. Of course each separate variety should be properly labeled, and to avoid the chance of mistakes, it is advisable to work upon only one sort at a time.

In spring, as soon as the soil is in good working condition, the grafted plants are set out in nursery rows. The usual method of planting is to open a trench and set them about 18 inches apart and cover so that the junction will be entirely below the surface. By making the cuts clean with a sharp knife, joining so that the inner bark of stock and cion will be in contact, and binding carefully with waxed cloth, there is little danger of failure. One great advantage of root grafting is that it can be done indoors, and at a time when outside work cannot be prosecuted. Trees started in this way will in favorable situations make as good a growth as from buds.

### Rotating Crops

In forming plans for the future improvement of the farm, a good rotation is of the first importance. The neglect of this is ruining the virgin soils of the country. A good plan—convenient, simple, and effective—is as follows: 1st year, corn upon a sod, limed in the early fall, and turned over either in the fall or spring, and the lime spread upon the inverted sod; 2nd year, a crop of oats, or a summer fallow, with all the manure spread in the fall; 3d year, winter wheat, with six quarts of timothy to the acre, at drilling, and six pounds of clover seed the following March; 4th year, a crop of clover for hay, and a second crop for seed; 5th year, timothy for one, two, or three years, according to the strength of the land.

The aim is to keep up the land to a productiveness of two tons of hay or more to the acre, and, if it falls below this, it is an indication that more lime and manure is needed.

A common rotation in Canada is: 1st, wheat; 2nd, clover for two years; 3d, fallow; 4th, wheat; 5th, oats; 6th, peas; 7th, a bastard fallow; 8th, wheat; making three crops of wheat in eight years. But the land runs down under this treatment without manure, and this must come in as a part of the rotation in any improving system upon ordinary land. And even upon the prairies and bottoms, where they get forty bushels of corn in constant succession, it would pay better to use manure and get eighty or ninety. In those states where grain is raised with less profit, manure is still more important and is the foundation of all successful husbandry. Manure should accompany every hoed crop, or should be used in large quantities once in a rotation of five years. Hay is a very valuable crop, and, with sufficient top-dressing or irrigation, land may be kept constantly in grass.

### Making Permanent Hotbeds

Hotbed sash should be constructed of softwood, and the sash bars should run in one direction only: lengthwise of the sash. The bars may be braced through the middle by a transverse bar placed through the long bars below the glass. The two ends of the sash should be made of sound timber, 3 inches wide at the top and 4 inches wide at the bottom end, mortised to receive the ends of the sash bars, and with a tenon at the ends to pass through the side pieces, which would be 2½ inches wide.

A permanent hotbed should be so constructed as to be heated either with fermenting manure or by radiating pipes from the dwelling or greenhouse

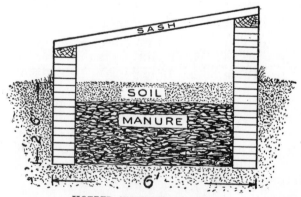

HOTBED WITH BRICK WALLS

heating plant. For a permanent bed, in which manure is to supply the heat, a pit 2 to 2½ feet deep, according to the latitude in which the work is to be done, should be provided.

The sides and ends may be supported by a lining of plank supported by posts 4 feet apart, or, what is better still, a brick wall 9 inches thick, as shown in the drawing, may be used. In either case the pit lining should come flush with the surface of the soil. The site for the pit should be on naturally well-drained land, and a tile drain from the bottom of the excavation should be provided to prevent the water from accumulating in the pit and stopping the fermentation of the manure during the period the hotbed is in use.

Standard hotbed sash is usually 3 by 6 feet. The pit, therefore, should be some multiple of 3 feet in length, and the width should be the same as the length of the sash, 6 feet. The plank frame, or the brickwork of the pit, may be extended above the surface of the ground sufficiently to allow for placing the sash immediately upon these permanent structures.

To provide heat for the hotbeds, make an excavation 5 x 16 feet on the surface, and about a foot deep. Lengthwise along this space lay three rows of tiling, one along the center and one about a foot from each side. The tiles should be 4 inches inside measure, and 1 foot long. These are placed end to end so as to fit closely, and the earth is pressed around them so as to hold every piece exactly in place. Then the excavation is filled with rich soil until level with the surface, excepting at the end where the tiles are left bare for a few inches. The board frame, 5 x 15 feet, is next put in place so as to leave 6 inches of each row of tiles projecting beyond the ends of the frame.

At the east ends of the bed, a hole should be dug 3 x 4 feet on the surface and 2 feet deep. In this hole a crude fireplace may be made of loose brick and the flue connected with the three ends of projecting tile. At the west end of the frame a brick chamber should be made into which the three tiles enter, giving them a common flue for outlet. Cover the top of this chamber closely, excepting a 6-inch circular hole, into which a single length of stovepipe is fitted. A sloping door is hung over the fireplace cavity to keep out the rain; and the earth is raised high enough around to prevent surface water from running into the hole. Bank soil about the frame. (You may happen to have on hand old storm window sashes of that size.) Of course the sashes slope to the south in the usual way.

When the fire is kindled in the fireplace, the smoke comes freely from the stovepipe. The tiles are covered with soil to a depth of about 6 inches. With a good fire, you can quickly warm up the earth on the coldest days of spring. And when once well heated, the earth and tiling hold the heat for a long time, provided the draft is closed. Unlike beds heated with manure, the heat supply can thus be regulated to suit the demand of the prevailing weather.

### Gate to Overcome Snowdrifts

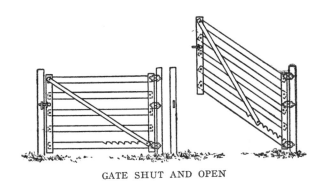

GATE SHUT AND OPEN

In the picture is shown a gate which can be readily adjusted to swing over snowdrifts. It is easily made from ordinary lumber. A 1 x 6-inch upright is used for the lower boards; 1 x 4 for the upper ones. The uprights at the hinge post are double 1 x 4, one piece outside and the other inside the bars. The upright at the latch side may be the same weight of stuff or slightly lighter, and fastened in the same way. Instead of nailing the bars to these uprights, bolts are used, one for each bar at each end. The lowest board is notched as shown, and the double brace used from the top of the latch post to the bottom of the hinge post. For the brace, 1 x 3 stuff is strong enough. They are joined near the bottom with a bolt, which engages with the notches when the gate is raised, as shown at the right.

### Rabbit Hunting

Farmers, as a general thing, regard all sportsmen as trespassers, as they are apt to cross their fields with little regard for the crops that may be underfoot. While the farmer may count upon all birds as his friends and look unfavorably upon those who would shoot them and thus destroy his important allies in the war against insects, he can not so regard the

are greedily devoured by the rabbits, as are all the small twigs within their reach, thus seriously lessening the fruit crop of the coming season. There is nothing favorable to be said of rabbits when alive; and dead rabbits at the proper season are very good indeed. The farmer who neglects by means of trap and gun to provide his table with what city people purchase as a luxury does not live up to his privileges. There is a singular prejudice with many against the use of the flesh of squirrels and rabbits as food—a prejudice which a single trial of a well-cooked, fat, young rabbit would at once remove. These animals, incidentally, are so generally called *rabbits* that it would be difficult to change the name to the more correct one—*hare*.

### Freezing Ice in Blocks

Where a pond or stream is not handy from which to get the year's supply of ice, blocks can be frozen in forms with comparatively little labor. A supply of pure water is essential. The forms are best made of galvanized iron of any size desired. A convenient size is 16 inches wide, 24 inches long, and 12 inches deep inside measure. The sides and ends should be made to taper ¼ inch, so that the frozen block will drop out easily. The top of the mold should be reinforced with wire for the sake of strength and durability. With a dozen or 20 forms, one can put up quite a supply of ice during the winter. The forms should be set level on joists or boards and placed a few inches apart. Fill them nearly full with pure water and let them freeze, which they will do in one or two days and nights in suitable weather. When frozen solid, turn the forms bottom-side up and pour a dipper of warm water on them, which will release the cake of ice. The form can then be lifted

rabbit hunter. To the homesteader, rabbits are properly enemies and ought to be destroyed. Though they are mischievous at all times, they inflict their most serious injuries when the ground is covered with snow, and the animals, being unable to find their usual food, attack the bark of young fruit trees, often completely ruining a young orchard. The frequency with which this loss is sustained, is great throughout the country. Not only are the trunks of young fruit trees injured, but when the snow is very deep and sufficiently crusted to bear the weight of the animals, the branches of low-headed trees are attacked. The plump buds on the lower branches

off, the ice put away in the icehouse, and the form filled with water again.

## A Fire Alarm

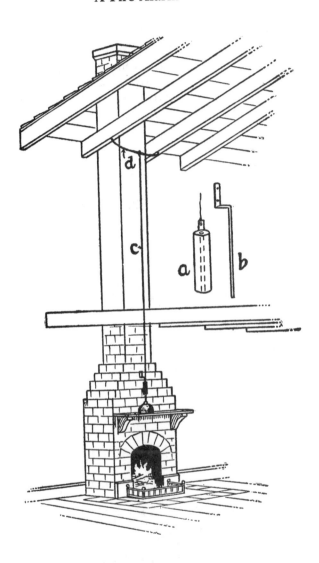

A handy device that will give an alarm in case the roof catches fire close to the chimney is shown in the illustration. Drive a nail in two rafters on a line with the face of the chimney, to which stretch a cord close to the chimney, so that, in case of fire, the cord will burn off and release the weight hanging to it, which in turn will drop on an electric button and ring a bell. (A dry battery and a bell are inexpensive, easily-purchased items.) Place these on a shelf above the fireplace. Place a piece of heavy wire, b, 10 inches long, as shown, and fasten to the wall or chimney for the weight, a, to slide on. The weight need be suspended only an inch or two above the bell.

## A Lamp for Cooking

A lamp may be utilized for cooking purposes in the following way: Make a tripod by taking three strips of wood of equal length, putting in one end a headless nail and making slightly slanting holes in the corners of a 6-inch triangular piece of board in which to fit them. A screw hook in the center of the board, on the underside, completes the device, which has only to be stood over a lighted lamp to be ready for work. A small stew kettle, or tin pail, hung on the hook, within a half inch of the lamp chimney, enables one to have a "pot boiling" in short order. If you have a large lamp with a round wick, it will give the heat of two or three common ones, and you can cook almost as rapidly as over a stove.

With an ordinary lamp, food can be heated, eggs boiled, or coffee made very quickly, helping wonderfully in the getting of a meal. This is also an easy and convenient way to heat baby's milk or water in the night, in case of sickness. Stood on a chair by the table, the device can be used to keep the coffee or chocolate hot during mealtime. A round piece of sheet iron, with chains attached to suspend it from the hook, is an additional help to hold a steeper for tea. There will be times when nothing will be wanted but a hot drink, which can be made over the lamp with less trouble than it would be to make a fire in the stove.

## A Temporary Smoking Device

If one butchers only once a year, it is not necessary to build an expensive smokehouse, for almost as good results can be obtained from a device such as

the one here illustrated. It is made by taking both ends out of a barrel and mounting it upon a box or above a fireplace in the ground. The meat to be smoked is hung from the sticks laid across the top of the barrel, the fire built underneath and the lid put on.

## Washing While Reading

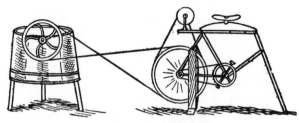

PEDAL POWER DEVICE

Here is a way of making play of washday. Perhaps some of our bright boys will try this to help mother. A friend of ours had an old bicycle unfit for use. He made a frame to raise the hind wheel from the floor, wound the rim with twine (tire being off), and reversed the seat. In place of the form he inserted a pipe (a stick would do as well). Then he took some old belting, cut it to 1 3/4 inches wide and about 10 feet long, and with that he runs the washing machine for his wife. He can read the paper while he washes, and he does not lose much time from field work either. An emery wheel can also be run with it by bolting 1-inch strips to the top part of the frame extending over the wheel and mounting a polishing head on the same.

## Use for a Tough Log

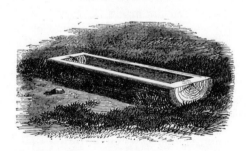

Most farm woodpiles have two or three old logs lying about which nobody cares to tackle with an ax or blasting powder and are too short for the sawmill. If straight, they will make good water troughs. Square the ends, mark off about 10 inches from each end, chop out the inside and trim the edges. An inside coat of oil or pitch tar will increase wearing qualities.

## Mending Glassware

Broken dishes and glassware may be easily mended as follows: Fit the pieces in their proper places and tie a string around the vessel to keep the parts from slipping out. Then boil the entire dish for two or three hours in sweet milk. This will firmly glue the vessel together, and it will last for years with proper care.

## Building a Dog-Power Water Pump

This sketch shows an arrangement for making use of the dog for carrying water. It simply consists of a wheel 8 feet in diameter and 18 inches wide, with room enough inside for the dog to walk around, where he acts as a tread power, which causes the pump to revolve. In southern California there are a number of these dog-power pumps, which are very

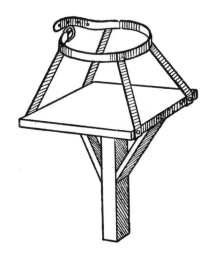

inexpensive to construct. A good-sized dog can easily earn his living in an arrangement of this kind.

## Building Milking Stools

**The Ever-Ready Stool:** A very convenient stool for use in milking the cow in yard or field is shown in the cut. It is merely a one-legged stool to which is attached four straps connecting with a broad strap that is buckled around the waist. The stool is quickly fastened to the milker and is always in a position so one can sit down anywhere. Such a stool with a short leg would also be useful in the garden. Of course, if one preferred four legs instead of one, the stool could be so made, but experience proves that the one-legged kind serves well.

STOOL TO HOLD PAIL

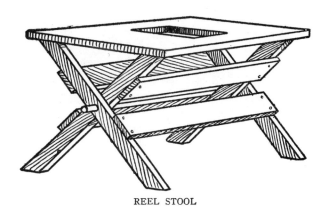

REEL STOOL

Milkers who have trouble with restless cows that invariably either upset the pail or get a quantity of dirt in it will find the stool shown here a remedy for their troubles. It is also very serviceable in fly time. The upright pieces forming the legs and ends of the stool are made of 2 x 8-inch pieces about 1 foot long. The supports for the bucket and the seat are made of inch boards. To secure rigidity it is best to put three-cornered blocks under the seat and bucket board as brace stays. The most restless cow is not likely to upset the bucket from this stool.

**Another Cheap Milking Stool:** A cheap and very useful milking stool is made of the reel from which barbed wire has been removed. Any similar industrial spool will do. Saw off the ends so it will set level, and cut a board to fit on top. Make a hand hole through the board as shown in the illustration and the stool is ready for use.

# FARM
# AND GARDEN WORK FOR

# February

Verdant fields, bright with white clover, or fresh springing grasses, together with the blossoming of shrubs and trees, make many days of February of the Gulf States and the far South among the most delightful of the year. Plowing for spring wheat and for other crops gives employment to the laborers and teams, and the season of field work fairly begins with the warm, drying weather usually occurring at this time of the year.

The Northern farmer buffets the winter usually for a good part of this month. He may look for deep snows, powerful rains, ice storms, and hard freezing weather with the thermometer below zero, and need not be disappointed if before the 20th the frost is all out of the ground south of latitude 41°, and bluebirds are singing. Nevertheless it will probably freeze up again, and the poor little birds will look blue enough.

The days are much longer, and they should show notably more work done than those of December or even January; nevertheless, there is comparative leisure and season for reviewing the past year's work and laying plans for the coming months, when so much hard labor will be demanded that the mind will not give itself readily to continuous thought. Whatever plans are made—on this very account, if for no other reason—should be put upon paper, so that when the time comes for their prompt execution, they shall not be forgotten. The season of field work, when it does come, will be likely to come all at once, and then you will feel as if every moment were gold, as if the horses and oxen, though doing their utmost, did not walk half fast enough. There-fore use the leisure of this month to get all ready for spring work.

## HINTS ABOUT FARM WORK

Over a good part of the country, it is neither winter nor spring; the frost may be out of the ground so that we can begin setting fences and doing some kinds of spring work, and it may come on and freeze again, and a second edition of winter in all its severity be upon us.

**Winter Work**—Make the best use of the snow to haul home the timber, fencing stuff, and boards from the sawmill or from the wood lot. Employ every hour-of daylight, when other important work is not pressing, in cutting.

**Firewood**—Make provision against a more hurried season, when every hour will be worth two or three hours of this time of the year. There is nothing that pleases the good wife better than a nice lot of clean, dry chips and light stuff, to make a quick blaze; and if she has to run to the woodpile, tear off splinters, pick up damp chips, and so spend five minutes out of the kitchen, just at the critical time when the dinner needs attention, the farmer must not complain if the potatoes burn in the pot and things go wrong.

**Ice, nice ice,** will keep splendidly on a floor of rails, under a heap of straw. Lay a floor of slabs on

three old rails as sleepers, the floor being 12 x 12 feet square. Cover it a foot thick with straw. Lay up a square pile of ice eight or ten feet high, of solid square pieces, having the spaces between the cakes well chinked in with pounded ice. Set posts, as for a high fence, two feet outside, all around. Board up with close-fitting 16-foot inch or inch-and-a-quarter boards, and stuff the whole, outside the ice, with straw. Put on a single-pitch roof of boards, inclined to the north, and fill the whole interior above the ice with straw. The ice will keep well, and should be used from the top only. It is well, before piling up the ice, to set two light posts, two feet from each corner, against which the ice may rest, so that the corners of the pile will remain firm.

**Manure** — The time for economizing in the use of bedding is late in the season, if ever. Early in the winter, use as much as you can in order to increase the manure pile. This month often offers a first-rate opportunity to work over all the accumulations of manure in the yards and cellars, to throw them in compact heaps, well laid up, mingling with them as much muck and litter as can be spared from the stores of bedding for use later in the season, and all the uneaten cornstalks, which are too apt at this time in the winter to disfigure the yards. Composts may be greatly enriched and their fermentation quickened by a mixture of hog and hen manure; but it is important that these should be pretty thoroughly disseminated through the whole mass in order to give it uniformity.

**Plows and Harrow** — Farmers living at a considerable distance from mechanics should have, not only good plows, but plenty of duplicate parts, that they can themselves attach in case of breakage: several

new shares, at least one new beam for each breaking-up plow, and several plow handles that may be adapted to the plows most used. Have wood ready to mend harrows if they are to be subjected to any trying work among stumps or on rough, rooty ground. Give a coat of paint to all tools of this class, being particular to work paint well into the joints, and it is well to give these spots several coats, so that water cannot get in. Paint tools only when they are thoroughly dry.

**Wagons** — When the sleighing is good, don't forget to put the wagons in good order.

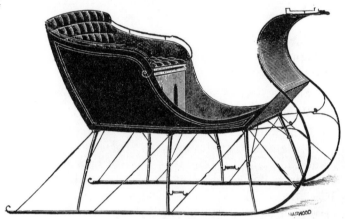

**Working Cattle** — Save the strength of the ox for the plow and for the heavy work; feed him a little grain; keep him in first-rate working order, and give just work enough to prevent his neck getting soft; then when the time for hard labor arrives, give good feed and all the work he can do. *Work the bulls!* They are healthier for it; they are easier and safer to handle; they are surer and better stock-getters. They are more intelligent than oxen and easier taught, if they do not learn that dangerous lesson that they need not mind unless it suits their own convenience.

**Cows** — Feed dry cows well; give them a daily feed of meal of some kind, corn meal and wheat-bran, or corn meal and oil cake, or some other milk-producing or fattening diet. You will get it all back when you begin to milk. Keep bovine stock of all kinds sheltered and warm. Do not expose them to the spring storms, which are more trying than those of the autumn and early winter.

**Young Cattle** should never stop growing until they come to full maturity. They will surely stop, and thenceforth have that stunted, weakly look so common among "scrubs," unless they are sheltered and so well fed that they do not lose flesh.

**Horses and Colts**—The same remarks are applicable to these animals as to bovine stock, except that the horse will thrive under much severer exposure than cattle if he has enough to eat and a shed to go under. It is, however, the worst policy to put the toughness of any animal to severe tests. Horses must be well fed for the hard work of spring. Great care should be taken that colds are not caught from exposure during sleighing excursions or after other sweating work; they are very apt to run into confirmed coughs and the heaves, especially at this season. Blanket only and always when warm, rub off *dry*, withhold food and drink, and litter freely. A horse stable should not be exposed to interior drafts.

**Sheep**—Have an eye to evidence of parasites, and apply a strong solution of carbolic soap, thrown into the parted wool, on the parts most affected.

**Salting Stock** of all kinds must not be neglected; irregularity is nearly as bad as entire neglect.

**Poultry** require close attention, especially if they are laying freely. Hens that are repeatedly checked in their laying by exposure to cold are likely to become diseased. If hens are sitting, they must be well protected and must not be interfered with, lest they remain in cold weather too long off their nests and the eggs get chilled. We know of no better feed for laying hens or young chicks than good wheat screenings.

**Reset Fences** and renew rails and posts wherever they are falling as soon as the frost is out of the ground and the weather is favorable. Staking and binding with withes answers a tolerable purpose, but is a very bad-looking way of mending a fence.

**Repair the Roads** by filling soft spots with stones, and covering them with good, sharp gravel, leaving the cart-paths and farm roads rounded up, free from water and as even as you can with the time and labor you have to put upon them.

**Ditching and Draining** may be undertaken at once and pushed at odd times, when the ground is too wet to plow.

## Hints About Horticultural Work

In arranging plans for spring work, do not lay out more than can be done thoroughly. Amateurs especially are apt to grasp at too much and take up a heavier load than they can carry. Laying out and planting are not all, but only the beginning; the labor and cost of cultivation and maintenance are to be taken into the account. Orders for trees and seeds sent the present month are more likely to be satisfactorily filled than if delayed until planting time.

### Orchard and Nursery

**Plant Trees** in those states where the season is sufficiently advanced to admit of it. In the North it is much better to wait until spring is well opened.

Young, recently planted trees are often much injured by exposure to cold, dry winds, as they are unable to take up moisture to supply the waste by evaporation.

**Grafting,** for the same reason, should not be done too early. If the cions are put in just as the tree is starting into growth, the chances of success are much greater.

**Nursery Trees,** if frozen in transportation as they are apt to be, are not likely to be injured if allowed to thaw very gradually. Cover the package with hay or straw so that the thawing may go on slowly.

**Injured Trees** are to be attended to as soon as the trouble is discovered. If any limbs have been broken by storms, remove them and paint the wound with a thick white-lead paint colored with lampblack or amber.

**Girdling** by rabbits and mice may now be discovered. Most trees injured in this way may be saved by proper care. Draw up a mound of earth to completely cover the wound, or if the place is too high for this, bind on a generous plaster of clayey loam; if this is mixed with cow dung it will retain its moisture better. If the injury is very severe, grafts must be inserted to establish a connection between the bark below the wound and that above it. Cut incisions with a chisel downwards, below the wound, and upwards, above it; then take twigs of the same kind of tree of the proper length, sharpen them to a wedge at each end, and insert the ends in the incisions; put grafting wax over the insertions, as in ordinary grafting.

**Cions** may still be cut. Pack them in sawdust; or, if put in a tight tin box and kept in a cool place, their own moisture will keep them plump and in good condition until it is time to set them.

**Washing** with some alkaline wash is of great benefit to trees, as it removes parasitic growths, loosens old bark scales, and dislodges insects. Homemade soft soap, thinned with water, and put on with a brush, is one of the best applications, or a moderately strong lye of potash or soda ash may be used. The effect is more satisfactory if the wash is used during a damp spell.

*Fruit Garden*

Do all preparatory work that the weather will allow; see under "Orchard" for sundry hints.

**Blackberries and Raspberries** should be planted as soon as the ground can be worked, as they start very early; the shoots will be much broken in handling them if delayed until they have pushed.

**Dwarf Trees** — and none other should be in the fruit garden — may have the general care given to

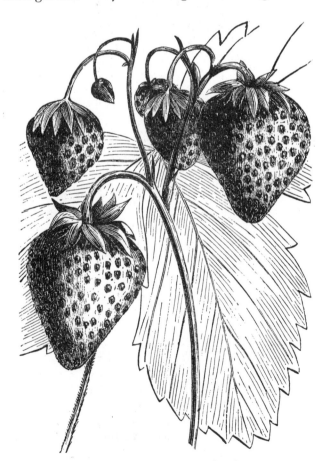

trees in the orchard; being small, they are more accessible, and it is inexcusable to neglect them.

**Strawberries** — Some good cultivators prefer to set them as soon as the frost is out of the ground, while others prefer to wait until later.

**Grape Vines** which were neglected may be pruned in mild weather. Cuttings made from wood that has been exposed all winter do not usually succeed so well as from that cut in the fall and properly cared for during the winter.

*Kitchen Garden*

The main consideration just now is manure, which will soon be needed not only for enriching the land but for hotbeds.

**Manure** — The heaps should not be so small as to freeze, and when the heat increases so as to cause an issue of steam from the heap, it should be forked over, and watered, if dry enough to need it.

**Cold Frames** — Plants in these will need more care and must have plenty of air and exposure by removing the sashes whenever the weather will allow.

**Hotbeds** — These, unless very early vegetables are wanted, need not be made, in the North, until next month. In Southern gardens they may be prepared and tomatoes, peppers, eggplants, cabbages, etc. sown in them. Shelter from wind should be looked out for, and, if necessary to make the bed in an exposed place, it will pay to put up a temporary fence to shut off prevailing winds.

**Straw Mats** are almost indispensable where there are hotbeds. See Hints for January.

**Poles** for peas and beans should be cut while there is leisure, trimmed and sharpened, and stacked near the place where they will be used.

**Root Crops** that were left in the ground all winter — salsify, parsnips, and horseradish — may be dug for sale or use whenever the ground is thawed.

**Rhubarb** may be forced by taking up the roots and setting them in boxes of earth in a greenhouse, or a few roots in the bed may be forced by covering with boxes or barrels around which is heaped a good supply of fermenting manure.

**Potatoes** — Plant some early sort as soon as the frost will allow.

*Flower Garden and Lawn*

There is plenty of planning and some work to be done. One of our best writers gives the advice to always have the garden look different each year. The advice is good and is capable of being followed even in a very small place. Take a single bed in a lawn. One year it may be gay with coleus and other "foliage plants"; in the fall, plant hyacinths, tulips, and other bulbs; in early spring, sow portulacas to make the bed gay when the bulbs have passed out of bloom. In a similar way each bed in a lawn can every year present some new feature. Of course in borders where there are herbaceous perennials, there must be some sameness in their appearance for several years in succession. Yet if these are so planted as to allow room for the introduction of clumps of annuals or bedding plants, a pleasing variety can be made and be different every year.

**Ornamental Trees** should have the same care as fruit trees. Most of them will repay manuring, and they need pruning whenever a branch disfigures the proper shape.

**Shrubs** may be pruned and thinned. Those that bloom on the new wood may be cut back, but those which have their flower buds already formed need only to be thinned when the growth is crowded.

**Seeds of Annuals** may be sown where there are facilities for keeping the young plants in good condition until time to set them out, but as a general thing sowing in hotbeds or in window boxes had best be left until next month.

**Plants in Cold Frames** must have their air on warm days or they will get drawn up by the increasing heat of the sun. Give water only when the soil in the pots is dry.

**Lawns** may be rolled as soon as the frost is out of the ground, and, if they did not have a top-dressing last autumn, give one now of good compost.

**Repairs** to woodwork of all kinds, and painting, are best done now. Paint trellises and other work needing it, using drab or some other subdued color in preference to glaring white or green.

**In the South** — Make walks, prepare borders, and set edging. Transplanting of trees, shrubs, and herbaceous perennials may be done, and the hardier annuals sown.

*Greenhouse and Window Plants*

Plants coming into flower need more water and a place nearer the glass. Prolong the bloom by shading from the hot sun in the middle of the day.

**Annuals** may be sown in the greenhouse, but it is a month too early where it is done in the window. In either case boxes are better than pots.

**Bulbs** in pots, as they go out of flower, should have the flower stalk cut away and the leaves kept growing until they naturally decay. Bulbs grown in glasses of water are not worth anything afterwards; those forced in pots may be turned out into the garden as soon as the frost is out.

**Air** is to be given whenever the weather will allow.

**Dust** — Mild days will allow window plants to be taken outside for a thorough showering; where this cannot be done with safety, a bathtub or sink will serve a good turn. Lay the plants on the side, when it can be done without injury, and shower from a watering can with a fine rose; in this way both sides of the leaves will be washed.

**Propagation** of bedding plants of all kinds should be going on. Our most successful growers use very short cuttings of tender and succulent growth.

**Potting** of plants that appear to be sickly may be done, cutting them back at the same time. It is not always necessary to put into a larger pot, but shake out the old earth from the roots and re-pot with fresh soil in the same pot.

# PROJECTS FOR
# FEBRUARY

## Making Maple Sugar

During the growing season, the maple, or "sugar bush," stores in its wood substances which are converted by the warmth of the spring, coming after the influences of the autumn and winter, into a sweet sap. The sugar is "cane sugar," identical with that of the southern cane, but mingled with so few impurities, which incite fermentation and other changes, that it is very easily obtained in condition of considerable purity. The purer it is, the lighter colored; and the more rapidly evaporated, the more it retains the pleasant flavor peculiar to it. Artificial clarification removes this flavor, and the perfectly pure white loaf sugar, which may be made, cannot be distinguished from that of the same quality from other sources.

It is always desirable to avoid injury to the trees by tapping; the incisons should therefore be made where they will do no damage to the timber — that is, below the cylindrical part of the trunk, where the sap will flow quite as abundantly as at any place above. There is nothing gained by cutting such large gashes as are sometimes made when trees are tapped. In fact, some of the most thrifty trees when hacked in such a manner commence decaying and continue to rot until the body is nothing but a shell. It is unnecessary also to make *deep* incisions either with center bits, gouges, or axes, as sap will flow as rapidly if one or two of the concentric layers of wood are cut through. The best way to tap a tree is to hew off the dead bark with a sharp ax, making a smooth place about as large as a man's hand. Then with a mallet and wide chisel cut two small convergent channels through the bark and into the wood in the form of

Fig. 1—TAPPING.

the letter V, and shown in *fig. 1.* Then, about 2 inches below the incision, make a gash with a 1½-inch gouge and insert a metallic spout made of stiff zinc or galvanized sheet iron. The spouts may be 10 or 12 inches long and made of strips 1½ inches wide, with one end ground or filed to a sharp edge. Cut a small channel in the bark from the V-shaped gash down to the spout. It is not necessary to cut through the bark when making this channel. The lower edge of the cut should be beveled downwards and inwards so as to conduct the sap down to the angle. There may be several taps made in large trees, and each yield as much as if there were but one.

The tools needed for tapping trees in this way are a mallet, a sharp 2-inch "firmer" chisel, a 1½-inch joiner's gouge, and a sharp ax or a carpenter's adze for dressing off the rough bark. Insert the spouts as low as the top of the sap buckets so that the wind may not blow the liquid over the side of the vessel. When domestic animals are permitted to roam in a sugar orchard, trees must be tapped several feet from the ground and the sap vessels suspended by hooks. The better way, however, is to keep all such animals in their appropriate enclosures, especially at this time of the year.

The best sugar makers all over the country are employing commercial evaporators. For those who cannot go to this expense and would still pursue a much better plan than the old kettle swung on a pole or set in a brick or stone fireplace, we describe a good homemade pan, or pair of pans *(fig. 2)*, one being used as a heater and reservoir of hot sap, and

Fig. 2.—EVAPORATING PAN.

the other as the evaporator. The sides and ends of the pans are made of 1½-inch planks of any kind of wood (though maple or beech is preferred), and the bottoms of iron or zinc. The sides of the reservoir pan should be at least 12 inches, and of the other 6 inches high. As sheets of iron and zinc are usually made about 26 inches wide, the dimensions of the pans should be at about an inch shorter and narrower than a sheet of the metal, so that the edges, after the bottom is nailed on, may be turned up with a mallet and nailed to the outside as well as to the bottom of the wood.

The pans rest at leat 3 inches on brick walls, which are 1 foot high and 18 inches apart. Bars of iron or pieces of old wagon tire support the bricks at the end. When everything is made of the size given, there will be ample room for the fire. The throat of the chimney should be about 18 inches wide by 4 in height. This size will correspond with the fireplace. The height of the chimney should be sufficient to carry all smoke, atoms of charcoal, and ashes beyond the pans and sap receptacles, as such substances falling into the syrup give it a dark color. A barrel or other closed vessel may stand, supported upon blocks or horses, so that the sap, which is strained into it through straw, may either be drawn directly into the pan, or, several barrels or hogsheads being used and set back from the fire, the sap may be conducted in leaders at pleasure into the large pan, from which it is dipped into the shallow one. Such an apparatus may be erected at a comparatively small expense where bricks and lumber are cheap. Metallic or wooden faucets may be inserted in the ends of the pans for drawing off the syrup, or it may be dipped out, which is the usual practice. There should at least be a shed over the pans, but a more spacious and better-built structure, with a tight roof and enclosed, so that the buckets, etc., may be locked up in it the rest of the year, is much preferable.

When the syrup is nearly as thick as molasses, take it from the fire, strain it through flannel, and let it stand till cold. Then pour it off from the sediment which will separate and place it in a kettle or deep pan over another fire. As soon as it becomes warm, but not near boiling hot, add a pint of water to each pailful of syrup, and stir thoroughly. When it boils, remove all the scum. Keep the fire under control, and when sugar will granulate freely in small quantities of syrup (such as would adhere to a stick dipped into it), or when a little cooled on the snow is brittle, it may be removed from the fire. As it thickens in cooling, it may be dipped into molds or well stirred until quite dry. "Strained sugar" is not boiled so long, and after it has cooled and granu-

lated, being transferred into false-bottomed tubs and kept at a temperature of about 70° more or less, molasses is drained off from it and a better quality of sugar obtained.

## Plans for a Cow Barn

Agriculture, as a rational system, is making constant progress. Old forms disappear, and better methods take their places. This will probably soon make the widely comprehensive American barn a thing of the past. We try to get everything under one roof— stables for horses and cattle, breeding pens and cow stalls, wagon and tool rooms, repair shop, even boiler and engine room sometimes. Besides, hay, straw, and grain are stored here, and in the cellar roots are kept and manure is accumulated and rooted over by pigs. This may save labor in some sense, but it has many evils. The danger from fire is not the least; the moist breath of the cattle rusts the tools; the dust from the hay, the threshing, and all that settles over everything and enters the lungs of the cattle. Exhalations from manure and from the livestock too often contaminate the fodder, and the cows and fattening cattle are subject much of the time to disturbing influences instead of the entire quiet which is most promotive of milk secretion as well as laying on of fat.

The barn for dairy stock should contain only provision for sheltering the cows and preparing their food, for storing hay and other forage, for grain and provender of various kinds, and for saving and composting all the manure. It should be throughout absolutely rat-proof and be defended from lightning and the highest winds. To accomplish these ends in the best possible manner, we give the accompanying elevation *(fig. 1)*, plans, sections, etc.

The cow floor, as indeed the manure cellar, should be protected against cold by double-faced stone or brick walls, with air spaces between inner and outer courses. The basement, or cellar floor, is for receiving and caring for the manure. The walls and piers are of any durable stone, well laid in cement. The floor is made of a cement concrete or grouting and slopes towards certain depressed points at which are pump wells, where pumps are to be set for distributing the liquids over the manure. Eight windows are provided on each side. Ventilating trunks (not shown in the diagrams) carry off the fumes of fermenting manure to the ventilators in the roof. There are openings in the floor above,

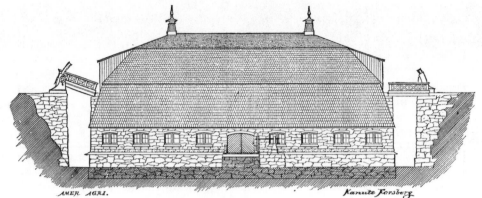

Fig. 1.—ELEVATION OF COW BARN.

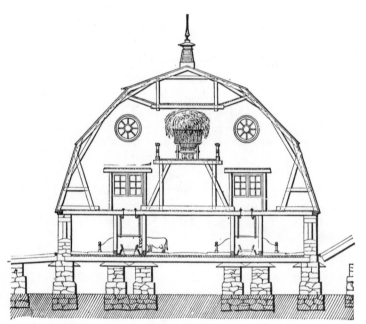

Fig. 2.—CROSS-SECTION OF BARN.

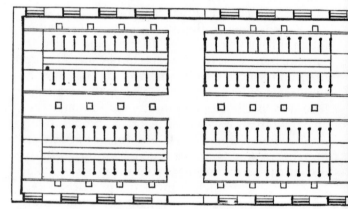

Fig. 3.—PLAN OF CATTLE FLOOR.

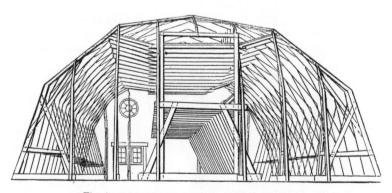

Fig. 4.—SECTION AND INTERIOR VIEW OF FRAMING.

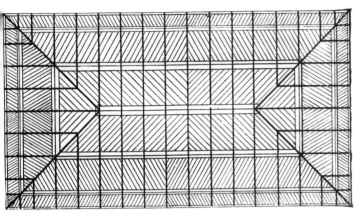

Fig. 5.—VIEW OF FRAME PARTLY BOARDED.

Fig. 6.—VIEW OF ROOF FRAMING, LOOKING UP.

through which the manure is thrown down. These must be arranged to close perfectly tight so as to keep the air of the cellar from rising into the cattle floor. The depth to which it will be desirable to excavate for this basement depends upon the formation of the ground. In the plan as drawn, there is a supposed excavation of 8 feet upon one side, the earth being used in part for filling out upon the other, and there is a 10-foot passageway all around the building. All the copings to this basement foundation, both outside and inside, as well as to the piers, are furnished with galvanized iron caps, a foot out from the walls, as a protection against rats. And for the same reason no stairs of any kind communicate from the basement to the floor above.

*Fig. 3* is the plan of the second or cattle floor. The two doors on the east and west sides are approached by slightly raised ways and two bridges, which are arranged to be raised at the outer ends 3 feet. This is to prevent rats from crossing. The bridges are lowered chiefly when the cattle are to cross, the men being able easily to help themselves across or to jump. There are two rows of stalls or stanchions on each side, running the entire length of the building, including some loose boxes for cows at calving time, and calf pens provided at both ends. This plan should be taken in connection with *fig. 2,* which is a section of the whole building. The manure traps are shown conspicuously; gutters for the urine, which is led through pipes to the pump wells, are

behind the stalls. There are water troughs, for the cattle to drink, and racks for fodder. Above the feeding passages are suspended cars or baskets, hung on rails or rods, for carrying the feed along to the cattle. Hay shutes, or trunks, are provided for throwing down hay or straw from the loft. These should have doors, which are to be closed when not in use. The floor of the cow stable should be double throughout—the upper floor, if not both, of tongued and grooved plank—and between the two boardings there should be a layer of paper or felt, well tarred, the upper planks being laid upon the fresh tar. This makes the floor practically water-and airtight. This story has also eight windows upon each side, besides the large end windows seen in *fig. 2.*

The hayloft is entirely a roof construction, as is clearly shown in *figs. 1, 2, 4, 5, and 6.* The timbers forming the strong braced arches are 6 inches thick by 10 wide, halved together, and the joints covered by two iron plates, one on each side, bolted together through the timber; they are braced by strong braces across the angles, as shown in the engraving. Each arch is formed complete before it is raised into position. The whole roof is diagonally boarded and well nailed. The lower two sections having a sharp slope are either shingled or slated; the upper roof is covered with the roofing. This construction of the roof, especially if it is properly anchored to the walls, makes the building almost absolutely windproof, even if exposed upon the open prairie. The location, as shown, is in a sheltered nook between hills or headlands. There is thus afforded a passageway for teams at the level of the middle division of the roof. Here there is the wagon floor, with room for four or five loads of hay, at least, to stand at one time, and they may be driven in at one end and out at the other.

## How to Set Up a Leach

It is more economical to make the common soap used at home than to buy it. The basis of good soap is good lye; and to have this, good ashes must be properly leached. The ashes of hardwoods are best, those of hickory being preferred to all others. Ashes must be kept dry while they are accumulating. So many fires result from ashes that we would recommend keeping them in a tightly-covered box in an isolated position not far from the house and that the box be always out of, and away from, all buildings.

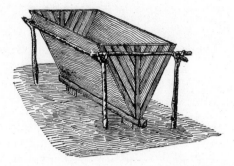

An excellent leach is shown in the engraving. A trough is made by hollowing out a log or by nailing planks together. It is open at one end. The length of the trough, from the inside of the closed end, is 5 feet. It is 6 inches wide at the top, 3 at the bottom, and 6 inches deep. Whether made from a log or with plank, hardwood should be selected. It is placed upon two rocks, or blocks, which raise it a foot from the ground, the open end being slightly the lowest. Set four forked stakes in the ground at the corners of a 5-foot square, the forks being 4 feet above the ground. Lay two poles in the forks, and cross-poles on top of these, and pin them together to make a frame 5 feet square. The sides and ends of the leach are made of boards, inserting one end in the trough and leaning the other against the frame. If it is desired to leach a large quantity of ashes (the more ashes the better lye), the boards can project a foot or more above the frame. Forming the sides is easy, but to form the ends is less so. The manner in which the end boards are cut and arranged is shown in the engraving. If possible, use boards of hardwood. The leach is now ready for the ashes.

Cut small, straight brush and lay it along the bottom of the leach, where it should form a layer 3 inches thick. Over the brush place a 2-inch layer of coarse straw. Next, carefully throw in a few shovelfuls of ashes. With a sprinkler or dipper, dampen the ashes until they will compact well, after which pound them down solid with a post-hole tamper or a maul. Much of the value of the leach depends upon the ashes being thoroughly compacted; therefore, add a few at a time. When compacted, each layer should not be more than 3-inches thick. Keep the ashes hollowed in the middle; when finished, this hollow should hold from three to six buckets of water. Add a good roof, and the leach is done.

### To Sharpen Scissors

Do you know that you can sharpen scissors, and easily, by passing the blades over glass jars? Take a bottle or jar, make believe you are trying to cut it (have one blade in and the other outside of the top of the bottle), and then allow the scissors to glide off the hard surface naturally, just as if you were trying to cut the glass. Use firm but not too hard pressure, and repeat the operation several times.

### Papering a Room

If a room has been papered several times, tear off all the loose parts you can, and, with a sponge and water, loosen what remains on the walls, removing as much as possible so as to have a smooth, even surface. If the room has never been papered, first go over it and fill all large cracks and holes with a paste made of whiting and water, or plaster of paris and water. When using the latter, mix only a little at a time, having it rather thin, and use quickly. Then, give the room a coat of sizing, which is made of common glue, three or four handfuls dissolved in a pail of boiling water. The sizing is applied with a large brush and should be allowed to dry overnight.

**Choose Judiciously:** For very sunny rooms, select cool-looking papers, such as blues, greens, and browns in various shades; while for dark rooms, pinks, reds, terra cottas, and yellows are best. When selecting papers, pay careful attention to the color scheme of your room, and don't have an inharmonious mixture which will offend good taste. Small, plain patterns are the most economical and the easiest to match. The cheap, trashy papers are not worth the trouble of putting up. No borders should be used for rooms having a low ceiling. For such, a striped paper of pretty design running right up to the ceiling is best. The ceiling may be papered in a plain or very small-patterned design to harmonize with the side walls, or treated with several coats of tinted calcimine or paint. A picture moulding of appropriate color is used to finish the side walls, being placed scarcely 1 inch from the ceiling. The ceiling, whether papered, painted, or calcimined, should be done first. It is a very difficult matter to paper the ceiling, and, unless you can have help, it would be better not to attempt it. Plain tints in paint or calcimine are always pretty and in good taste. If, however, you want to risk papering the ceiling yourself, get some handy body to help you.

**Paste and Tools:** The paste is made by simply boiling flour and water together and adding a very little alum, salt, and glue—about a tablespoon of each to a pound of flour. It should be a consistency

thick enough to apply easily, and not so thin that it will run. Provide yourself with a good-sized paste brush; another one (a whitewash brush will do) to use dry over the paper; sharp scissors and a knife; plenty of clean rags; two barrels; two long, smooth, clean boards, each about 10 inches wide; and a step-ladder. Make a long table by placing the two barrels about 8 or 9 feet apart and on top of these the boards.

**Trimming and Cutting:** The first thing to do is to cut the necessary number of strips of paper long enough to allow for waste in matching, and lay them all face downward on the "operating" table, one on top of the other. Next spread the paste evenly over the top (or first) strip of paper, being very sure to have the edges well pasted. Then turn the top and bottom parts down, bringing the pasted sides together so that they meet and none of the paste part

is exposed, and carefully trim off the edge on one side with large, sharp scissors. Lift up the part thus trimmed and folded and mount the ladder, which should previously have been placed convenient to the place where you intend to begin operations. The largest wall space is best, next to a door or window.

**Hanging the Paper:** Now take hold of the top end which was doubled over (it will open and hang by its own weight) and adjust it to its proper place on the wall. Then, with a large clean rag in your hand, rub downward, (never up or sideways) and take great care to keep the edge straight. If you find that you didn't start straight from the top, loosen the paper and do it over again. A "straight eye" is needed to do the work neatly. Don't rub too hard, and always rub downward, doing a little part at a time, and lifting the paper occasionally so that no air bubbles are left under it. When the upper part is done, dismount from the ladder, undo the folded part at the bottom of the width, and proceed in the same manner to adjust it to the wall. When you are sure it is on straight and smooth, trim with a sharp knife along the baseboard. Then give the strip another smoothing by going all over it again with a dry, clean brush. Proceed in this way until all the full-length parts are covered, and then match in the small spaces over and below the windows and doors. All the matching must be done with great care.

## Removing Fence Posts

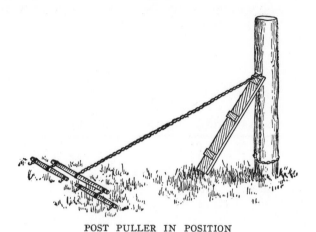

POST PULLER IN POSITION

An easy and practical method of pulling fence posts, by which all digging and hand labor is eliminated, is here shown. Take a plank 4 feet long and 1 foot wide and make a V-shaped notch in one end, nailing on several crosspieces to prevent splitting. This plank is used to change the horizontal draft to the vertical. Place one end of chain around the post close to the ground. Incline the plank against the post so the lower end of the plank will be about 1½ or 2 feet from the base of the post. Place the chain in the notch of the plank, start the team, and the post in a few seconds will be clear of the ground.

## Homemade Sleds

Here is a pair of sleds which have neither mortises, tenons, nor iron about them (except, necessarily, the shoes, kingbolt, and the coupling clevises). They can be made without any other tools than an ax and an auger. They sit low to the ground and are easily loaded and difficult to upset, and the cost to a man who can use an ax is about four days' work. The runners are hewed from small oaks or sugar maples, which have a natural crook at the root. They should be 2½ or 3 inches thick and as deep as desired. Blocks are pinned onto each runner to receive the beams.

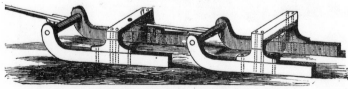

HOME-MADE WOOD OR LUMBER SLEDS.

The hind beam should be 8 inches thick, the front beam about half that thickness, the holster being the same or an inch or so heavier. The beams and blocks are bolted to the runners with 1¼-inch oak or hickory pins, well wedged at both ends. The tongues are fitted in with wooden wedges, which come well up from the roller, and two ½-inch pins should be put through both the wedges and tongue sufficiently rigid without braces, unless some careless teamster drives around too short sometimes, when the tongue is just as apt to break as to be wrenched from its place if well wedged. In case the sleds are wanted shod, we would recommend cast-steel shoes, ⅛-inch thick, to be put on with 3-inch wood screws, the holes being countersunk so that the screwheads may be quite flush with the shoe. A steel shoe is light and will not "stick" in frosty weather, as a cast shoe will. One can build such sleds and shod them with common bank iron, ⅛-inch thick, which comes cheaper than the steel, and for ordinary use is nearly as good. But for heavy work, such as drawing logs, timber, or lumber steadily every day, the steel shoes are the cheapest in the end. These sleds are very durable if taken care of during the summer, and a coat of crude petroleum put on will increase their durability.

## Propagating Plants from Cuttings

A saucer used to hold water below flowerpots or even common kitchen saucers or plates are filled with sand (any kind that is most convenient) and the cuttings are inserted just thickly enough to touch each other, then watered until the sand turns to mud. The first condition of success is that the sand must be kept in this half-fluid state until the cuttings are rooted, which will be in from ten to twenty days, according to the condition of the cuttings. The second condition is the temperature of the greenhouse or room in which they are placed. The best temperature is from 70 degrees to 75 degrees, but it may range from 50 degrees to 80 degrees. If placed in the greenhouse, the saucers should stand on a stage or shelf fully exposed to the sun; if inside the house, then in the lightest and sunniest spot and never shaded, for, so long as the sand is kept in a state of mud, the most tender cutting will not wilt. But once allowed to dry, the whole operation will be retarded, if not entirely defeated.

When rooted, the cuttings should be potted off

at once into good soil, in the smallest-sized pots, and kept well watered until they begin to grow. The best cuttings to use are what we term "young wood"— that is, the young shoot in the succulent state, before it attains its woody or hard character. In this way, roses, geraniums, fuchsias, carnations, verbenas, heliotropes, etc. (in fact almost any cutting) will root, without a loss of more than five percent.

FARM
AND GARDEN WORK FOR

# March

The coming of this month brings the renewed stir and activity of pressing work or the preparation for work soon to be undertaken. March is a month of work from New England to Texas. The early part is usually the last of the winter, even in Maine, and over most of the North farmers are hauling manure, plowing, setting fences, and engaged in other field work before its close. Where much snow has lain, winter grains and fields newly laid down to grass will be benefited, but where the ground has been bare, the deep freezing of the soil, and the exposure of the plants to both cold and heat before it thaws, will be likely to injure both grain and grass and render the application of some "hand manure" very desirable. After so severe a winter, an early spring is anticipated. This is rejoiced in by most farmers, but it is accompanied by many more dangers to fruit trees and field crops than when the cold holds on and the warm weather, coming later, is subject to few or no great fluctuations of temperature.

Loamy or clayey soils should never be worked before they are so thoroughly dried as not to pack before the plow in pasty clods; and no seeds, except those of grass and clover sowed upon winter grain, should be committed to the soil before it is warm and mellow. The error of too early plowing is a common one; everybody wants to be at work in the spring, and no one really feels as if he had begun farming before he smells the fresh earth and sees the long furrows turned. So we get the manures spread and the plows at work, often enough when the plowman's feet are loaded with pounds of sticky

clay, and water even stands in the furrows in the low spots. This is all wrong, for thus we burden ourselves with the care of rough, cloddy fields which will hardly get in good tilth before autumn.

## HINTS ABOUT FARM WORK

The most important work any farmer does is to:

**Lay Plans** for the coming season. If possible think of every important thing, and keep a memorandum of whatever is deemed most essential and the order in which it should come. In case of necessary absence, the foreman or any intelligent hand can go on with the work without any supervision if a definite plan is made and talked over beforehand. The responsibility thus thrown upon an employee is a stimulus to faithfulness to which an intelligent man almost always responds. The circumstances of different farmers are so various that it is impossible to even hint at a plan of operations applicable to all. With many, a regular system of rotation of crops and manure leaves the principal work of the farmer all planned beforehand. Others decide in the autumn or summer previous, and others still delay until spring even the decision as to what fields to put under plow and where to put their manure. The aimless course is almost sure to bring delays and disappointments which are readily ascribed to *the weather*. He who works with a steady aim attains the greater success with much less labor.

**Animals**—The maintenance of animals in the stable or in the yards at any time of the year is unnatural, but, if they have a great abundance of food and considerable range, the conditions surrounding them approach those that they are subject to in the wild state. The amount of food animals exposed to the weather will eat is enormous, and even then they never come out in more than fair condition. We think every spring that it is almost absurd to reiterate our condemnation of farmers who expect, as a matter of course, to have their cattle "spring poor." This condition of a man's stock tells of exposure, lack of good food, and of very serious losses to the farmer himself—losses both of fodder wasted and of cattle injured in their productiveness for the rest of the year, or the rest of their lives.

**Working Stock** should be fitted for hard labor by increasing their grain and accustoming them gradually to severer demands upon their strength and endurance. Horses' shoulders are apt to gall, and oxen's necks will become sore if they have done little work during the winter. Look out for such troubles, and bind on wet cloths at night, greasing the spots when the yoke or harness is again put on; but above all have well-fitting yokes and harness.

**Milch Cows**—Now is the time when rutabagas and mangels will tell on milk production. Cows coming in this month should have succulent food, if possible. Half a bushel, or even a peck, of roots will make a marked difference in the yield of milk, and soon after calving it will pay over and over again to feed oil cake, from one to three quarts daily. Soak until all the lumps are broken up, and pour the gruel on cut corn stalks or hay.

**Calves**—It is more humane, and better policy besides, to take away the calf, which is to be removed in a few days at farthest, as soon as it is dropped. The cow "takes on" less, and the calf does not mind the separation at all. It will learn to drink from a pail readily. Its diet at first must be its dam's new milk, and then any sweet milk; after the first week it may be changed gradually to skimmed milk with a little oil-meal gruel, or a thin porridge of wheat middlings mingled with it—the quantity of meal being increased as it grows, and that of milk lessened. Scours may usually be checked by a little scalded fine-flour porridge, and constipation by oil-meal. Young calves should be fed four times a day, dividing the periods equally between 5 or 6 o'clock in the morning and 9 or 10 at night. After a few days, three times a day will be enough.

**Sheep**—Examine the flocks carefully so as to be sure that each sheep gets its share of grain or roots. Give ewes near yeaning pens where they are not crowded, littered with short straw, trodden firm. Early lambs are well worth extra care in raising. If found chilled, they should be brought to the house and warmed at the fire or by a warm bath and rubbing. A mild milk punch sometimes has an excellent effect.

**Swine**—Breeding sows should be placed, isolated, in warm, well-littered pens several days before farrowing. Feed roots as a guard against constipation. Raw potatoes are excellent. Charcoal dust with a portion of ashes is uniformly good, and by all menas throw them a few fresh sods to root over and chew. A thorough carding is also beneficial, and, if a man pets his pigs and really desires to have the young litters in the very best condition, he will do all he can to have the sows not only well-fed but in the very best health.

**The Currycomb, Card, and Brush** are among the best friends of the farmer and his stock, especially when the animals are shedding their coats. Every horse, young and old, should have a good grooming daily, cattle twice, and hogs once a week. Carrots appear to have a remarkable effect upon the coats of cattle and horses. Four quarts a day is enough, if fed with other roots, grain, bran, or oil cake.

**Buildings**, the foundations of which have been disturbed by the frost, should be at once settled to their proper bearings. The present is a good season for outside painting and any repairing.

**Manure**—That not intended for immediate use may be forked over and laid up in good-sized heaps, well trodden down, to undergo another fermentation before its use in May or later in the season. Manure that cannot be plowed under, harrowed in, or in some way immediately incorporated with soil, should not be spread in the field, but left in heaps till it can be. Exposure of a day or two to the sun and wind is often a serious detriment. Top-dressings of animal manure upon grass or grain are of comparatively little avail in the spring. Ashes, phosphates, fish manure, guano, bone meal, etc., if purchased at reasonable rates, are economically applied at this season.

**Pick up Stones**—As soon as the surface is thawed, the stones will be loosened and may be picked up and laid in heaps, or at once loaded into wagons or boats, and removed. Many hands make light work at this business, and half a dozen neighbors' boys may be hired to work for a few days and they will

make fun of the job. Mowing land, newly plowed ground, and fields of winter grain should certainly be gleaned over. A stone which is fast may often be loosened by being struck with another, and those which the boys cannot start will most of them yield to a few blows from a pick.

**Fences**—When the ground is loosened by the frost coming out and the land is still too wet to plow, all hands may be set at fence making—resetting posts, renewing rails, staking, bracing, etc. The material needed, and that for new fences, should have been prepared from fall-cut wood during the winter.

**Soiling**—Rye will be the first crop ready to cut for soiling. It will respond quickly to a dressing of 100 or 200 pounds of guano, which, if applied just after the frost leaves the ground, will probably not only add considerably to the crop, but will bring it on notably earlier. If cut so as to allow it to make a second growth, the top-dressing may be given at the time of cutting. Oats, sowed as early as the ground is fit, at the rate of 4 bushels to the acre, are regarded as the best crop to follow fall-sowed grains.

**Field Work**—*Clover* and *grass seed* may be sown on the winter grain. *Grain* and *grass* fields may be rolled as soon as the frost is out, thus resetting the roots laid bare by the action of frost and wind and sinking the small stones. Plowing and harrowing may be done when the ground is dry enough.

*Potatoes* may be planted on warm, early land, using good-sized seed not cut small, and if cut at all left some days to "heal" before planting.

**Spring Grains**—It is generally best, north of latitude 40 degrees, to sow in April, but, where the ground is warm and can be thoroughly prepared beforehand, it is well to get all kinds, even peas, in as early as possible. *Peas* and *oats* sown together are an excellent crop for feeding green, or for cutting and curing before ripe enough to shell, to be fed in the straw, or when ripe, to be thrashed and ground together for feed.

**Work for odd times**—The weather and other things will cause unavoidable delays, but few compared with those coming from our own improvidence or thoughtlessness. Always have work for odd times: clear up around the house and barn; work over manure; prepare composts of hen manure or privy soil for corn, or for top-dressing grain or grass; collect chip dirt where old wood piles have stood; make ditches to spread the wash of highways over the grass; get out pea brush and bean poles, trimming and sharpening them ready for use; and clean out the well and cistern, if necessary.

**Prepare for a Good Garden**, which should be the pride of every farm. Read the hints under "Kitchen Garden," and if there is a probability that it will be well looked to, make a hotbed, and sow lettuce, radishes, early cabbages and cauliflowers, peppers, tomatoes and eggplants. Cucumbers, melons, and squashes, started on pieces of sod, may be removed to the open ground when danger from frost is past.

HINTS ABOUT HORTICULTURAL WORK

The time for performing the different operations of outdoor work is well known to those with experience. To the novice we would say, do not be in too great a hurry; after the frost has gone, the ground must drain and dry and get in working order. Set out all hardy trees, shrubs, and plants as soon as the soil can be made fit to receive them. Sow seeds of hardy vegetables, peas, turnips, carrots, cabbage, etc. as soon as the frost is out and the ground can be worked. For tender plants, such as squashes, melons, tomatoes, etc., the time for corn planting—well established in every locality—is the safest guide.

*Orchard and Nursery*

One of the first things to be done is to care for:

**Girdled Trees**, which should be attended to as soon as the injury is discovered. The manner of treating them was given in last month's "Hints."

**Order Trees** from the nursery at once if this has not been done. If planting with a view to selling fruit, have a few kinds that are known to succeed in the locality, rather than many but little-known ones.

**Plant** as soon as the soil can be thoroughly prepared. If not ready to set the trees as soon as they arrive, unpack and

**Heel-in** at once, taking care to put the different kinds so that there will be no confusion of names.

**Pruning at Planting**, and indeed pruning at all, has been much discussed, but we have seen nothing to convince us that it is not both advisable and necessary. Cut back at least one-third of the branches of the tree before setting.

**Deep Planting** is injurious; the tree should be set no lower than it stood in the nursery, allowing for the settling of the newly disturbed soil.

**Grafting** is not to be done until the buds upon the stock show signs of starting; the cherry and plum should both be grafted very early.

See notes of January and February for other work which may yet to be done.

*Fruit Garden*

**Planting** of all kinds is to be done as soon as the soil is in good working order.

**Grape Vines** that were not pruned last fall should be attended to. In planting young vines, cut them back to two or three buds, and then allow but one of these to grow the first year. Much of the failure

with grapes is due to planting a long vine and allowing it to grow as it pleases.

**Grape Cuttings** are best kept out of the soil until it gets thoroughly warmed to some depth.

**Currant Cuttings**, as well as those of the Gooseberry, are to be planted as soon as the ground is ready. In setting these, as well as other cuttings, have the earth well packed around their lower ends, even rammed down firm against them.

**Currant and Gooseberry Bushes** should be transplanted as early as the weather will allow, as should

**Blackberries and Raspberries**; these should be cut back and the growth started from buds at or near the root. If the canes are not cut back, some fruit will be borne the present year at the expense of the future welfare of the plants. In the West these fruits are grown in hedges; the plants are set two or three feet apart in the row, and when the raspberries are a foot high, and the blackberries two feet, the shoot is pinched, and the side shoots are pinched when they are a foot long. It is said that in this way a very large crop of fruit is obtained, and the plants become self-supporting.

**Strawberries**—Set as early as the plants can be had; one foot to 18 inches, or two feet for the large growing sorts, is the usual distance between plants for garden culture.

**Trees** in the garden will need the general care indicated in this and previous months under "Orchard."

## Kitchen Garden

If the preparatory work is not well along, it will not be because we have not given frequent injunctions to collect manure, procure seeds, repair tools, and consider all the ways and means beforehand!

**Preparing the Soil** should be done at the earliest practicable moment, but not until it is sufficiently dry. In properly drained gardens the work can be done much earlier than in others. Deep plowing and subsoiling are best for a garden large enough to allow this kind of work. It is advisable to have no trees or bushes in a kitchen garden, or, if they must be there, let them (as well as such permanent plants as rhubarb, asparagus, etc.) be so placed as not to interfere with the free and frequent working of the portion devoted to vegetables. In small gardens deep spading must be resorted to.

**Hotbeds** are to be made and the seeds sown. It is much more economical of heating material to place it in an excavation. Dig a trench 2 feet deep and of convenient size for the sash on hand. Drive down stakes, and board up the sides of the pit, the boards at the rear being 18 inches and those at the front (facing the south), 12 inches above the surface. Provide cleats extending from side to side for the sashes to run upon, and board up the ends. Fill the trench with fermenting manure, distributing it evenly and beating it down with a fork, or use one-third or more leaves with the manure. Put on 6 inches of rich, light soil and place on the sashes. The bed will become very hot, and, when the heat declines below 100 degrees, the seeds may be sown. Sow tomatoes, peppers, eggplants, early cabbages, etc. in rows crosswise of the bed and about 4 inches apart. Cover small seeds very lightly.

**Cold Frames** are much safer for the inexperienced than hotbeds. Place a frame over a well-prepared spot of light, rich soil; put on the sash; and at night cover the sash with mats or shutters. In a few days the soil will become well warmed, when the seeds may be sown the same as in a hotbed.

**Air and Water** must be properly given in either hotbeds or cold frames. The water should have the chill removed and be applied from a fine sprinkler. Give air every day when not too cold.

**Planting on Sods**—This simple but useful contrivance may be new to some. Get a good bit of pasture sod, and lay it on a board, grass side down; then with a knife cut it into pieces about three inches square. In the earth of these sods the seeds of any of those plants that are not easily transplanted may be sown. Place the whole in a hotbed or cold frame. Cucumbers and melons seem to delight in this treatment. At the proper time the sods are planted out without disturbing the roots of the plants. It is well to put a half-dozen seeds in each, and thin out to two or three. Some hills of early corn, and even potatoes, may be had in this way.

**Plants in the house** may be started in common boxes.

**Cabbage Plants** and others that have been wintered in frames must be freely exposed, and generally the sashes may be removed altogether.

**Asparagus** is to have the litter removed and some good manure carefully forked into the beds; give a dressing of salt. Sow the seeds early for new plants in rows a foot apart, and make new beds.

**Rhubarb** needs the same treatment, except the salt; divide old roots and make new beds, setting the portions of root, with a bud in each, 3 or 4 feet apart each way, according to the size of the variety.

**Sow Seeds** of beets, carrots, spinach, salsify, onions, leek and early turnips in rows 15 inches apart and cress and lettuce in rows a foot apart.

**Radishes** may be grown by themselves in rows a foot apart, or be sown bewteen the rows of beets.

**Peas** — Sow some of the early sorts, putting the seeds 3 or 4 inches deep.

**Potatoes** — Plant good early sorts.

**Onions** — Sets are to be planted early, 4 or 5 inches apart in rows a foot apart.

**Parsnips and Salsify** that have remained in the ground over winter should be dug before they grow.

**In the South** the tender vegetables may be sown (such as sweet corn, beans, and okra,) and sweet potatoes may be planted.

## Flower Garden and Lawn

The heavy work of preparing the soil, etc., should be pushed along whenever the weather will allow.

**Paths** should be thoroughly done; provide for good drainage and a solid roadbed.

**Lawns** are too often slighted; as with paths, the best part of the work is out of sight. Deep working, draining, manuring, and leveling are all requisite to a good lawn.

### ASPARAGUS WORTH GROWING.

ONE-HALF THE AVERAGE SIZE.

**Trees** of all deciduous kinds may be transplanted.

**Hardy Shrubs** are to be transplanted; clumps of these often grow so dense as to need thinning out.

**Tender Shrubs** that have been protected during the winter should not have the covering material removed before the weather becomes settled. The alternation of warm days and cold nights that occurs in spring is often more injurious to such plants than the continued cold of winter.

**Uncover** beds of bulbs, but have a little litter handy to throw over them in case of sudden cold.

**Perennials** of most kinds that have been 3 or 4 years in a spot do the better for dividing and replanting.

## Greenhouse and Window Plants

**Propagation** for a supply of plants to use for bedding purposes can now go on rapidly. Where there is a greenhouse and a gardener, no instructions are needed, but in the absence of these,

**Saucer Propagation** is the great resource of the amateur. A shallow dish of sand, always kept wet — *in the condition of thin mud* — allows for the rapid multiplication of most plants. We have tried it with things of the most diverse nature and know that it will succeed (1) if the cuttings are sufficiently succulent, (2) the sand is kept thoroughly wet, and (3) the saucer is exposed to full light. As soon as the plants make root, they must be potted in light and rich soil.

**Camellias** bear all needed pruning. The only time the camellia can be forced is when it is making its growth. Rapid growth and early formed buds will give early flowers next autumn.

**Plants in Cellars** are to be brought forward according to the season. Exposure to light, water, and heat will soon start them into growth.

**Insects** will increase with the season. Prevention by fumigation is better than cure. Make a smoke of tobacco in the houses at least twice a week.

# PROJECTS FOR
# MARCH

## Plain Directions for Grafting

Grafting is simply taking a twig from one tree and planting it in the limb of another, the conditions of success being that the *inner bark* of the two must be in perfect contact and that the point where they join must be so covered that neither the cion nor stock will become dry.

**Materials**—The cions should be cut before the buds begin to swell and be preserved in damp earth in a cool place. They may be buried in the cellar or out of doors. If taken late in winter or early in spring, the upper portion of the cuttings should be rejected as this is frequently winterkilled or has its vitality impaired by the severe cold. Exercise care in the selection of varieties and keep the cions properly labeled after they are cut. Prepare a supply of waxed cloth according to the directions given for root grafting in January. Some use grafting wax without the aid of cloth. To prepare this, the composition directed for the cloth is thoroughly melted, poured into water, and when sufficiently cool, is taken out and worked in the hands, in the same manner as candy, until it is of a uniform character throughout. The hands may be rubbed with tallow to prevent the wax from sticking to them. Grafting clay, made by working together clay or strong loam and cow dung, is sometimes used with success.

**Tools**—A fine saw with the teeth set rather wide will be needed for taking off the limbs. For splitting the limbs in cleft-grafting, a chisel, stout knife, or a grafting knife may be used. *Fig. 1* shows the common form of grafting knife, consisting of a steel blade fastened to an iron back, which is turned up at the end to furnish a wedge with which to open the cleft. Where this is not used, a wedge of hardwood will be needed. A wooden mallet will be required and also a sharp knife to prepare the cions. In crown-grafting, an iron bodkin *(fig. 2)* is used to lift the bark. This is in the shape of a half-rounded wedge and may be made of a half-round file, heating and slowly cooling to soften it and then grinding it smooth. A substitute may be readily made from hardwood.

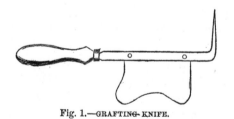

Fig. 1.—GRAFTING-KNIFE.

Fig. 2.

**Practical Operations**—The renewal of a tree should not be done all at once, but extend through three, or at least two, years, beginning with the upper part. In renewing the head, regard should be had to the future form of the tree, recollecting that a small cion will ultimately become a limb and that an overcrowded head (as well as one too thin) is to be avoided. The limbs are usually sawn so as to leave only about 6 inches in length for the reception of the grafts. In sawing, care should be taken that the weight of the branch does not break it off before it is completely severed as this would strip away the bark from the lower side and leave an ugly wound. The limb should be held firmly until it is completely cut through, and it is safest to cut a ring through the bark with the knife at the place where the saw cut is to be made. The rough surface left by the saw is to be smoothed by paring with the knife or drawing knife, and a split is to be made for the reception of the grafts. Place the chisel, knife, or grafting tool across the end of the butt, and, with a few moderate blows of the mallet, split it to the extent of an inch or two. A cion is prepared by cutting its lower part to the shape of a long wedge *(fig. 3)*, taking care to have a bud (*A*) at the base of the wedge. It is customary to make the edge of the wedge opposite to this bud slightly thinner than the other. The cleft being sprung open by means of a wooden wedge, or the turned up portion of the grafting tool, the cion is inserted with the bud *A* outward, taking care that its inner bark and that of the stock come in contact. In stocks an inch or more in diameter, two cions are usually placed, one of which is ultimately cut away. When the opening wedge is withdrawn, the cions are held quite firmly. The whole wounded portion must then be covered with waxed cloth. Tear off a strip long enough to go two or three times around the limb and wide enough to cover the split and to

double over and cover the end of the butt. The strip is to be wrapped closely around and fitted nicely about the cions so as to form an air and watertight covering over all the wounded portions (*fig. 5*). It takes longer to describe than it does to perform the operation, and a little practice on a few limbs taken off for the purpose will give the needed facility in working. Those who make a business of grafting usually prepare the cions first and hold them in the mouth while splitting the stock. The waxed or grafting cloth is the easiest of application, but some prefer to use the wax alone. Waxed cloth is prepared as directed above, in convenient-sized rolls, and, in use, a small portion is pulled off and smeared over the cut portions by means of the ball of the thumb. A piece of tallow should be used to grease the hands if either the wax or cloth are disposed to stick to them. When small stocks are cleft-grafted, only one cion is used and about half the stock is cut away in a sloping manner as shown in *fig. 6*. A cut of this kind heals over more readily than one made straight across.

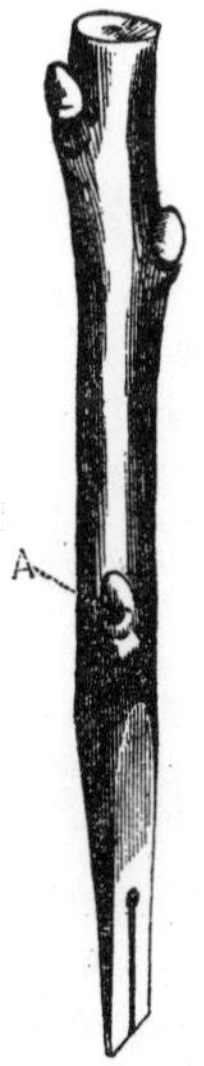

Fig. 5.—BANDAGE.

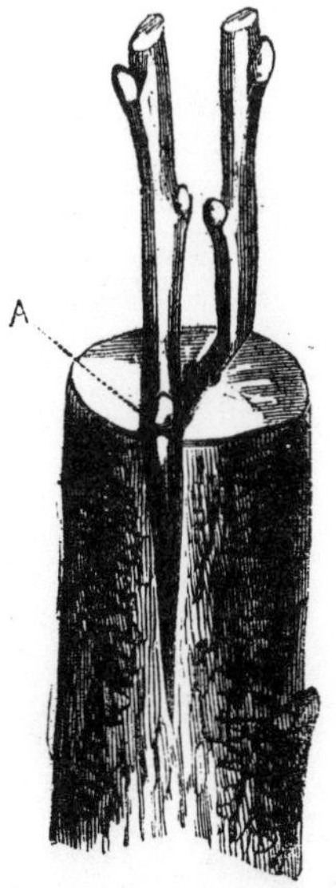

Fig. 6.—SMALL STOCK.

**Crown-Grafting**—In cleft-grafting a split is left which never fills up; to obviate this, many practice what is called *crown-grafting*. The stock is prepared as already directed, but not split. The cion, instead of being cut as in cleft-grafting, is shaved down on one side only to form a half-round wedge with a shoulder, like *fig. 7*, with a bud at *A* as before. To insert the cion, the bodkin (*fig. 2*) is forced between the bark and wood of the stock so as to lift the bark (no matter if it cracks), and on being withdrawn the cion is pressed into the opening thus made, its cut

Fig. 3.—CION.

Fig. 4.—CION INSERTED.

Fig. 7—CION
FOR CROWN-
GRAFTING.

Fig. 8. CROWN GRAFTED.

## Splitting Firewood

In most parts of the North many farmers are busy a portion of the time, from January to April, in cutting and hauling their firewood for next year. For the most part, it is sawed, split, and piled during the wet and stormy weather of March and April, when workmen cannot engage in field labors. This is a good practice and worthy of adoption by scores of slipshod farmers who commence a year beforehand to prepare their firewood for a year to come, but who are never able to get it split and piled in time to allow it to become well seasoned before it is to be burned.

There is much bad management with firewood. Allowing it to remain for several months exposed to the weather after it has been cut and split fine enough for the stove is a very bad practice. Its quality will be injured, more or less, and it will never make as much heat as though it had been piled under an open shed as soon as split and before it was seasoned.

The labor of splitting firewood for stoves may be greatly facilitated by using a splitting bench,

portion being toward the center of the stock *(fig. 8)*. Two or three cions may be introduced, according to the size of the stock; then cover the wounded portions with cloth or wax as before. Grafting should be done just as the trees are beginning to start. It is not well to do it too early, as the cions are exposed for a long time to the cold winds and are apt to die. The grafts should be looked to after they are set to see that the binding or the wax covers do not become displaced.

which is represented by the illustration. It is made in the following manner:

Procure two small logs or round sticks of wood, about 3 or 4 feet long and 6 or 8 inches in diameter. Connect the two logs with a 2-inch wooden round near each end, as shown by the engraving, so as to form an opening about 10 or 12 inches square. Place this frame on four strong legs driven firmly into the logs in the underside. Place billets of wood in the bench, standing on one end, and apply the ax. The object of the bench is to keep the wood erect while it is being split.

When a splitting bench is not used, the workman is obliged to set up the billet every time a stick is split off. Consequently, he will spend as much or perhaps more time in simply setting up his sticks in a proper position for splitting than he will in splitting them. After a billet of wood has been placed in the splitting bench, a man may split three or four of them fine enough for the stove about as soon as he will be able to split *one* stick without using such a bench. The height of the bench should be about two-thirds the length of the wood that is to be split.

A splitting bench of a different style may be constructed by using the crotch of a tree, with a stick fastened across the two branches. In using any kind of a wood splitting bench, care must be exercised not to allow the ax to pass through a stick so far as to permit the helve to strike on one of the sides of the bench, as one careless blow would break it. Let the blows be applied in such a manner that the edge of the ax will pass through the upper end of a billet of wood and strike the side log.

Wood splits much more readily in the direction up from the root of the tree than when the blow of the ax is downward. In other words, to split a chunk place it upside down—contrary to the direction in which it grew. It is much easier to split by slabs than to try to cleave through the center. This means to split off pieces near the edge.

For splitting wood most economically, use a device as shown in the drawing. Take a 2 x 8-inch plank about 3 feet long and an upright of the same material about 20 inches long. Set this upright at an angle of 20 degrees and use a brace of the same material. The sharp points shown in the drawing are wire nails. Set the wood against these spikes in splitting it.

### Laying Out a Garden

As a vegetable garden is not for ornament, the plan should be the simplest possible and made with a view to facilitate working. The garden illustrated here contains an acre, and, in representing it on so small a scale, the paths and borders are necessarily made too large in proportion. The borders are occupied by small fruits as indicated in the plan. A gate at *C* opens near the house, and another at *D*, near the barn, is wide enough to admit a wagon.

*A* is a bed 16 feet wide, running from the house entrance to the foot of the garden; this is devoted to radishes, onions, beets, etc., which are all planted in rows across the bed. At the upper end of this bed is a hotbed (*H.B.*), near the house since it requires frequent visits. Then comes a rhubarb patch (*R*), 5 hills

### Another Way to Split Wood

WOOD SPLITTING DEVICE

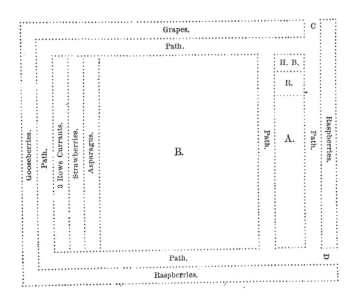

square, which affords an abundance. Below the rhubarb this long bed has no subdivisions; one article follows another, without loss of space. For the use of a good-sized family, 25 rows of beets are needed, the same of onions, 10 of parsnips, 5 of carrots, and 3 sowings of radishes, 8 or 10 days apart, and 3 sowings of radishes, 8 or 10 days apart, 8 rows at each sowing. The parsnips should be next to the rhubarb, to be out of the way in the spring or fall if you wish to plow or spade the bed. This bed affords room for any new thing and for early squashes or cucumbers.

Corn, early potatoes, sweet potatoes, tomatoes, cabbages, snap beans, cucumbers, and melons occupy the next space (*B*). All these are planted in rows running through from north to south and are worked by a plow; the paths afford turning places. Twelve rows of corn at two plantings, and one each of tomatoes, snap beans, and cucumbers are sufficient. All the permanent things—strawberries, asparagus, etc.—are placed together.

### Storing Water

An easy way to make a reservoir at the spring is to throw up a bank, perhaps laying a wall first, founding it below the surface. Should the soil be such that water percolates through it, face the soil with loam on top and puddle it well. If this leaks, face it with

clay and puddle the clay. These rules apply to all dams made of stone and earth.

Pipes entering reservoirs should enter at the bottom and the soil be well puddled around them to prevent the water working through beside the pipe. Each pipe must have a strainer over its supply end and have no air holes in its entire length.

A good strainer can be made from a piece of large pipe punched full of holes. One end may be flattened or turned over and the other drawn on over the end of the water pipe. Let nobody suppose that simple, inexpensive arrangements are faulty because primitive. If constructed correctly and in line with natural laws, they are not only all right, but are preferable to fancy, complicated devices that get out of order easily or in a year or two and require a master mechanic to put them into working condition again.

### A Barbed Wire Tightener

Here is a device easily made and very convenient to use in tightening barbed wire when stringing it upon the posts. Cut out a piece of inch board in the shape shown in the picture with a notch to let in the face of a hammer. Insert a long bolt at the point indicated by the light dotted lines to prevent splitting. Fasten

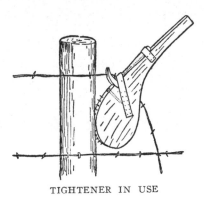

TIGHTENER IN USE

on the hammer with leather straps. The sharp brads should stick out about half an inch. Carefully finish the handle so that it will be smooth and not hurt the hands when you are using the device. It should be made of tough hardwood.

## A Safe Way to String Barbed Wire

One of the most satisfactory ways to unreel barbed wire is to make a contrivance similar to the one illustrated here. Fasten a short piece of plank to the front end of a "stone boat" or drag. Bore a 2-inch hole in this plank and set the spool of barbed wire on top. Run a piece of pipe about 5 feet long through the spool and let the bottom end rest in the hole made in the plank. Attach the drag to the rear of your farm wagon and have an assistant sit in the wagon and hold the top end of the pipe. If the wire becomes kinked, the assistant simply lets go of the pipe and the spool rolls off the boat without breaking the wire.

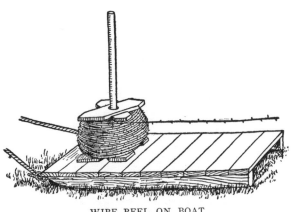

WIRE REEL ON BOAT

## How to Catch an Owl

Owls are very destructive to poultry, especially in the breeding season, and are much more dangerous than hawks, inasmuch as they pay their visits to the roosts in the night. There is no effectual safeguard against their visits unless you have the hennery made owl-proof. Most farmers make their roosts under an open shed, or even upon the trees, which are as free to birds of prey as to the hens. Chickens are very delicate food for young owls, and sometimes a dozen will be missing from the perch in a night and their feathers and claws will be found the next day in a neighboring owl's nest. Old hens will be taken and their heads eaten off and the carcass dropped under the tree, quite too heavy for the owl to carry off. Not a moment should be lost when these depredations occur. Tie the dead fowl upon the limb or the perch where it was accustomed to roost, and shut up the other fowls. The dead fowl should be tied in a roosting position so as to seem alive to the owl. Place a small mousetrap on the back of the hen and fasten it to a neighboring limb. The owl will generally make his appearance the following night, and in swooping down upon the back of the hen will find his claws securely caught in the trap.

It should be noted, of course, that this wise bird that plunders in the night is the enemy of chicken farmers only. He is in every other respect one of the farmer's best friends since he is an indefatigable killer of mice. The remedy above, therefore, should be employed only by the chicken farmer so threatened by owls that he is at the "end of his tether." Any why not build an enclosed hennery instead?

## Three Simple Board Fences

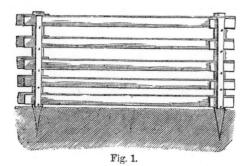

Fig. 1.

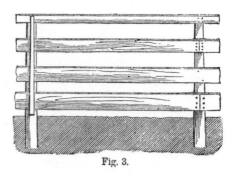

Fig. 3.

*Fig. 1* is a straight board fence, 4½ feet high. Its advantages over the common board fence are as follows: It is substantial, tasteful, economical, easily built, easily moved, and any length may be taken out like a pair of bars. If the posts heave out, they can be driven down again. No nails are driven through the boards; consequently, the lumber is not injured for any other purpose; and on flowed lands the boards may be taken out in the fall and put in again in the spring. The materials are as follows: *Boards,* chestnut or pine, 11 feet long, 6 inches wide; *posts,* chestnut or oak, 7 feet long, round or half-round, split or square, sharpened and driven 2½ feet into the ground, 10 feet apart; *cleats,* chestnut or oak, 4½ feet long, 2 inches wide, 1¼ inch thick; *nails,* one six-penny nail to each board.

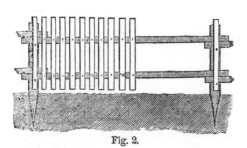

Fig. 2.

*Fig. 2* is a straight picket fence, 3 feet 10 inches high, tasteful and economical. *Posts,* 6 feet long, 10 feet apart; *rails,* 11 feet long, 2 x 3 inches; *pickets,* 3 feet 10 inches long, 3 inches wide, 1 inch thick; 2 seven-penny *nails* to each length. To rebuild either of these fences where decayed, split open the old rotten posts to get the nails, and then set up the lengths and fasten them with nails and cleats to the new posts.

*Fig. 3* is known as a running or strip fence. *Posts*—Chestnut timber is preferred. The posts are sawed 7 feet long, 4 x 5 inches at the bottom, and 3 x 4 at the top, and all set 4 feet 2 inches above ground, 8 feet apart. They should be cut in winter when the sap is down, for they will thus be lighter to cut and handle, and dry out quicker. They may be set as they grew, or reversed, whichever way they will saw to the best advantage. *Boards*—For strips, employ hemlock, sawed one inch thick and 16 feet long. Two courses of 7-inch strips at the bottom, 3 inches apart, and two courses of 5-inch strips, 8 inches apart, starting 5 inches from the ground, will make the fence 4 feet 2 inches high, as required. A cap rail or strip is necessary for strength, but gives the whole a neater appearance. If used, it may be sloped to turn rain more readily. No fixed rule is necessary for this. Each board will require 6 ten-penny nails, driven 1½ inches from the ends and edges. Break joints, by all means, to secure strength, and a batten is absolutely indispensable.

## Raising Evergreens from Seed

Seedlings of the evergreens are the most difficult to manage of any that come under the care of the propagator. The seeds abound in an oily, resinous fluid that quickly becomes rancid and destroys the germ if they are taken from the cones a long time before using. The seeds of most species may be preserved for several years if allowed to remain in the cones until wanted for planting. Most kinds germinate easily, but the critical season is when the true leaves are being developed and before the stem becomes firm and woody. At this period the propagator should be on the alert to guard against sudden changes in the atmosphere or an excess of moisture. *Damping off* is the bane of young evergreen seedlings, and the most experienced hand not infrequently finds himself at fault to counteract it. A sprinkling of sulphur will destroy the various fungoid growths so destructive to young evergreens, and dry sand counteracts the effects of too much moisture in the soil.

The fundamental principle in growing conifers is to plant at the *very earliest moment* in the spring, as no amount of care or forcing by artificial heat will compensate for lost time. Some of the more hardy species will succeed in our variable climate without resorting to glass coverings: as, for instance, the arbor vitaes, Norway spruce, Austrian and Scotch pines, red cedar, etc. In the case of these, we select a sheltered spot and prepare the ground in the preceding autumn by carefully pulverizing the soil and incorporating a fair proportion of sharp sand with it, but never using stimulating manures. A coating of ashes is excellent. The following spring, as soon as the soil is in a suitable condition for the operation, shallow drills may be drawn out, and the seeds thinly sown. The soil should then be gently beaten down with the back of the spade, and nothing further will be necessary until the appearance of the seedlings, which soon occurs after a few warm days. We very much question whether any benefit results from deep and frequent cultivation of the soil between

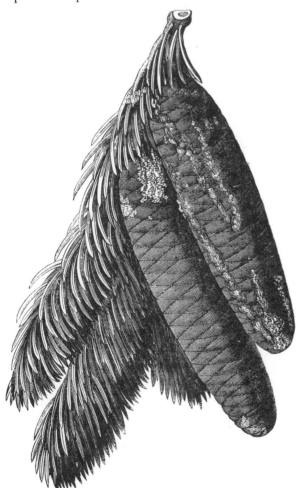

the rows, as our own expeience has been exactly the reverse. Young evergreens appear to need a compact soil to counteract the tendency to dampen off, and they will survive the first summer more readily if the weeds are pulled without the use of the hoe.

Such species as produce berry-like fruit should have their pulpy covering removed by washing as soon as gathered, and the seeds placed in boxes of sand or sowed at once in beds where they are to remain. If allowed to become dry, they will frequently lie in the ground for two and even three years before germinating. This applies to the yews, junipers, and red cedar.

With the rarer kinds of evergreens, the following contrivance has been used with excellent success. A cold frame is raised above the bed by placing a brick flat on its side, under each corner. After sowing the seeds, the sash should be placed on, and a thin coat of whitewash applied to the glass to break the direct rays of the sun, after which an occasional slight syringing will supply all needful moisture.

This plan insures a free circulation of air, a moist atmosphere, and partial shade. Sometimes one becomes possessed of a few very rare seeds, upon which he desires to bestow extra pains. In such cases prepare some turfy, sandy soil, and fill large pots within one or two inches of the rim. Sow the seeds in the autumn, as soon after gathering as possible, and place a pane of glass on the pot. The pots must then be set in a cool greenhouse or pit, secure from frost. Under the staging is a suitable spot. Towards spring the seed leaves will commence making their appearance, and moisture must be withheld as much as possible—never, however, allowing the plants to actually suffer. When the young seedlings are well established and show signs of producing their true leaves, they should at once be pricked out into single pots and placed in a cool, shady place for the remainder of the season. In summing up the requirements of evergreen seedlings of their growth, we may say that in all cases they must have a *free circulation of air, shade, moisture over the plants. but not in the soil, and an early planting.*

# FARM AND GARDEN WORK FOR

# April

April is one of the most indefinite months; March work holds on into it, even though May weather prevails. Besides, there is almost always a great deal of work which inopportune rains will postpone and again postpone, quite into next month. There should be an early division of work thus: dry soil work, rainy day work, and work for fair days when the soil is wet; this makes three good divisions. Nothing should interrupt the work in the field and garden while the soil is in good condition for working. With proper diligence all that needs to be done indoors, or that can be done on rainy days, or while the soil is too moist to work, may be accomplished without infringing upon the good days for field work. If plans are not well matured for the summer campaign, lose no time before forming them. If there are seeds to buy, tools to provide, or anything of that kind to do, delay not. If we begin the season with good "help," good teams, good tools, good seeds, all the manure we can get, and the best plans we can make, after doing all we possibly can we may rely upon Providence for sunshine and showers and fruitful seasons.

## HINTS ABOUT FARM WORK

Review what was said in March with regard to winter grains, grass, soiling, and the working of wet soils.

**Double Cropping** — Land to be suited for raising two crops in one season must be rich, in good tilth, and free as possible from weeds — in fact, like a good garden. Early potatoes, peas, onions, early cabbages, or any early soiling crop may be followed by cabbages, rutabagas, common turnips, pickles, etc. Onions will leave the ground for carrots, which should have been sowed at the last hoeing between the rows, and cabbages may be set out before the potatoes are dug.

**Animals** — Let stock of all kinds have frequent carding and some hours of sunshine daily. Only in the South will the grass be forward enough to be pastured without danger to the crop. The temptation will be great to turn cattle upon the fresh meadows in case forage is scarce, but it will be much better both for the stock and the pasturage to feed a month longer, perhaps, on corn stalks. The first lands that are fit to turn stock upon are unreclaimed bogs, where the coarse grass growing in tussocks has been burnt off. Such grass is sweet and juicy early in the spring, and eaten with zest after the dry fodder of winter; but it soon becomes wiry and hard and will be refused by the stock. If fed off close when it first starts, it will keep on growing and furnish considerable feed. Nevertheless such land is very unprofitable property.

**Horses** shedding their coats may have a quart of oil meal fed to each daily with cut feed or on a peck of carrots. Feed work horses well. If kept steadily at work, calculate to feed so well that they will not fall off at all in flesh. Daily thorough grooming is worth four quarts of feed a day at this season, even for farm horses. Mares near foaling must be well fed, relieved from severe labor, and as their

bred of fullblood sires, by all means secure them; they grow faster and fatten more easily.

**Chickens**—There are some useful hints to follow. Several painful diseases are apt to attack fowls in wet springs, of which the worst are the roup, and that disease so close akin to it as to be confounded with it—swelled-head. Both are brought about by uncleanly apartments, and both are highly contagious; although the previous preparation of the system by exposure to wetness and filth seems to be an almost essential condition. A cold will run into roup if any roupy fowls are about the yard. In bad weather, give an iron tonic, say a teaspoonful of tincture of iron, wet up in a quart of corn meal, to a flock of twenty. About a tablespoonful of red pepper may be mixed with it to good advantage.

time approaches given roomy quarters in loose boxes. A box 10 feet square is none too large. A slightly loose condition of the bowels in breeding animals is always favorable and should be induced by feeding roots, oil cake or flaxseed.

**Oxen**—Feed in proportion to work required, card often, give long noonings, and a chance to feed but not to fill themselves. Cattle, like all ruminating animals, eat fast and do their chewing afterwards. An ox that is put to work with his paunch full of unmasticated food is lazy, at least, and probably more liable than otherwise to be hurt by hard work.

**Cows and Calves**—Refer to last month's hints; we have little to add here. Calves that are beginning to nibble grass a little may be tethered by the fences, where the grass starts green and sweet, and will thus learn to pick up a good living as soon as turned to pasture. Never let the scours run a day.

**Sheep**—Take extra care of the lambs; if stinted in their earliest growth they never catch up. The flock will need close watching to see that no ewes become gargety and their lambs lack milk, that none refuse to own their young, and that no lambs are hurt or sick. Provide fresh water regularly, if not constantly, and by no means neglect salt.

**Swine**—See hints for previous month. If the stock kept is not bred upon the farm, look out early for such pigs as you will need. If these can be had

In fact, this is one of the best preventives of disease, encouragements to laying, and promoters of health, which the poultry breeder can use. Taken early, these diseases may be cured by stimulants and cleanliness, but after the first stage they are usually fatal. Coops for hens and chickens should be placed on clean turf, where no chickens have been, at least since early last spring. Old coops should be well cleaned and whitewashed, and the water furnished to chickens should be so covered that they cannot foul it nor step in it, and protected from the dirt which the old hen throws in all directions by her scratching. We believe absolute cleanliness, on fresh ground, to be a perfect prevention of the gapes.

**Turkeys and Ducks**—Turkeys hatch and care for their own young best. Ducks' eggs, however, ought always to be put under hens. Keep ducks shut up until 8 o'clock every morning, or until all have laid. They lay an egg a day, if well fed, and will steal their nests and hide them where they are hard to find if allowed their freedom. When the eggs are regularly removed, they will not want to sit, but keep on laying until midsummer. Otherwise they sit as soon as they have a nest full of eggs.

**Buildings** — As soon as the weather is warm and settled, open and clear out cellars, both in house and barn, whitewash thoroughly, and stop rat holes and cat holes. Roots still on hand may be put in barrels or boxes so that the bins may be cleaned. Outside painting may be done now, and a better surface may be formed than if the work is done when the wood is thoroughly dry.

**Draining** may often be done in the spring better than at any other season, and spring draining has this great advantage: the filling has all the summer to settle, and there is much less danger of the surface water washing in and gaining direct access to the tiles than when the draining is done in the fall. On this account it is advisable to do the draining on side hills after the heavy spring rains have passed.

**Barnyard Manure and Composts** — Where manure has any value in the estimation of the farmers, nobody has enough. Nevertheless, the prevailing notions about it are so crude that few take the pains they should to increase their manure both in quantity and quality. Manure the land well, or not at all. It does not pay to put on a sprinkling and get half a crop. Manure will secure a reward for labor that can be gained in no other way. Begin the season by making arrangements for saving manure, and thoroughly composting it with muck, sods, or with other vegetable matter later in the season. Manure for use on land intended for rutabagas or other crops sowed in summer should be put in compost heaps and worked over once or twice before it is

used. Poultry-house manure mixed with soil or muck should be frequently worked over and made fine for use upon corn in the hill.

**Liquid Manure** — The leachings of the barn yard, which ought always to flow into a tank especially prepared for them, are among the most valuable additions to a compost heap. Not a particle of it should be allowed to waste or wash away when rains cause an overflow. It will pay well to have a sprinkling cart to carry the liquid upon the lawns or fields, and it is especially useful upon the garden. During a moderate rain, or in showery weather, is the best time to apply it on all well-drained soils.

**Spring Grains** — Wheat and barley should be pickled in a strong brine and dried with lime before sowing to destroy the smut. Sow as early as the ground is brought into fine order, using about 5 to 7 pecks of wheat, 2 bushels to 2½ of barley, and 2½ of oats. The later the grain is sowed the more seed should be used. Heavy, plump seed, free from weed seed, is of prime importance. No rank, heating manure should be used, but fine compost or applications of commercial fertilizers.

**Peas** — The crop should be sown early. In light soils put the seed in deep. It should go upon soil manured last year and free from weeds. A common

practice is to scatter the peas by hand liberally in every third furrow. The furrows should be not more than 4 to 6 inches deep, the depth depending on the soil. Broadcast sowing and drilling are more commonly followed, the latter practice being usually preferred on warm ground. Peas and oats sowed together is a favorite crop with many good farmers, but, as nearly a full crop of each may be produced, the land must be mellow and rich.

**Root Crops**—Sugar beets, mangels, parsnips, and carrots may be sown as early as the ground can be well prepared. These crops can hardly have too rich or well-worked soil, yet they will reward labor on soil which is far from being either as rich or as mellow as it might be. Be sure of good seed. Sow in straight drills so far apart as to allow of horse cultivation. Carrots may have the drills closest, but these should be at least 2 feet apart; 30 inches is none too far for the other roots named. Roots require a good deal of labor, but is well spent.

**Potatoes**—The earliest varieties are the ones for early planting. Plant good-sized seed, cutting the largest potatoes, and aiming to have the pieces fully as large as hens' eggs. Let the cut pieces dry a day or two before planting. Plant close, one piece in a place, and not less than 4 inches deep in dry ground.

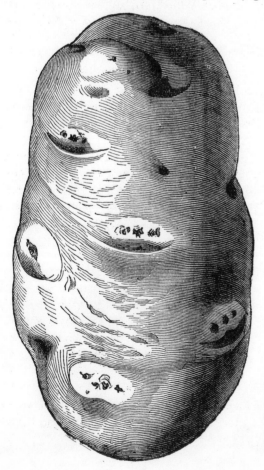

Cover with a plow ridging up a little over the rows, and lay all flat as soon as the plants get above ground with a wooden-toothed harrow, an iron one on its back, or with a bush harrow.

## Hints About Horticultural Work

As a matter of convenience we arrange these notes under different heads, though we are well aware that many have but one garden for small fruits, vegetables, and even flowers. It is better to grow those things so than not at all, but it is on many accounts preferable to have separate compartments set off for the fruit, kitchen, and flower garden. The manuring and frequent working of the soil, so necessary to the production of the best vegetables, is not practicable where permanent beds of fruits are in the way, and while we appreciate the love for flowers that will have them under every disadvantage, we much perfer to see the onions grow at a distance from the tulips. Enthusiastic cultivators are often in a hurry to be at work with the first mild days of spring. It is always best to wait until the soil is in "working order" and will crumble rather than clod when turned by the plow or spade. Work must often be pushed, but never badly done; better do less and do it well.

### Orchard and Nursery

**Plant trees** as soon as they are received. Cut injured roots smooth and shorten the tops. Make a hole broad enough to allow the roots to be spread; throw on some fine soil and work it in among the roots with the fingers so that no hollow places will be left; put on more soil and press it down with the foot, and the tree will not need staking to support it, although a stake to each tree is very useful in laying out the ground before the tree is planted and afterwards in enabling its position to be more readily seen in cultivating.

**Grafting** is to be done upon the plum and the cherry before the buds have started. Other trees may be worked after the buds have swelled.

**Root Grafts and Cuttings** are to be planted in a rich, mellow bed as soon as the soil can be prepared.

**Seeds** of all kinds for raising your nursery stock should be sown as soon as possible.

**Insects** have been sufficiently commented upon in previous months; continue to destroy them.

### Fruit Garden

If constant pleading would effect it, every farm would have a fruit garden, and every farmer's table would have an abundance of fruit. A few neglected currant bushes and a run-out strawberry patch too often supply all the summer fruits. We mean a fruit garden which shall be planted and cared for as furnishing necessary food rather than a luxury. Have strawberries, raspberries, blackberries, etc., not by the stinted tea-saucerful, but a big soup dish, heaped at that, at every meal. There is health, comfort, and economy in a fruit garden. So have one. Half an acre or an acre to a good-sized family is not too much, and let the children do all but the heavy work. If limited in means, begin with strawberries and currants. Choose a good soil near the house, manure and plow it thoroughly, and plant these, at least, and as many more as can be had.

**Strawberries**—Eighteen inches apart in rows two feet apart is a good distance. Set as early as possible. If any blossom buds appear this year pick them off. Keep the ground clear of weeds by use of the hoe, and cut the runners off. The plants will form large stools and next year give a good crop of fruit. Beds that were covered last fall should have the straw or other mulch removed from over the crowns.

**Currants** are easily raised from cuttings, and rooted plants may be had at nurseries. Cuttings should have been made earlier, but in many places will do well if put in now. Old and neglected bushes may be made to produce better fruit and more of it by cutting out a good part of the old and stunted wood and leaving an open, well-balanced bush. Spade in good manure around them.

**Blackberries and Raspberries.** See last month's notes.

**Gooseberries** are propagated the same as currants.

**Grape Vines** that have been covered should be placed upon the trellis. If there is room for anything in your fruit garden, plant a grape vine of some kind.

**Figs** may be tried by those who have sheltered places in a mild climate; cover them in winter.

### Kitchen Garden

No matter how rich the garden may be thought to be, most things will be benefitted by more manure. Regular market gardeners use from 50 to 100 tons of stable manure or its equivalent to the acre. See last and previous months for hints on preparation of the soil, hotbeds, cold frames, etc.

**Plant in rows**, as far as possible, as this is much more convenient in working than the old-fashioned way of dividing up the garden into small beds.

**A marker** will be found very convenient in laying off the rows. It is made like a heavy wooden rake, with teeth 12 inches apart on one side and 9 inches apart on the other. By dragging this along the prepared ground, lines for planting are marked.

**Seedbeds** will be needed by those who do not use glass for starting their plants, and for plants for later crops. The soil should be rich and light, of a nature that will not become compacted or caked. Many failures with seeds are due to the inability of the delicate plant to force its way through the heavy, baked soil. Sow here all plants that are to be transplanted, such as cabbages, celery, sweet herbs, etc.

**Varieties**—It is of great importance to have good seeds of good kinds. Do not delay getting at once all that may be needed.

**Asparagus and Rhubarb**—Remove the litter, and fork in a good dressing of manure. In places far from the sea a liberal salting is beneficial to asparagus. Make new beds as previously directed.

**Beans**—Plant bush sorts as soon as danger of frost is past. Limas should be left until the ground is warm.

**Beets and Carrots**—Sow early sorts in drills a foot apart, or in 2-foot drills with radishes between.

**Cabbages and Cauliflowers**—Transplant from cold frames and from hotbeds; in the latter case, the plants must be properly hardened by exposure. Sow seeds in the open ground in well-prepared beds.

**Celery**—Sow in seedbed in rows 8 inches apart.

**Chives**—Divide clumps and number new plantings, putting the small bulbs 6 inches apart.

**Cress or Peppergrass**—Sow a small quantity every ten days to keep up a supply. Dust the young plants with slaked lime if insects trouble them.

**Cucumbers** may be had quite early by planting seed in frames from which other plants have been removed, giving, of course, plenty of manure.

**Eggplant**—Sow seeds in hotbed, which should have a covering of mats on cold nights.

**Garlic**—Sets obtained by breaking up the bulbs are planted 6 inches apart in foot rows.

**Horseradish**—Put the sets in manured trenches and fill in as the plants grow in a good way. You may also put sets between the early cabbages to occupy the ground after that crop comes out. Drop straight pieces of roots in holes made between the cuttings and at the same distance that they are apart. Let the top of the set be at least 3 inches below the surface. Never plant crowns if pieces of root can be had.

**Herbs**—Sow in seedbed where the ground is dry and warm: sage, thyme, sweet marjoram, etc.

**Leeks** need a fine, rich soil. Sow in foot rows.

**Lettuce** should be kept in constant succession. If plants have been wintered in cold frames, set them out a foot apart each way. Sow seeds in seed bed.

**Mustard**—Put out sets as directed last month. Seeds are to be sown as soon as the soil is ready. Plenty of good manure is required, and it is best to make the bed each year in the same place. Sow fresh seed in foot or 15-inch drills.

**Parsley**—Sow in open ground or in cold frames.

**Parsnips**—Use last year's seed only; sow only in rich, deep soil, in drills 15 to 18 inches apart.

**Peas**—The distance will depend upon the height the variety grows. Dwarfs will do a foot or 18 inches apart, while those requiring brush will need to be 3 or 4 feet or more distant.

**Peppers**—Sow in hotbed and treat like eggplant.

**Potatoes**—Plant only the early sorts in the garden. Use good-sized seed, and drop in manured drills that are a foot apart.

**Radishes**—Light, warm, and rich soil is necessary. They may be sown between rows of slower crops or by themselves. Sow a portion every ten days.

**Salsify or Oyster Plant**—Treat the same as carrots.

**Spinach**—Cut that which has been wintered for use and sow for a fresh supply in 18-inch drills.

**Swiss Chard** is a beet, the leaves of which make excellent summer greens. Cultivate like beets.

**Sweet Potatoes**—Better buy plants, if but few are wanted. They are started by putting the potatoes in a hotbed and covering with about 2 inches of rich compost. Give water and air as needed.

**Tomato** plants in hotbeds when large enough to handle may be potted and placed under glass or

HENDERSON'S EARLY SNOWBALL CAULIFLOWER.

pricked out into another hotbed. Seed may still be sown under glass, or for late crops in open ground.

**Turnips** — Sow early sorts as soon as possible.

**Hotbeds** will need special attention to keep the plants from hurrying. Water, if needed.

*Flower Garden and Lawn*

Much of the work indicated in previous months is still to be done. Get all rough work out of the way as soon as possible, and have all transplanting of ornamental trees and shrubs, excepting evergreens, done as soon as may be. See last month's notes about lawns. Push all heavy work, such as making of paths and the laying out of borders, and get it out of the way.

**Borders** need to be carefully forked over, first giving a coat of well-decomposed manure, and

**Edgings** made. Box may be reset and grass edgings laid. We wish someone would make a nice tile edging. Bricks set diagonally may be used as a substitute along paths where there is much travel.

**Herbaceous Plants,** where they have stood two or three years, will often need dividing; do this early. Seeds of perennials may be sown.

**Hardy Annuals** may be sown when the ground is dry, but tender ones are best left until May unless they can be started under glass.

**Bedding Plants** should not be put out too early. They are generally subtropical things, and a cold spell gives them a check, if it does not kill them.

**Forced Plants** — In cities and towns, plants that have been forced are often offered for sale. As a general thing they are worthless for future use, although for present gratification they are often worth the price asked.

**Climbers** — The hardy climbers are great favorites with us, and we would introduce them wherever it is possible — on verandas, fences, and to cover unsightly objects. Our woods supply the Virginia creeper, moonseed, waxwork, and others, and the nurseries have a long list of the exotic ones.

**Roses** — Where there is room, have plenty of June roses, but in restricted gardens the China and tea varieties will give the most satisfaction as they bloom all the time.

*Greenhouse and Window Plants*

Warmer days will allow more free ventilation. Sudden changes will occur, and during cold and damp spells heat will sometimes be needed.

**Propagation** of plants for outdoor planting should be pushed, as with the increasing power of the sun this now becomes much more difficult.

**Pot off** plants, using light, rich soil, as fast as they are fairly rooted in the cutting bench.

**Half-hardy Plants,** carnations and roses, may be planted out as soon as the soil can be prepared.

**Seeds** — Sow the tender annuals in boxes to get strong plants ready for the open ground.

**Dahlias** — Start by placing in heat. Cut off the sprouts with a bit of root, and pot. Rare sorts may be propagated from cuttings of the shoots.

**Tuberoses,** for outdoor blooming, should be potted and started in heat the last of the month.

**Insects** flourish in these spring days, and fumigation with tobacco stems and other means of prevention and destruction must be attended to.

**Water** will be needed more frequently now. Do not let growing plants suffer for the lack of it.

# PROJECTS FOR
# APRIL

## Making Homemade Lime

The application of lime improves the mechanical texture of heavy soils, and thus will frequently compensate for its use if the lime can be obtained cheaply. In many localities, the farmer can burn the lime he needs and thus obtain it at a much less cost than the market price. It is not necessary to build a kiln of masonry. The cheapest kiln is made by digging an excavation in a bank, as shown in the engraving. If much lime is to be burned, it will pay to line this excavation with brick and place an iron grating across near the bottom, beneath which the fire is made. Whether the kiln is so made or is constructed in only a temporary manner, it must be banked up in front with earth after the limestone is placed in it. Where the iron grating is used, it should project out in front as far as the bank of earth will permit, while under it is placed a sheet-iron door to close the furnace and regulate the draft. A platform is built just above the projection of the grating to support the earth backed against the rock. The top of the heap is covered with earth, leaving a hole in the center for a chimney. When the kiln is only temporary, an arch of large rocks takes the place of the iron grating, and the sides of the kiln are lined (as the rocks are laid in) with large stones instead of brick. It will take four or five days, with a good fire, to burn the kiln sufficiently.

Lime may be burned by piling the stones in a conical heap above ground. Large stones are used to make an arch under the heap, and the cavity

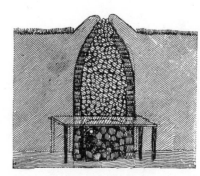

A LIME "KILN."

below the arch is filled with fuel. Immediately above the arch is placed a layer of dry wood, then a layer of stones, next a layer of wood, and so on until the heap is completed. The stones are laid rather loosely, and the entire heap is covered with earth to the depth of at least a foot to retain the heat, leaving an opening at the top for the escape of smoke. It will pay to insert a short, sheet-iron chimney in this opening to increase the draft, as a hot fire is needed. The draft is regulated by opening or closing the doorway under the arch. Do not disturb the heap until it is perfectly cool, and, if the lime is not to be used at once, it should be protected from rain by a roof and from surface water by erecting a low bank about it. Where limestone boulders can be gathered in sufficient quantities, the cost of lime will be very little, and, even when the rock must be quarried, burning lime will frequently yield handsome returns when the weather does not permit regular farm work.

## Pulling Tree Stumps

The accompanying illustration represents a very convenient and efficient stump puller for such stumps as are not very firmly rooted, and especially for those of which the small roots have decayed. It will be seen by the engraving that a strong chain is first placed around the stump with a rolling hitch, and the other end is then fastened to the large end of a stiff pole, 20 or 30 feet long, and a team is hitched to the small end, and driven in a circle around the stump until it is turned or twisted entirely loose. About the only expense of such a stump puller will be a strong chain with two very heavy hooks. When the stump is a small one, let the chain be passed twice or thrice around it before it is hitched to the pole. By cutting off a portion of the large lateral roots, a green tree of large size may be uprooted in a short time, especially where the principal roots do not strike very deeply.

## Four Ways to Make Hard Soap

No. 1 — Pour 4 gallons of boiling water over 6 pounds of washing soda (sal soda) and 3 pounds of unslaked lime. Stir the mixture well and let it settle until it is perfectly clear. It is better to let it stand all night, as it takes some time for the sediment to settle. When clear, strain the water, put 6 pounds of fat with it, and boil for 2 hours, stirring it most of the time. If it does not seem thin enough, put another gallon of water on the grounds, stir and drain off, and add as is wanted to the boiling mixture. Its thickness can be tried by occasionally putting a little on a plate to cool. Stir in a handful of salt just before taking it off the fire. Have a tub ready soaked, to prevent the soap from sticking; pour it in, and let it settle until solid, when you will have from the above quantity of ingredients about 40 pounds of nice white soap.

No. 2 — Dissolve 1 pound concentrated potash in 2 quarts of boiling water in a small kettle by itself. In another kettle, boil about 5 pounds of clean fat, or tallow, or its equivalent of soap grease with 2 gallons of soft water. As soon as the grease is melted, gradually add the dissolved lye from the small kettle, about a gill at a time, until all the lye is used, constantly boiling and stirring over a slow fire until the whole becomes thick and as transparent as honey. During the process, sufficient water should be added occasionally to replace what has boiled out. If using fresh grease, add 4 ounces of salt. Let it stand till it gets cold, then cut into bars, and put away to dry.

No. 3 — Hard soap is made the same as good soft soap, by the union of grease and strong lye; the clearer the grease, the better the soap. They are boiled up together; when they boil up thick, then add salt in the proportion of 2 quarts to 8 gallons of soap. Let it boil up thoroughly, set it away to cool, when it can be cut up and dried and ready for use.

No. 4 — Take about 12 quarts good soft soap, add 1 teacupful of fine salt, bring to a boil while stirring, and set away until cold; then strain and put it on a board to dry. Cut it up and turn while drying.

## How to Whitewash

Procure fresh-burnt lime—not slaked lime. The large lumps are best. The fine portions and small lumps will not make a wash that will stick well. For this reason, lime that has been burned several months is not as good as that just from the kiln. Put a pound or two into a vessel, and pour on boiling water slowly, until it is all slacked and is about as thick as cream. Then add cold rain water until it will flow well from the brush. Stir often when using it. A few drops of blueing added will give it a more lively color. One or two tablespoonfuls of clean salt, and one-fourth pound of clean sugar to a gallon of the wash will make it more adhesive. If the walls have been whitewashed, let them be swept thoroughly, and, if colored with smoke, wash them clean with soapsuds. A brush with long, thick hair will

hold fluid best when applying it overhead. If a person has the wash of the right consistency and a good brush, he can whitewash a large parlor without allowing a drop to fall. When it appears streaked after drying, it is too thick and needs diluting with cold water. Apply the wash back and forth in one direction, and then go crosswise, using a paintbrush at the corners and a thin piece of board to keep the brush from the woodwork or the border of the wall-paper. Coloring matter may be mingled with the wash to give it any desired tint. To make a light peachblow color, mingle a small quantity of Venetian red. For a sky-blue, add any kind of dry, blue paint, stirring it well while mixing. To make a wash of a light straw-color, mingle a few ounces of yellow ochre or chrome yellow. The coloring matter should be quite fine to prevent its settling to the bottom of the vessel.

## Cultivating Flax

The subject of flax culture may be properly considered under three parts: One, the preparation of the soil; two, the seed, the growth, and culture of the plant and harvesting; and three, the rotting and dressing for market. The first two parts belong particularly to the tiller of the soil and these are our primary interest. Flax is grown sometimes for the seed only, and sometimes for both the seed and lint. The seed yields a drying oil of the best quality for painters' purposes, the residue being oil cake which is used for feeding stock; and the straw yields lint of two qualities called flax and tow. Flax is the long, straight fibre, and tow consists of the short and tangled fibre which separates in dressing the long lint. Sometimes, however, the entire fibre is prepared as tow.

**Characteristics of the Plant:** Flax has one very important characteristic, an understanding of which is of great practical advantage. When a flax stem is growing alone, it will throw out numerous branches, many of which will be as large as the main stem, as shown by the accompanying engraving, *fig. 1.* Each of these will produce other branches, all of which will yield seed. On the contrary, when the seed is sown thickly, each seed will produce only a straight stem, without any branches, with but little seed. The practical point is to decide before the seed is sowed whether the purpose is to raise flax for the seed chiefly, with coarse tow in connection, or principally for the fibre. (See paragraph on seeding in another place below.)

**Soil:** Flax will flourish well on any soil that will yield good crops of cereal grain, and some soils that do not produce abundant crops of certain kinds of grain will produce an excellent crop of flax. Flax likes a deep, fertile, and mellow loam, and on such a soil a heavy crop of both seed and lint may be produced, provided there is not an excess of water in the soil. These river bottoms and uplands where the predominating characteristic of the soil is black muck, if fertile enough to produce heavy grass, will yield a good crop of flax fibre and a small crop of seed. But, if the soil is in a good state of fertility for

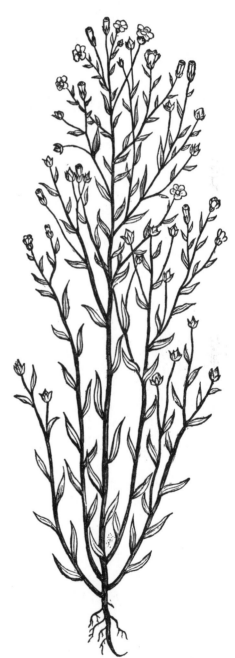

Fig. 1.—FLAX PLANT GROWING ALONE.

70

yielding potatoes, oats, corn, or rye, the yield of both seed and fibre will be large.

**Preparing the Soil:** There is no kind of grain for which the soil needs as much preparation as is required for a good crop of flax. Not only will the seed be better, but the fiber also, when the flax is grown on soil that is very fertile and has been kept clean by thorough cultivation. Preparation of ground should begin, if at all possible, at least three years before planting a crop. This area is used in the preceding years for the cultivation of corn, barley, oats, winter or spring wheat, and red clover. In October or November of the third year, the soil should be well plowed. Where black muck predominates in the soil, or where it is a very porous, sandy, or gravely loam, or a light alluvial deposit, it should not be plowed in late autumn, but rather in' August or September. In the following spring, as soon as the ground has settled and become sufficiently dry, it is plowed. After that it is harrowed twice and rolled previous to sowing the seed.

The great object in harrowing and rolling before sowing is to have the surface of the ground as smooth and uniform as it can be made so that the flax may get an even start and grow more uniformly. If the seed is sowed on an uneven surface where there are lumps, sods, and little furrows and holes, much of it will be buried too deep, and consequently, the growth of the straw (and fibre) will not be uniform, and the seed will not mature alike. Thoroughly rotted manure is quite as essential for flax as it is for wheat. Clean culture, a deep soil thoroughly pulverized and in a good state of fertility, will always produce a good crop of both lint and seed if the season is at all favorable for other crops.

**Seeding:** After the soil has been well prepared for the seed, let it remain about ten days, when nearly all the seeds of noxious weeds will have vegetated. Now, on the day that the seed is to be sowed, give it a thorough harrowing for the purpose of destroying the little weeds that have appeared in the "seed leaf." In case lumps of earth or small stones are harrowed up, the surface must be rolled. And while the surface of the soil is fresh, let the seed be put in as speedily as possible.

The correct quantity to seed depends upon the object for which the flax is raised. If we desire to obtain the largest yield of lint, we must sow the seed very evenly, and as thinly on the ground as it will grow and not throw out branches, as shown in *fig. 1*, but having the branchless habit shown in *fig. 2*. If the object is simply to raise seed and coarse tow, it

may be sowed very thin — say from half a bushel to one bushel per acre.

Fig. 2.—THICK SEEDING.

All writers on the subject agree that seed should be sowed when the soil has settled and is warmed by the influence of the sun, and the weeds and grass have begun to spring up, and the leaves of trees begin to unfold. If sowed too early in the season, much of it is likely to be stunted; late frosts are very apt to injure it, more or less; and noxious weeds are sure to get the start of it, unless extra pains have been taken to destroy them. The very best time, with reference to the condition of the soil, is soon after a shower when the small lumps of earth will crumble at a very slight touch, and the entire surface is friable and "lively." Then it will germinate in a few days, get the start of weeds, and keep the ascendency through the season.

Flax seed is a very slippery grain to sow by hand. Unless a man takes great care, the seed will be sowed very unevenly. As it is so very slippery, however, it is not practicable to sow it with a grain drill nor with any kind of broadcast seed-sower that we have ever met with. After the soil has been harrowed as directed above, mark out the ground two ways, in lands about 18 feet wide. This breadth is wide enough to sow at one round, or at two casts. Let the seed be soaked in warm water about two or three hours and then rolled in plaster or gypsum. Then count the land both ways, and make calculation to sow a given quantity of seed on each land, each way.

Fig. 3.—BRUSH-HARROW.

Flax seed requires but little earth to cover it deep enough to vegetate in a short time, and by depositing it all on a smooth surface where several seeds will not be gathered into depressions in the soil, it will all vegetate alike, will stand evenly on the ground, and pull easily, may be cut close to the ground with scythes, cradles, or horse mowers and the straw and lint will be of a uniform length and quality. The practice recommended is to "bush in" the seed by drawing a brush harrow by hand (*See fig. 3.*). With a suitable brush, one man can brush in four or five acres per day and do the work well. Such a harrow covers a strip about five feet wide, and an active man or a strong boy would cover the seed nearly as fast as he could do it with a team, and much better.

The accompanying illustration, *fig. 4*, represents five young plants of flax, three of which are three or

Fig. 4.—EFFECT OF DEEP AND SHALLOW SOWING.

four inches high, the seed of which was covered about half an inch deep. The seed of the one at the left hand was buried nearly two inches deep; and the one just in the seed leaf was buried still deeper. The illustration is designed to show the importance of covering all the seed of a uniform depth in order to have all the stalks as nearly of a uniform length as practicable. When some of the seed is buried too deeply, these plants that spring from such seed as may be covered only half an inch deep will get the start of the other by several days' growth, which will produce stalks of various lengths.

**Weeding:** If the soil has been prepared, and the seed put in at the time and in the manner directed, very little weeding will be required. If Canadian thistles, dock, wild mustard, or other noxious weeds should show their heads, let a careful man, shod with two or three pairs of old woolen socks, remove them when the flax is eight or ten inches high. The object of covering the feet with something soft is that in this manner the plants may be injured as little as possible. The weeds should be cut off close to the surface of the ground, gathered in the arms, and carried to a pile—not thrown down. If pulled up, much of the flax will be rooted up with them.

72

**Pulling:** When the bolls have assumed a brown color, and the leaves have died for one-fourth the length of the stems at the butt ends, and the stems have changed from a dark green to a light yellowish color, then the flax is fit to pull or to cut. At this stage of growth, it will yield more and better fibre than if cut at any other period. Should the soil be variable in its character, the flax will ripen unevenly, and the ripest portions may be pulled first. When flax is allowed to stand until all is dead ripe, the seed will be of a superior quality, but the fibre will not be so heavy, strong, or soft as if cut earlier.

When flax is pulled by hand, each laborer takes a strip about four feet wide, and either spreads it in a swatch behind him, or throws it down in gavels, or binds it himself, as far as he pulls it. The flax is grasped just below the bolls with both hands and pulled up with a sudden jerk. If it is pulled slowly, a much larger quantity of earth will adhere. As soon as one handful is pulled, it is set on the ground close to the standing flax and held with one hand, while the other gathers as much as can be held conveniently; then both hands grasp the whole and pull. When enough has been pulled to make a gavel as large as the puller can grasp with both hands, it is "butted" once or twice on the ground to even it. The gavels should be set up north and south so that the sun may shine on both sides of the stook in the course of the day. (*See figs. 5 and 7.*) Before the gavel leaves the hands of the puller, he should strike it once or twice on the ground or on his foot to knock off the dirt. After it has lain in the sun from half a day to a day, it ought to be turned over to sun both sides. As flax will hang together if in a continuous swath, it is better to leave a space of two or three inches between the spread gavels. When it is bound as soon as pulled and set in stooks, it will require from one to two weeks to cure before it will be fit to stack or mow. The question is frequently asked, why is it not as well to cut flax as to pull it? The fibres of flax diminish in size, tapering out at the root of the plant. It will, therefore, run much smoother when spun and will form a cleaner and smoother thread than if the fibre is cut in two. If, however, the stalks can be cut within an inch of the root, nearly the entire length of the fibre will be secured, as well as part of the advantage of this tapering of the fibre.

**Stacking:** It is not always convenient to put flax in a barn, and it is important to keep it where hay seed, chaff, and straw will not be mingled with it, and where mice and rats will not work. The best way of stacking it is to make a long stack-bottom by placing three poles, sticks of timber, or plank side

Fig. 5.—STOOK OF FLAX.

Fig. 6.—STACK OF FLAX.

Fig. 7.—GAVEL.

by side, from two to three feet apart, according to the length of the haul, and one foot above the ground; and then lay two courses of sheaves with the tops together, and with one course above another as represented in *fig. 6*. The ends of the stack may be carried up square, without any posts or stakes. In order to give the sheaves a good pitch, the heads of a few of the top courses may be laid on each other. Then cover it with canvas or with boards as represented in *fig. 6.*

**Threshing:** When flax is bound in small sheaves, we used sometimes to take a bundle in both hands and strike the heads on a large stone or plow turned upside down on the barn floor. Sometimes the seed was threshed off with flails. If the sheaves are not too large, the best way is to whip it out on a large boulder. Strips of canvas or blankets should be hung up on three sides to keep the seed from flying beyond the floor. This is superior to using a flail as this instrument will break the stalks, more or less, which works an injury to the fibre.

Further steps in the use of fibre are undertaken by a flax merchant. There are various means used to "rot" the fibre and to make it pliable, to dissolve the mucilage that holds the fibre and woody parts together so that they will separate readily as soon as the flax has been dried.

## Watering Livestock

If water has to be supplied to stock by pumping or if the animals must be driven to the trough or brook, aside from the great expense, in time there are other losses felt keenly by the thoughtful farmer. Besides, the duty of watering the animals, if left to irresponsible parties, is more likely to be neglected than perhaps any other in the whole routine of farm labors. The remedy for all this trouble is a supply by means of flowing water in the barn and stockyard. Hence the arrangement may be fashioned that is shown in *fig. 1.*

The leader, which may be a branch from, or the terminus of, the pipe that comes from the spring or elevated cistern, comes up from the ground at the post under the tub, and a short piece of rubber tube connects it with another piece of metal pipe, which delivers the water at the top of the tub. The post is of oak or cedar, made with a sharp edge at the upper end, which receives the weight the tub when full. Over this edge the rubber connection lies. The tub is balanced upon a frame, as shown, and, when nearly full, it presses with sufficient force upon the rubber tube to close it. Thus the tub can never remain long empty, neither can it overflow, and the water is never flowing except when there is need.

Fig. 2.—WATER FOR FOWLS.

Another application of the same principle is seen in *fig. 2,* where a wooden tube conducts the water from a barrel along near the chicken coops. Near each coop a hole is bored in the pump tube, and a cork inserted in which is a glass or tin tube or a bit of pipestem. The tube may be made to fit watertight in the cork by melting a little wax around it with a hot iron. Over this tube or pipestem a thin rubber tube is drawn, which is laid upon the board, and, passing under a squeezer, discharges the water into a pan at one end of the board, which is counterbalanced by a brick or stone at the opposite end. Should a chick, perchance, perch upon this brick, its weight might cause the water to overflow in the pan; hence a board is nailed over it to prevent such a catastrophe.

Fig. 1.—WATER FOR STOCK.

### Trapping Moles

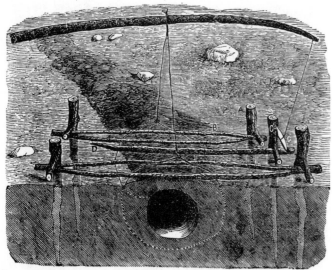

HOLLAND MOLE TRAP.

and set in less time than it takes to write out a description of it and of how it works.

### How a Stone Wall Should Be Built

Stone is by no means an unmixed evil on a farm. Being indestructible, it is an excellent material for fences, and, when properly laid up, stone walls are not disturbed by a frost which will thrown over post and rail or board fences, or draw out the posts so as to seriously weaken them. To build a stone wall some skill is required. The foundation should be dug out a foot deep and the earth thrown upon each side, which serves to turn water from the wall. Large stones are bedded in the trench, and long stones placed crosswise upon them. As many whole stones as possible should be used in this place, and if such stones are scarce, some pieces of 4-inch plank may be used occasionally. The stones are then arranged as shown in the engraving, breaking points and

WELL LAID WALL.

distributing the weight equally. Any small spaces should be filled with chips broken off in dressing the larger stones, so as to make them fit snugly. As it is a work that will last a century, it is worth doing well.

### Helps in the Garden

In laying out and planting the vegetable, fruit, or flower garden, there are several convenient imple-

The trap is made of rough sticks which can be cut from any kind of brush, a string, and a few feet of fine wire. The illustration shows the manner of setting the trap. The mole run is trodden down to close it, and across it is placed the forked stick (*B*) about a foot long, which is held down by a hooked wooden peg (*A*), driven into the earth at each end. About two inches from this stick and parallel to it another one is similarly placed. Between the two is the trigger (*D*), a stick placed between the two forks. One end of this has a notch cut in it and passes under the crotch of a hooked peg. At the end of a spring-pole, only part of which is shown in the engraving, is fastened a string, to which is attached the little catch (*C*). Both ends of this catch are wedge-shaped, and one end is placed in the notch in the trigger, while the other catches in a corresponding notch cut in the hooked peg. It will be seen that if the trigger is slightly lifted, the catch will be loosened and the spring-pole will fly up. Two pieces of wire, each with a loop in the lower end, are attached to the pole. These loops, which should be the size of the run, are so buried that the mole will pass through them. The earth is scooped out between the arms of the forked sticks and the loop placed in and covered with earth. If the mole comes in either direction, it springs the trap and is caught and held fast by the wire loop. The trap is much less complicated than may seem from the description and can be made

ments which can be made with little trouble and which will greatly facilitate work.

**A Garden Reel**—This is to hold a line which is to serve as a guide in running straight lines from one point to another. Iron ones are sold at the seed stores, but a homemade one will answer as well. *Fig. 1* shows the shape. The sidepieces (*A, A*) are made of curved limbs or may be worked out of straight stuff, about ⅝ inch in diameter and 12 to 15 inches long. The crosspieces (*B, B*) are 2 inches wide, ½ to ¾ inch thick, and 1 foot long. These have holes near the end through which the sidepieces pass and project above and below for about an inch. The center stake (*C*) is 2 to 2½ feet long, 1 inch in diameter where it passes through the crosspieces, and with a shoulder below the lower crosspiece, from which place it gradually tapers to a point. A pin through the upper end of the center piece, above where it passes through the upper crossbar, will prevent it from slipping out. The best cord is a small hempen one, of a length suited to the size of the garden; and, if tarred, will last all the longer. One end is fastened to one of the sidepieces of the reel, and the cord wound up by turning the frame by means of the handle (*D*), the other end being fastened to a sharpened pin (*E*), which is made about 18 inches long, and of the size of *C*. All parts of the reel should be made of hardwood, and with careful use it will last for years. To use the reel, thrust the stake portion firmly in the ground at one end of the bed or other work to be laid out, and walk off with the pin to the desired point. Drive the pin into the ground, then stretch the line tight, and secure it by taking a turn around the projecting corners of the frame of the reel.

**A Marker**—Very convenient for making drills at equal distances. *Fig. 2* shows the usual form. A piece of scanting has a handle fastened to it horizontally and well braced. Teeth of hardwood, about 18 inches long, rather bluntly pointed, are fastened at the distances required for the rows. It is convenient to have three sizes, with the teeth at 12, 15, and 18 inches apart. To use the marker, set the line as a guide and run it with the first tooth next to the line; afterward the marker is guided by running one tooth in a mark previously made.

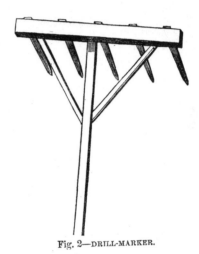

Fig. 2—DRILL-MARKER.

**Compasses**—A pair of rude compasses can be made of lath or light stuff, about 3 feet long, fastened together at one end by a screw so that the points can be set at any required distance. This is convenient in spacing off distances at which to set plants in rows. The line being stretched the length of the row, the spaces can be marked off very rapidly by the compass. It is very, very useful also for striking circles or curves.

**Plank**—A plank a foot or 15 inches wide, and long enough to go across the beds, will be found very useful in sowing many seeds. Lay the plank square across the bed, and, with a small stick or the finger, make a scratch or drill, using the edge of the plank as a ruler. Sow the seeds, then turn the plank over and put in another row. By turning the plank carefully, the rows will be just as far apart as its width and thickness, and the plank serves to stand upon while sowing, thus avoiding any trampling of the bed.

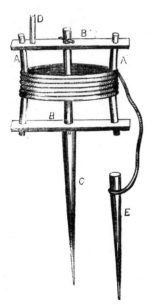

Fig. 1—GARDEN REEL.

# FARM AND GARDEN WORK FOR

# May

The average temperature grows warmer, and our cold storms are less cold in May than in April, yet they are cold enough. Seeds will rot in the ground; the plows will be dragged through the pasty soil and mold it into clods, which will stand in mementos of indiscreet haste; sheep will shiver and snuffle, and lambs will die for lack of protection. We judge these and other things will happen, because it always is so. There is no need of their occurring, or very little, at any rate. May is always unreliable, except for storms and showers of rain. Sometimes we have many days of fine, clear, dry weather, but usually everybody is tired of seeing it rain. Proper efforts having been made, there need be little delay in the more important labors. Year by year, one's practices should improve; year by year, the farmer's reasonings should be more accurate and his judgment better. This month the great bulk of the corn crop and more than half the potato crop is planted, much wheat is sown, as roots of all sorts, except those of the turnip family.

### HINTS ABOUT FARM WORK

**Last Year's Mistakes** are to be avoided. Take time to do all kinds of work thoroughly and well.

**A Watch on the Markets** — We have almost always either something to sell or something to buy; hence it is always well to watch the fluctuations of prices and take advantage of them, if possible.

**Labor will Pay** — Hire more labor. Take risks of this kind. If work is well planned and judiciously carried out, the more there is done, the better off you will be. If money at interest pays, that spent for labor ought to pay fifty percent better.

**Working Stock** — Groom horses daily and thoroughly; rub them dry if they come wet to the stable either from perspiration or rain. Feed regularly, and, when cool, give water. It is well to let a pail of water stand where the horse can drink during the night if it wishes to. Oxen should be well-brushed every day likewise. They are healthier for it, and endure more fatigue. If hard-worked eight hours a day, it is all that should be expected of oxen. Give long noonings and good fodder.

**Cows** — When there is a good strong growth of grass, turn the cows to pasture, but not before. Calves, wearing muzzles, may run with their dams without danger of their sucking. Cows "coming in" on full feed often make more milk than their udders have capacity to retain if milked but twice a day. Neglect to milk oftener causes not only the loss of a pint or two which leaks out daily, but induces a tendency of the cow to secrete less, entailing a loss through the year.

**Bulls** — There are hardly enough good full-blood bulls of all kinds for farmers in every part of the country to be able to secure their services. Never, *never* send a cow to a grade bull.

**Sheep** — Keep them off the pasture until there is a good stock of grass. Mow off the brush, if this has not been previously done. The sheep will keep down the young growth, and kill the bushes. Shearing may take place before the settled warm weather of June, provided the naked animals can have warm, sheltered sheds and good feed until accustomed to the change. If the fleece is to be washed on the sheep, by all means delay shearing until warm weather. If wool is to be tub-washed, or if sheep are to be washed in tanks from which the water may be drawn off and distributed over the land, much valuable manure may be saved. Nothing could do better for grass.

**Spring Grains**—As a rule, it is best to let at least oats and barley go, unless they are sowed by or before the first week in May. Wheat may be put in a little later on soil very well prepared, but do not neglect the preparation, except on rich land; apply fine manure, plowed under lightly; harrow thoroughly, adding to the seed dressing of guano, superphosphate, fish guano, or bone meal.

**The Corn Crop**—Be sure of your seed. It should be early, uniform, and adapted to your land. Manure heavily; plant all, except very large kinds, in drills, rather than in hills with rows running both ways. A heavier stand is thus gained, and the ground well filled with roots. Be careful to have the rows very straight, and, to this end, use a marker. North of latitude 40°, be in no hurry about planting—if the crop is in by the 20th or 25th, it is early enough, and replanting will not be necessary.

**Roots**—Beets and mangels ought to be sown early. The soil should be in the best order it can be put—deeply tilled, and well manured, and the rows placed 2 feet apart, so that they may be worked by horsepower. This distance is about as small as will do for field culture. The plants cover the soil well, and as large crops are gained as when the rows are closer. Parsnips may be sown in rows equally distant, but the seed should not be so deeply placed, nor should the sowing be done before the soil is warm and dry. Rows of carrots may be placed a little nearer together—about 20 inches apart is best on most soils—though, in the garden, they are often 16 to 18 inches apart.

**Potatoes**—Finish planting before the middle of the month; it is unsafe to delay longer, though, if the season be a wet one, June-planted potatoes may do tolerable well. Manure at the first or second hoeing with ashes and plaster, lime, or some concentrated manure, cast in small handfuls upon the plants, if backward, or the soil not rich.

**Tobacco**—The seedbeds may need watering with liquid manure towards the end of the month. See that they are weeded thoroughly and thinned.

**Soiling Crops**—In this climate there is no summer soiling crop equal to corn. If the ground is very highly enriched, it may be sown early this month, but otherwise sow when the main crop is in, or about the same time. Drill it in rows 2½ feet apart, sowing any large, sweet variety.

**Grass and Clover** may be sown upon winter and spring grain early in the month with very good results. Sown alone on well-harrowed fallow soil, they will do well also. Old "hidebound" or mossy meadows, full of weeds, or bare of grass, may have new life put into them by a thorough tearing to pieces with a harrow, giving a dressing of 25 or 30 bushels of lime, followed by yard manure or compost and a fresh seeding with clover and grass.

**Weeds**—The warfare begins this month—push it forward. Whenever you can find a root, kill it. Remember, weeds may be killed in the seed leaf by thousands, with the same labor and less thought than will be required to kill them by scores after they have grown. When very small, even stirring the soil in moist weather kills many; when large, unless great pains are taken, though uprooted, a slight rain will revive them, and they will mature seed as if transplanted for their own good.

**Birds and Insects**—Some birds may still be attracted by birdhouses, though most have their nests already built. Do everything possible to encourage a feeling of security on their part. They are our best allies in the warfare against insects of all hurtful kinds. Look out for the nests of the tent-caterpillar; destroy when the worms are housed.

## HINTS ABOUT HORTICULTURAL WORK

This month will bring a press of work. If the season has been an early one, the young seedlings of some crops will need attention, and if the spring has been a late one, with chilly nights and cold rains, much of the work set down for last month must be done now. In late seasons, nothing is gained by hurrying. Wait patiently until the soil is in working condition.

### Orchard and Nursery

**Tree planting** is generally over, but where trees have been heeled-in and shaded, they will be in a good condition to set out.

**Grafting,** if done after growth has commenced, will need care not to injure the trees. The bark at this time easily slips, and there is danger of peeling it if the limbs are not cautiously managed.

**Cions**—If any valuable cions have been left over that could not be used in grafting, they should be set out like cuttings. This will keep them plump and moist until the bark will run on the stocks, when they may be used to furnish buds for insertion just as buds of the present season's growth are put in. Worth remembering.

**Cultivating the Orchard,** especially if a young orchard, is necessary to get a good thrifty growth.

Very few will cultivate the ground for the sake of the young trees alone, and it is well to put between the rows of trees such crops as require manure and frequent working. Potatoes, carrots, or whatever will leave the soil in as good condition as to fertility as it was before may be used.

**Mulching** cannot be too frequently advocated. It prevents the soil from drying and becoming hard and keeps down weeds. Almost any litter will do. Leaves from the forest are excellent. Sawdust is sometimes used, but is objected to by some on the ground that it undergoes fermentation and becomes sour and injurious to the trees. It will pay to mulch bearing pear trees, if for nothing else but to save the fallen fruit in good condition. Those near the coast use "salt hay." Bog hay, sedges, and the like, will answer equally well. If no mulch can be had, the next best thing is to stir the surface of the soil frequently. The mellow, recently stirred surface soil keeps that below from drying rapidly.

**Nursery Trees**—Those budded or grafted last summer will be disposed to throw out suckers from the stock. These are to be rubbed off as soon as they appear; do not let them get large enough to require to be cut away. The same care must be given to small or large stocks grafted this spring.

**Seedbeds** must be looked to. Young seedlings, even those of our hardiest trees, are very readily injured by the hot sun. The beds may be shaded by a lattice-work of laths, a rough frame covered with evergreen boughs, or any other contrivance may be used that will break the force of the sun.

**Insects** will begin their work as soon as there is any young growth to work on and, if not checked, will continue it to the injury of the trees. Don't stop to write the garden editor to ask what shall be done, but kill the insects when first discovered by some means. Destroy, in particular, the tent-caterpillar. Where this has been done thoroughly, there will be but little trouble. Where it has been neglected, they will not "fold up their tents like the Arabs," but keep spreading them all the time. Wherever a nest or tent is seen, no matter how small—and they are very conspicuous when the dew is on them in the morning—do not rest until the nest is destroyed. Bend down the limb, climb the tree, get a stepladder, or in some way reach the nest, and pull it out and crush the young brood. Some use swabs charged with soft soap, petroleum, or other substances. These will do if faithfully applied, but to our notion there is nothing as sure as pulling the nest off by hand and putting it under foot. The squeamish may wear gloves. Borers are to be probed or cut out. We haven't much faith in squirting any preparation into their holes. The curculio will now begin its work, and must be met at once. Avoid all vaunted remedies and washes, but follow the only sure plan yet known—jarring the trees, catching the insect on a large cloth, and killing it. The white grub will often make sad havoc among seedlings and young nursery stock. When a young tree in the row wilts, dig down and find the borer and kill it. Lice or aphids will appear on the young growth. If the trees are small, bend down the ends of the infested twigs, and immerse them in tobacco water or quassia water.

*Fruit Garden*

Many of the hints given in this and the previous months under the head of "Orchard and Nursery" have an application here, and need not be repeated. Finish up all uncompleted planting, and keep the surface of the soil always free from weeds. A pronged hoe, or hoe fork, will be found preferable to the common hoe.

**Grape Vines**—Those grown with horizontal arms will need to have the ends of the arms bent downwards, to cause all the buds to start equally. With vines planted this spring, allow but one bud, which should be the strongest, to grow. Two buds may grow from vines planted last year.

**Layers** may be made by bending down a cane of last year's growth, placing it in a trench 6 inches deep, and fastening it there by means of hooked pins. When the buds have started, and the shoots have made a few inches' growth, gradually fill the trench with soil.

**Currant Bushes**—The currant worm appears this month and next. No better application has been suggested than dusting with the powder of white hellebore. Keep the ground well cultivated, or put a heavy mulch between the rows.

**Strawberries**—Where the winter mulch still remains on, it should be parted over the plants if not already done. Set plants, and, if they show any blossom buds, remove them. Beds without mulch should have the surface thoroughly cleaned, without moving the soil so as to disturb the roots; then put on a thick mulch of bog or salt hay, straw, tanbark, or whatever is most convenient.

**Insects**—Hand-picking is the only remedy for rosebugs, as it is for the leaf-rolling caterpillars.

### Kitchen Garden

This month usually brings the first products of the garden. Those who had the forethought to have winter spinach have enjoyed that delicious vegetable ever since the snow disappeared, and so with salsify, horseradish, and others. But from this spring's sowing, even in the most favorable situations, radishes, lettuce, cress, and, it may be, early turnips and carrots, are the first returns received from early-sown seed. To our notion, no vegetable that comes afterwards is eaten with half the zest as these, the first fruits of the garden.

**Asparagus**—It is a good thing to have a bed just now; it, like all other good things, costs some trouble and forethought, but whoever has an established bed has a ready supply of a most delicious and healthful vegetable. Cut according to the weather, once in two or three days, or even daily. Use a sharp knife, and be careful not to injure the numerous buds still on the plant.

**Beans**—Plant as soon as danger of frost is over. If the first planting has done well, put in another for succession; if it failed, replant. Limas should not be put in the ground until the cold rains are over. Set poles 6 or 8 feet high, 4 feet apart each way, in warm, light, rich ground. Put 5 or 6 beans around each pole, pressing them into the soil eye downward, and covering an inch. Limas that have been started in hotbeds on sods may be set in the open ground as soon as the weather is settled.

**Beets and Carrots**—Weeding and thinning are to be done as soon as the plants are large enough to work. A slight supremacy of the weeds is very injurious to the carrot. Although the above applies to early-sown seed, sowing of beets and carrots may still be done. Where the ground is moderately moist, it is sometimes an advantage to sprout the seeds. Soak them in water over night, pour off the water, and keep the moist seeds covered in a warm place until they sprout. When the germ shows itself, dry off with lime, and sow.

**Cabbages, Cauliflowers,** and the less cultivated broccoli, brussels sprouts, and kohlrabi are to have

much the same treatment. Kohlrabi does best sown in place, and the others transplanted. The early crop should now be well started and will need frequent hoeing. A heavy sharp rake or a hoe fork is better to work among the plants than an ordinary hoe. Keep the ground stirred often, and the weeds will be kept down. If insects appear, use lime. Sow seeds of early and late sorts in open ground. Do not forget to have plenty of the delicious Savoys.

**Celery**—Sow, if not already done. As soon as the plants are large enough, keep them weeded and the soil loose around them. Turnip-rooted celery, prized by many for soups and salads, may be sown.

**Cress or Peppergrass** is to be sown every week.

**Corn**—Put the seed into the ground as soon as it is safe.

**Cucumbers**—In the North generally, this month is early enough to start the seeds on sods, under glass. When ready to set out, put them in well-manured hills. Sow seed in similar hills when the weather gets warm. Use a surplus of seed.

**Eggplants** in the hotbed or frame are to be potted as soon as large enough, or transplanted to another bed and kept under glass until cold nights are over.

**Herbs**—Sow in seedbed sage, thyme, summer savory, sweet marjoram, etc. The plants will be ready to follow cabbages, peas, or other early crops.

**Leeks**—Sow in rich soil, as directed last month.

**Lettuce**—Sow and transplant when large enough.

**Melons** are treated the same way as cucumbers.

**Onions**—Sow and plant sets as heretofore directed. Weed the beds clean from the start.

**Parsley**—Sow early in beds in the open ground.

**Peas**—In hoeing, draw the earth toward the stem. Give brush to the tall sorts before they fall down.

**Peppers** are warm weather plants and need the same nursing during their early growth as eggplants.

**Potatoes**—Hoe or otherwise stir the ground as soon as the tops can be seen. A dressing of ashes applied at hoeing time is a great help.

**Radishes** may be had in abundance by making successive sowings. They may be put among slower growing crops or used to fill spare corners.

**Rhubarb**—Allow recently-set plants to retain all their leaves until they become well-established. Remove flower stalks, but pull them; a quick sidewise pull will separate them very quickly and neatly.

**Spinach**—Sow, if not already done, and thin that already up.

**Sweet Potatoes**—Make well-manured ridges, about 30 inches apart at the top; and when cold rains are over, set the plants 15 inches apart. Set them down to the first leaf, and in very dry weather water the holes before putting in the plants.

**Squashes** need warm weather; treat as cucumbers.

**Tomatoes**—Put out the plants when safe to do so 3 or 4 feet apart, according to the variety. In gardens, some kind of a trellis or support for the vines adds to neatness and improves the fruit.

*Greenhouse and Window Plants*

There is no set time for bringing out plants; it must be governed by the season and the nature and condition of the plant. So many plants have been injured by injudicious sudden change in removal to the open ground that some of our best cultivators prefer to leave them indoors altogether.

**Plunging** plants means bedding the pot in the soil of the border without removing the plant. When this is done, a flat stone, coal ashes, or other matter should be put at the bottom of the excavation to prevent worms from finding their way through the hole in the pot into the ball of earth.

**Turning out** means that the ball of earth is to be removed from the pot and planted in the border. Many things that are turned out to fill up the borders are not taken up again, but a new and much more vigorous stock is propagated from cuttings.

**Camellias**, and other broad-leaved evergreens, should be placed under a lattice-work where they will be shaded during the heat of the day.

**Window Plants** which are neither plunged nor turned out in the border need shelter from the sun, plenty of water, and care in respect to insects.

**Ivy** that has been kept indoors may be set in a shady place, or the plants may be turned out. Do not allow the branches to lie upon the ground.

# PROJECTS FOR
# MAY

### How to Pitch Manure

As pitching manure is laborious work, it is important to render the labor as easy as possible by the exercise of skill in handling the fork or shovel. The accompanying illustration of a laborer pitching manure with a long-handled fork will illustrate the manner of performing easily with skill what is usually done by main strength.

To pitch easily, thrust the fork into the manure and make a fulcrum of one knee for the handle to rest on. Then a thrust downward with the right arm will detach the forkful from the mass of manure and elevate it from one to two feet high by the expenditure of little muscular force. By using a fork like a lever, as here represented, a man can pitch larger forkfuls, and more of them, with far less fatigue than he can without resting the handle across his knee. When manure is pitched with a short-handled fork, the force required to separate the forkfuls from the mass, as well as for lifting it on the cart, must be applied by the muscles alone. This often renders it fatiguing and backaching labor. Moreover, when a man pitches with a short-handled fork, he applies his force at a very great disadvantage since he is required not only to lift the entire forkful with one hand, but to thrust downward with the other one sufficiently hard to balance the force expended in detaching and elevating the forkful of manure. Consequently, the arm nearest the manure must expend muscular force sufficient to raise the weight, say, of two forkfuls.

This principle is quite as applicable in using the shovel as the fork. By resting the long handle across one knee when shoveling, keeping the arms stiff, and the body erect and straight, a slight thrust of the body and knee will force the shovel into the earth with the expenditure of little force. These suggestions, and the illustration, will enable anyone to expend his muscular force to the best possible advantage in using both manure forks and shovels.

### Building Sod Walls

There is no other material that the prairie settler can obtain so easily, and at so little cost, which will serve to give as much warmth and comfort to man and beast through a long, cold winter as sods. A thick, well-laid sod wall will make a far more comfortable building for stock—warmer in winter and cooler in summer—than any other material easily accessible.

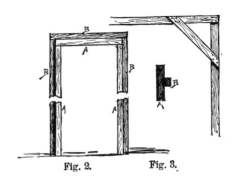

Fig. 1.—BARN PROTECTED BY A SOD WALL.

Fig. 2.　　　Fig. 3.

sods. Door and window frames should consist of 2-inch plank and be built into the walls; a strip about 2 inches square should be firmly nailed around the outside, near the center of the plank, as shown in *figs. 2 and 3, A* indicating the frames, *B* the strip. The sods, where they come against the frames, may be cut to fit around this strip and firmly pounded down. The frames will then stay where put, and wind cannot get around them—a considerable advantage.

If a barn built of lumber is covered with heavy tarred felt or tarpaper, well secured with laths or battens, and then sodded up on the outside as shown in *fig. 1,* the time and labor required in its construction will be repaid many times in the amount of fodder saved in keeping the stock through winter. A sod wall on the north and west sides of the dwelling house adds greatly to the comfort of its inmates. If a bed of mellow soil is made at the foot of the wall in which some climbing flowers or some roots of the Virginia creeper and bittersweet are planted, and the vines trained to cover the wall, it will not be an eyesore by any means through the summer, and the additional comfort it will give through the winter will atone for any unsightliness.

A sod wall should not be built close against a building, but a space of about 4 inches left between the wall and the siding; an occasional sod projecting against the building will serve to steady the wall. If well laid and pounded down, and if the sides or ends where the sods join each other are cut smooth and true to make a close joint, and the outside is pared down evenly with an axe or hatchet and covered over the top so as to shed rain, such a wall will last a number of years.

In building a barn of sods, the roof should be supported by posts, otherwise its weight will cause the walls to settle and rack them out of shape. When supported on posts and well braced, as shown in *fig. 1,* should the walls settle they can easily be raised to the original height by a few additional layers of

## Sowing Seed Evenly

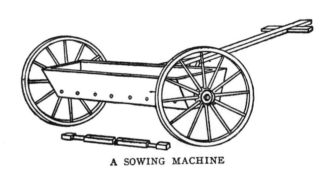

A SOWING MACHINE

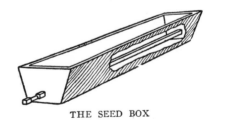

THE SEED BOX

These drawings show the construction of a wheel seeding device that can be easily made at home. The axle is tightly fitted into the wheels so that it turns when the wheels do. This agitates the grain or other seed and helps to keep the seed runing out of the holes at the lower backside of the box. The quantity of flow may be regulated at pleasure by making the holes large or small and increasing or diminishing the number of holes.

It may be found desirable to have a considerable number of holes and then having plugs for alternate ones, perhaps, which may be removed to make the seeding thicker. From 4 to 6 feet is suggested for the length of the box. Any old wheels will do if they are not too heavy to be easily drawn by hand.

## Growing Mushrooms

Comparatively little attention is given to the culture of mushrooms in this country. Those who do grow them meet with a ready sale for their crop. Quite a number of fungi are palatable, but the mushroom, *Agaricus campestris,* is the only one cultivated to any extent. The eatable portion is the reproductive part (equivalent to the flowers and fruit of other plants). The plant itself consists of whitish threads, which, under favorable circumstances, run among dung or rich soil, and when the plant acquires sufficient strength it throws up the mushrooms which appear above the surface. These threads (botanically called *mycelium*) can be dried and retain their vitality for a long time; when put into a bed of warm dung they start into growth and increase very rapidly. A block of dung and earth containing an abundance of these threads is called "spawn," and, by means of this, mushrooms are propagated.

The beds may be made in the cellar, under the stage of a greenhouse, or under any shed. A sufficient quantity of stable manure must be collected first. The greater part of the straw is shaken out and if the droppings are very wet, they are allowed to dry a little. The dung is then laid to form a bed about 10 inches thick, beating it down pretty firmly. Holes

are then made in the surface of the bed some 6 inches apart, and a piece of spawn about the size of a hen's egg is put into each and slightly covered. The bed is then covered smoothly with earth from the pasture or garden to the depth of 1½ inches. The temperature of the bed is tested from time to time by thrusting a stick into it; allow this to remain in the bed for a while; pull it out and the temperature can be ascertained by feeling it. When the heat rises to about 75 degrees, the bed should be cooled by making holes with a stick about a foot apart which are to be filled up again in two days. When the temperature of the bed declines to 55 degrees, it should be covered with 2 or 3 inches of the litter shaken out from the manure. If the bed gets dry, remove the litter and water thoroughly with lukewarm water from a watering pot having a fine rose, and then cover it again. If all goes well, the mushrooms will show in 5 or 6 weeks. They appear at first as little round buttons, but rapidly increase in size, and usually reach their full development in 48 hours. The illustration shows the mushroom in all stages, from the button to the fully-developed specimen.

## How to Drop Potatoes

For the purpose of facilitating the hard labor required in carrying and dropping potatoes, we include the accompanying illustration of a man in the act of dropping them. A wide leather strap, or, what is better, a strip of webbing with a hook attached to each end, is thrown over the neck and the basket of potatoes hung on the hooks. A basket or pail that will hold half a bushel is sufficiently large to contain as many as a laborer will desire to carry at once. The top of the basket should be about even with one's lower ribs. When a basket is carried in this manner, both hands are free to be used in dropping a row on each side, which can be done about as quickly as one row when the basket is carried on one arm according to the usual custom. By this manner of carrying a basket, all the severe fatigue of the arm and shoulder is avoided and a laborer can always walk erect, which is much easier than to support a weight on one side. When potatoes bound from their proper places they may either be put in place with the foot of the man who drops them or with the hoe when covering.

## Windmills for Farm Work

The advertising pages of agricultural periodicals display many newfangled windmills with patented "improvements." But the old-fashioned mill remains unaffected by patent rights and is just as useful as ever—and so simple that a mechanic who can construct a simple waterwheel or wagon wheel is competent to make one. Here is pictured a windmill which is in everyday use, which costs very little, and which may be constructed to do light or heavy work, as desired. The frame on which to mount it may be of timber, as in the engraving, or it may be a

stone or brick building if a substantial machine for heavier work is desired. The power is constructed in the shape of arms—shorter or longer, according to the power needed—fixed to a center wheel or hub, which is mounted and keyed onto an axle. Sails are carried on these arms, of sailcloth or heavy sheeting of a triangular shape, which are fastened closely to one arm and by a cord at the corner (shown at *a*) a foot or less in length to another. This gives sufficient inclination backward to the sail to gain the motion required with a front wind. On the axle is a crank wheel *(b)*, which moves the rod to be connected with the pump, or it may be connected by means of pulleys and bands to get an upright rotary motion needed for grinding, or a pair of miter wheels will give a horizontal rotary movement. A frame *(c)* is carried on a circular table, on which it may be revolved so as to enable the sails to be presented fairly to the breeze. A box *(d)* at the rear end of the frame is weighted with stone to balance the weight of the arms and sails. A pin passed through holes in the circular table retains the frame in the postion needed and keeps the sails faced to the wind.

The construction of this mill is so simple, and it is so easily managed, that all those who desire a cheap power for churning, pumping water, and irrigating land will do well to study it out. A mill with arms 6 feet long may be made to do work equal to one-fourth of a horsepower if all the working parts are well fitted and kept well lubricated, as all machinery should be. When out of use, the sails are untied and removed, or they may be furled and clewed to the arms until again required.

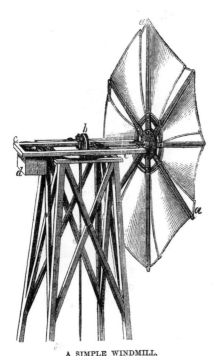

A SIMPLE WINDMILL.

## Building an Earth Closet

An earth closet may be placed in any convenient room. The closet may be partitioned off in a shed, in a barn or other outbuilding, or it may occupy a small room in the house without unpleasant results. The material required is dry loam—not sand, but good soil, the stiffer the better. Dry this earth thoroughly by spreading it on a platform of boards in the sun. When dust dry, pass it through a sieve to remove lumps, etc., and store in barrels or boxes in a dry place. Where coal is burned, sifted ashes will answer in place of dry earth, but wood ashes must not be used. For the closet itself, self-acting ones, in which the weight of the person liberates the dry earth from a hopper, may be purchased if preferred, but a simple and inexpensive closet may be made at small cost that will perform as well as the most costly affair.

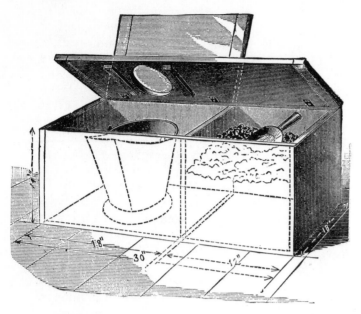

This simple earth closet was designed by a sanitary engineer of New York City. It can be constructed at slight cost by any householder. The body is a plain pine box. Its sides are not over 14 inches high; its depth is 18 inches, measuring from front to back, and its length is about 30 inches. It is divided into two compartments, one 18 by 18 inches, and the other 18 by 12 inches. The larger of these compartments has no bottom; the smaller has a tight bottom. On top there are two covers. The lower cover, hinged to the upper edge of the back, extends across both compartments. In this is cut the seat, of the usual pattern, over the center of the larger compartment. The upper cover is hinged to the lower one and may be raised independently. It is made the size of the larger compartment only; both covers have a little overhang to facilitate lifting them. Such a box, if made by a carpenter, will not cost very much. But, if time allows, make it yourself. The receiving vessel is a galvanized iron coal hod, as large as will stand in the larger compartment with the covers down. The smaller compartment is filled with dry earth, coal ashes, peat dust, or whatever else is used as a deodorizer, and a little hand shovel or scoop is laid in. The closet is then ready. Once in use, it will never be given up.

## Weeding and Thinning

An excess of seed—at least of all the smaller kinds—is usually planted. Aside from the difficulty of sowing just the quantity needed to furnish the required plants, there are good reasons for the practice. With plants that are feeble at their first start, like carrots, a quantity of seed is needed to break through the weight of soil and insure a fair stand. When the plants are fairly up, then comes thinning, or, as the English call it, singling.

How much soil each particular plant requires we do not know with precision, but doubtless most of our roots are allowed to stand too thick. The larger the leaves of the plant the farther apart the roots should be. Onions, with slender leaves, may be crowded, while beets do better grown far apart. It must be recollected that the development of the root depends entirely upon the amount of healthy, active leaf surface. Whatever, the importance of attending to the matter of weeding and thinning early cannot be underestimated.

Whatever tool or machine may be found useful for cleaning between the rows, there is a certain amount of work that must be done in the row itself. For this no machine has yet superseded the hand. The work must be done as soon as the plants have made a few "rough leaves," i.e., those beyond the seed leaves. There have been weeding hooks and weeding chairs and other contrivances to facilitate the operation, but the best way is to go down on the knees astride the row and work with both hands, thinning, and removing every weed, no matter how small. The operation of hand weeding may be facilitated by the proper use of the hoe. By employing the hoe, the plants in the rows, weeds and all, are cut out at intervals so as to leave little clumps or hills at proper distances. The amount of hand weeding is thus reduced, as the work is now confined to these little hills. Do it early, for weeds grow as fast as the crops and in a cold rain seem to grow much faster and get ahead of the crops and choke them. As soon as the plants are large enough to handle, go at them; delays are dangerous. Onions and carrots especially need the earliest attention.

## Making and Maintaining Tools

A farmer ought to be a tolerable mechanic and make, as well as mend, a great many things. Rainy-day work is often advantageously that of the jack plane and drawing knife.

**Harrows**—A very good "A" harrow can be made at home, and its construction is obvious from the illustration. The bolts (dotted lines) are both neces-

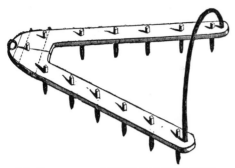

Fig. 1.—HARROW WITHOUT THE CROSS BEAM.

sary, not only to prevent the head opening, but to stop any tendency to twist. They are five-eighths iron bolts with nuts. The shorter and front one passes through the strap staple, on which is the draft ring. The teeth may be of iron or of wood; if the latter, 1½ inch oak pins are best. Holes should be bored diagonally in the ends of the harrow to receive the ends of a bent pole reaching conveniently high for the plowman to lift the harrow without stooping. Harrows are much used for giving potatoes and corn the first one or two hoeings. In hoeing corn, the crosspiece in an "A" harrow is in the way, the front part of the implement running usually high enough to clear the plants. In the one figured this difficulty is obviated. In hoeing corn the front tooth is always removed.

Fig. 2.—WHIFFLETREE.

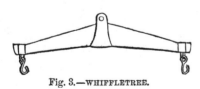

Fig. 3.—WHIFFLETREE.

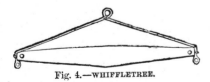

Fig. 4.—WHIFFLETREE.

**Whiffletrees** — It is very easy to make a whiffletree. The one shown in *fig. 2* is of 1¼-inch ash, with a 3/4-inch hole near each end to take a rope trace. A form more convenient, because adapted either to leather or chain traces, is shown in *fig. 3*, the trace hooks being attached to iron bands. *Fig. 4* represents a very strong whiffletree. Eyes in which to fasten trace hooks are made in the ends of an iron rod of suitable length and strength; and eye or loop is made in the center, and the rod riveted, as shown. The ends of the rod are either bent a little and braced apart by a stout piece of oak wood (being let into grooves in the wood and held by staples) or made with eyes to receive the ends of the wooden brace. In the former case, shown in the cut, the brace should have a bolt through each end to prevent splitting. In this form, lightness is consistent with great strength. The size of both iron and brace must be proportioned to the draft likely to be applied.

## How to Stake Out Stock

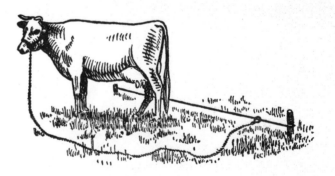

A convenient and simple staking contrivance so that no harm can come to the animal is to drive two stakes several feet apart and stretch a rope or wire on which a ring is placed. To this ring fasten the halter strap. The animal can graze up and down on both sides without tangle or injury. The ring slides, and the stretched wire will give some.

## Dog and Sheep Power for Churning

Where there is much churning to be done, a dog power (a contrivance utilizing the power of dogs) is truly a labor-saving device. There are several different kinds; the best, perhaps, is a "tread power," like the ordinary one-or two-horse tred powers. These, however, are rather costly, and can only be made by experienced mechanics. There are forms, however, which may be easily made by anyone familiar with the use of tools. Two of these are represented in the accompanying engravings. They are worked upon

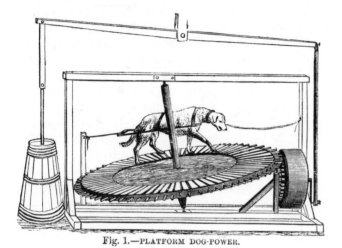

Fig. 1.—PLATFORM DOG-POWER.

Fig. 2.—WHEEL DOG-POWER.

very different principles. The revolving platform (*fig. 1*) is set at such an angle that, though the weight of the dog causes the turning, it is, after all, by his strength of draft that the machine is effective. The animal must be harnessed in some simple way and attached to some fixed object. The harness figured has no advantage over the simpler one by which the arctic sledge-dogs are attached to the vehicles they draw. This is by means of a broad collar band and a small rope or thong passing from it between the legs and held in position by a bellyband. The plat-form power is made as light as possible, consistent with strength. There is a frame made, supported upon the shaft by means of crossbeams pinned to it,

braces beneath, and a rim in which pins are set to act as cogs, meshing in with flat ones in a drum. The churn may be operated by a crank and walkingbeam, as shown, or, if a rotary churn, by a band running upon the drum. A track must be made for the dog by nailing radiating cleats upon the platform. Any arrangement to lessen friction, like friction wheels and iron sockets and bearings, will be of essential service. The platforms are usually 7 or 8 feet in diameter. The drum should be a little swelled in the center to prevent the band running off.

The wheel power is a little more difficult to make, but has some advantages. It is operated by the weight of the animal, his labor being exerted precisely as in running up a hill—as a squirrel runs in his cage. A heavy block is sometimes suspended from the axle to hang down behind the dog, and crossbars may be nailed to the arms or spokes to prevent his jumping through. The wheel is either made only wide enough for one dog to run in, or wide enough for two to run abreast. Friction rollers, in this case, are also very useful. The wheel is hung in a frame that will not shake with its motion, which is sometimes quite irregular. It is made with bent rims fastened to the spokes, and boards are nailed to these.

The greater the diameter, the easier and slower will the wheel turn. Eight feet is about the right size, and the wheel should be banded with common hoop iron nailed on. A 3/4-inch iron rod makes the best axle, and this should be keyed fast in the wheel, while the ends should run in metal boxes, which may be oiled.

Dogs, sheep, and goats are used in these and similar "powers." Goats are rather light, but active and hardy, and the exercise does them good, especially if they are ordinarily kept stabled.

### Grapevines in the Garden

Any soil which will raise good corn will do for grapevines. The chief thing to be avoided is a wet soil. Such difficulty must be overcome by draining, or, if this is not practicable, excavate the soil to the depth of 2 feet or more and put in a layer of brick, stones, and rubbish to serve as a partial drain. If the soil is in good condition, no manure need be used at planting, but, if it is poor, add a quantity of well-decomposed manure or compost or use about 2 quarts of bone meal to each vine, mixing it with the earth around the roots. A large supply of coarsely-ground bones, mixed with the soil, will furnish a lasting supply of vine food. The soil should be throughly pulverized to the depth of 20 inches or 2 feet. Make the hole about 5 feet in diameter, with the bottom 4 to 6 inches deep in the center and 8 to 10 inches deep at the circumference. In the center of the hole set a strong stake, 4 or 5 feet high. This should be placed before planting the vine so as to avoid injuring the roots in setting it afterwards. The vine should be well-rooted. To prepare it for planting, cut the roots back to at least 2 feet, and, if they are not as long as this, cut off a portion of their ends at any rate as this will cause them to throw out small fibrous branches. The top of the vine should be cut back to two or three buds. Set the vine in the

and press it down firmly with the foot. When the vine begins to grow, rub off all but the strongest shoot and keep this tied to a stake during the season.

In autumn, the single cane produced is cut back leaving three buds of new growth, and the next year two buds are allowed to grow. If the vine is a strong one, it may be allowed to bear a few bunches of fruit; if weak, the blossom buds should be pinched off to allow the whole strength to go to make wood. The vine in autumn will appear like *fig. 1*. Of course the canes each year are supported by tying to stakes. The following autumn the canes are cut off above the lower two buds if the vine is to be protected. Or, if left exposed, prune above the third bud and cut back to the second one early in spring.

The next year's growth is represented in *fig. 2*, and a vine of this size will bear from 12 to 20 bunches of fruit and will need only a single stake for support. In pruning this vine in autumn, cut away the uppermost two canes entirely and shorten the others to

Fig. 1—2nd YEAR.

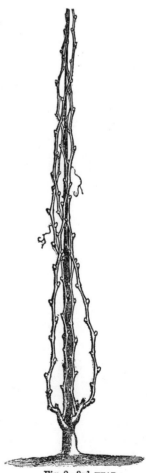

Fig. 2—3rd YEAR.

center of the hole close to the stake; spread the roots out to their full length and distribute them evenly, and then cover them with surface soil, working it in carefully around the roots. Then fill up the hole

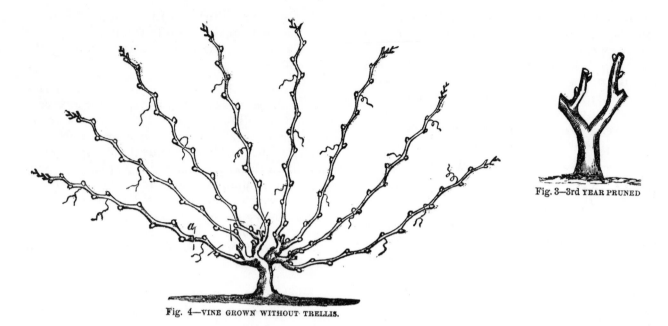

Fig. 3—3rd YEAR PRUNED

Fig. 4—VINE GROWN WITHOUT TRELLIS.

two buds each if protected, or to three if not, as before. The vine when pruned will appear as in *fig. 3*, and this manner of pruning may be repeated each year if the space is confined. Or, if there is room for a trellis, instead of removing two of the canes entirely, all four may be cut back to two buds, and these will produce eight canes as in *fig. 4*, which may be disposed on a trellis and will give from 30 to 40 bunches of fruit. This vine has four short spurs producing two canes each and may be pruned according to circumstances. If double the number of canes can be grown without crowding, then prune each cane to two buds, and next year sixteen canes will grow. If, however, eight canes are all that are needed, then cut away the upper cane on each spur and shorten each of the others to two buds.

### Horseshoe Lever

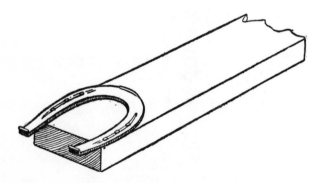

A handy lever for prying up boxes or barrels may be made by nailing an old horseshoe on the end of a 2 x 4, letting the ends of the horseshoe extend about an inch or two beyond the end of the timber. A more finished device may be constructed by cutting the upper part of the lever down to the form of a rounded handle. A horseshoe should be selected with fairly long and well-sharpened heel calks.

### An Elevated Clothesline

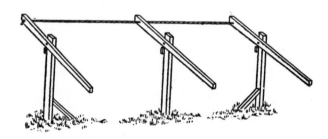

The good homesteader will not fail to assist his hard-working wife. This device will help to remove the "blue" from washday Monday. Heavy posts should be set for the ends, 3 feet in and 3 feet out of the ground. It is not necessary for the center post to be as heavy as the end ones. Have the posts clean and smooth so that they will not soil the clothes when blown against them. Take a piece of 2 by 4-inch hardwood 5 feet long for the lever. Fasten to the post near the top with a 3/4-inch bolt, 2 feet next to the line and 3 feet for the lever. A block holds the lever in position while the clothes are being put on. A button holds the lever upright when the line is hoisted.

## An Easy Way to Pole Beans

Set posts at convenient distances apart and stretch a wire at the top. This may be done as soon as ground is plowed. Plant and cultivate one row on each side of the line until beans begin to vine. Then set poles slanting, tying them together where they cross at the wire. This braces the whole row, and beans can be cultivated with the hoe. Hills 3 feet apart in rows with one vine to a hill are better than two vines.

## Protecting Newly-Set Plants

Plants newly transplanted always demand more or less protection from the blighting effects of too much sun and wind. It is best achieved by making a shelter such as is shown in the cut. Two 10-foot poles and two 3-foot pieces of any convenient thickness for the crosspieces, with four 14-inch weather strips for the legs, constitute the frame. In the middle of it two hooks should be inserted on each side, and upon these the covering fastened, which can thus be adjusted very quickly. The covering may consist of burlap or any kind of rough sacking.

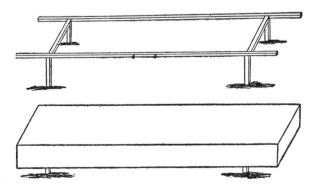

Being so simple and economical to make, it is advisable to have enough frames to protect the number of tender plants that are set out in a garden at one time. They possess other advantages than sheltering the young things from the direct rays of the sun. They allow slow evaporation, and so keep newly-watered ground moist for hours, whereas if exposed to the sun and wind it would soon become dry and caked. On windy days, it is only necessary to let the sacking down on the windward side of the shelter. In case of frost, the protection that they afford is of inestimable value.

## Moving a Large Tree

To move a large tree one may find it very satisfactory to use a rig similar to that shown in the picture. Make a three-sided standard of 2 by 4-inch stuff. Loosen the dirt around the roots of the tree and wrap the tree firmly at the base with old carpet or burlap to prevent injury. Place the standard firmly in the ground, and tie the crosspiece to the body of the tree with strong rope to each side of the standard, and hitch a horse to the other end. With a slow pull, the tree can be drawn onto the drag and then hauled to the new location. It can be placed in the ground again by using the standard in the same way it was used to load it upon the drag.

RIG FOR MOVING TREE

MEEDER-CHUBB SC

# FARM AND GARDEN WORK FOR

# June

What a glorious month June is! We have much more of sunshine than in any other month, and this is usually accompanied by heat and moisture in such degrees that the whole country has an atmosphere like a greenhouse, and vegetation of all kinds makes its most rapid growth. The chilly days and cold nights of May have past; the backward corn now makes amends for its tardy development, loses the sickly yellow hue, and puts on the bright green of health. Wheat pushes up its bearded ears, and the clover heads make the meadows rosy. Long dormant seeds are warmed to life, and plants spring up unbidden wherever the fresh mould has been stirred. The pastures are in their best condition, and the distended udders, full pails, thick cream, and golden butter make us glad. Fruits are ripening, and fresh vegetables appear in increasing variety upon the table. It is the month of roses, and with the queen of flowers comes a charming throng—some bearing chalices of beauty, others vials of odors—to crown with radiance and fragrance the measure of the month.

June is not playtime. Work, hard work, is the order of the day. All this energy of nature must be directed, checked, taken advantage of, utilized. If corn grows, so will weeds. Every additional pound of milk makes more work for us in the dairy. In almost every area of labor, the farmer may have more work than he can do, and, to accomplish well the most important, all the labor must be thoroughly systematized.

## HINTS ABOUT FARM WORK

**Buildings**—There are certain things which can be better done at this season than at any other. The barns are nearly empty. They must be prepared for the new crops of hay and grain. If a barn should need shingling, this ought be done when it is empty so that the nails which fall may be cleaned up. We know a case of a cow which died from swallowing nails in the hay. These were found in a large mass in the animal's stomach. Haylofts and bays should be cleaned, and all the hayseed and rubbish removed before any hay is placed in them. Old hay is good, but it is best not to allow it to accumulate from year to year.

**Working Animals** must be well fed if one expects them to work well. Oxen worked all day turned into the pasture for the night without grain of any kind cannot be expected to do much work. Give horses thorough daily grooming. A gill of oil meal, mixed with the feed at each meal, will give a glossy coat and is an excellent ingredient in any mixed feed given to them or other animals.

**Cows** are now at pasture, and the fresh grass adds greatly to the flow of milk and to its richness and color; but this should not lead us to withold all grain. A small quantity of oil meal or cornmeal, or the two mixed, say one quart divided between the morning and evening, should be given.

**Manure** — If cows are yarded or stabled, a very large quantity of manure is saved. We are too apt to look upon the manure crop as the harvest of the winter. With reasonable forethought and diligence the manure heaps will grow quite as fast in summer. Summer has one great advantage — fermentation takes place much more rapidly; hence accumulations of vegetable matter, fresh, or in form of muck and peat, if composted with stable manure, ashes, or lime, very rapidly ferment and ripen into homogeneousness, ready for use in the autumn.

**Swine** are widely employed as the summer manure makers, and they are worth so much more as rooters than "tamed" that it is not worth while to "ring" or "tame" them until they are penned to fatten. Confine them where they may have, conveniently, sods, weeds, and all sorts of green rubbish thrown to them to work over. If upon the manure of other stock, encourage diligence by scattering occasionally handfuls of corn about the heap. If muck or sods are used in the compost, swine will often tread it so hard as to arrest fermentation.

**Butter** — June butter is considered the best made during the year. Good butter makers pack it to keep the whole year. There is no difficulty about it if the buttermilk is thoroughly worked out, the butter salted one ounce to the pound, and worked again after standing 12 to 24 hours. It is packed in layers in firkins, with a thin layer of salt on the bottom, and salt between each layer. The butter must be packed airtight, if possible — that is, without holes — and pounded down flat and solid. The less butter is handled, the better, and the lower the temperature at which it is worked, provided it is soft enough to work thoroughly, the more waxy and firm it will be. If the tub cannot be filled at once, cover the butter with a strong brine.

**Green-Fodder Crops** — Sow corn in drills, 24 to 30 inches apart, for a succession of green fodder. This will keep up the flow of milk and add greatly to the butter and cheese returns of the summer, especially if the pastures are a little overstocked or the season is dry. Millet may be sown any time this month, for seed as well as for green fodder. Hungarian grass, a variety of millet sown for hay on land in fair condition only, will ordinarily yield a crop of two tons of good hay per acre.

**Pastures** may be benefitted by top-dressings at any time, especially if close cropped. They respond at once if wash from the highways is turned upon them. Never overstock, but provide early green-fodder crops to feed out before the fields are so far denuded as to be liable to injury from drought.

**Mowing Lands** — Clover which is clean enough for seed should be cut early, when first coming into bloom. Top-dress with fine manure, ashes and plaster, or guano and plaster, and a good crop of seed will be as sure as a crop of corn. Cut mixed grasses for hay, beginning when clover is in full bloom, before the heads brown, and cutting those fields first which have the most clover. Cure as much as possible in the shade — that is, in the cock (conical piles) after thoroughly wilting in the sun. If the ox-eye daisy abounds in the grass, it is most important to cut it for hay before the stalks harden, and for the future welfare of the farm it is more important to cut it before the seeds are so nearly mature that they will ripen in the curing of the hay.

**Root Crops** — Carrots and rutabagas may be sown to as good advantage between the 1st and 20th of June as earlier, considering the pressure of other work and the slight difference a few weeks make to these crops. Sugar beets and parsnips will make a fair crop, also, if put in as late as the first, but sowing should not be delayed after that time.

**Field Beans**—This crop is generally planted before the 20th, if possible. Use only fresh, tender seed. Two-year-old seed will surely disappoint.

**Cabbages** can hardly be overrated as an economical article of cattle food. The only objection to raising cabbages as a dependence for green fodder in winter is that their market price is usually so great we cannot afford to feed them out; but the same objection holds with regard to many other articles of human food. Set out the varieties after the middle of the month, in good soil, well manured with fine compost and top-dressed with lime.

**Hoeing Corn and Potatoes**—All tillage of these crops goes by the name of hoeing, though done with harrows, cutlivators, or plows. The harrow should be used upon potatoes until they are fairly up and the field is green. After this, light plows and cultivators do the work. There is no crop which requires more thorough weeding than potatoes, and none more generally neglected and more damaged by them.

### HINTS ABOUT HORTICULTURAL WORK

It usually makes but little difference how unfavorable the spring months have been. The middle of June generally brings matters in the different departments to about the same point. The skillful gardener will have replanted where the cold rains have brought failures and made up by extra care the delays caused by untoward weather.

*Orchard and Nursery*

**Shoots** will push on old and young trees just where limbs are not wanted. Remember that the now tender shoot will soon be a hard, woody branch. A slight rub will now remove it, but if left a year, the knife must be used. Rub off these shoots when young and save cutting hereafter.

**Pruning** may be done this month, especially if large limbs are to be removed. Cut the limb close to the one from which it starts, and do not leave any stubs. Pare the wounds smooth, and brush them over with melted grafting wax.

**Grafts** will need looking to, and if two were inserted where one would be better, remove one of them. If some of the shoots on a graft are getting the advantage of the others, pinch them back.

**Budded Stocks** will often push such vigorous shoots as to need staking until they become strong.

**Cultivation** in the orchard has a twofold effect—it destroys the weeds, and leaves the surface in that light, mellow condition which enables it to answer the purposes of a mulch. Young orchards, with crops between the rows, should be cultivated with as much an eye to the trees as to the crops.

**Mulching** around newly planted trees should be put on before dry weather comes on. It is especially beneficial to cherries and other stone fruits.

**Seedbeds** will need shading, as noted last month. Young evergreens will often rot or "damp off" without any manifest cause. Sprinkling fine sand or dry earth over the bed will often check it.

**Thin the Fruit**—It is not often that this is done as thoroughly as it should be, and it is seldom that a tree bears a decent crop which would not have been better had half of the young fruit been removed.

**Insects** will demand attention this month. See notes given in May. One great trouble with insects is that they are left too long without molestation, and most people do not notice their ravages until the mischief is done. Whoever loves trees will be frequently among them and observe the condition of each. A colony of caterpillars may often be disposed of in a few minutes, which, if left for a week, would prove a troublesome enemy.

**Borers** mostly lay their eggs this month; these are usually deposited on the bark of the tree near the ground, and the young grubs when hatched eat their way into the tree. Be sure that there are no grubs already in the tree, and some of the many preventives may be used. One of the most efficient of these is to wrap the trunk at the base with stiff paper, drawing away the earth around the tree, and replacing it to cover the lower edge of the paper.

**Curculio** is only effectually managed by jarring the trees and catching the insects. On large trees a limb may be sawn off to leave a stub which may be struck with a wooden mallet, but small trees can be easily shaken by a sudden jar with the hand.

**The Slug** which appears on the leaves of pear and cherry trees is killed by dusting with slaked lime; it is said on good authority that dry dust of any kind will answer the same purpose.

**Plant Lice**, often troublesome on trees, are killed by the use of an infusion of tobacco or of quassia.

## Fruit Garden

**The Insects** mentioned above, and others, will need close attention here; they are more easily managed in fruit garden, as the trees are, or should be, dwarfs. Much can be done by hand-picking, which is, indeed, the only way of managing some of the larger insects that infest the grape.

**Currants** will need care to protect them from the currant worm. Many useless shoots will appear upon the bushes which may be rubbed out. Green currants often bring a higher price than ripe ones, and where this is the case it is better to dispose of a portion of the crop in the green state.

**Strawberries** will now demand attention. The rows should be mulched, if not already done. Straw of coarse hay is best. Sawdust and tanbark soil the fruit. Keep the runners cut where close culture is practiced, and pull up large weeds.

**Blackberry Bushes** should have the new growth pinched at the height of 4 or 5 feet to make them throw out side branches for next year's fruiting.

**Grape Vines**—The future success of the vine depends upon getting a good strong cane to start with. Superfluous buds will appear which should be rubbed off. Young vines will be apt to be injured from overbearing, and one or two bunches are enough to a cane. If mildew appears, use sulphur. Keep the young growth tied up to the trellis.

## Kitchen Garden

Do not let disappointment from rotting of seeds, killing by late frosts, or bad luck of any kind prevent you from trying again. Those who have been deterred by a press of work from giving proper attention to the garden can do considerable work even now. It is true the products will not be early, but they will be better than none. Seeds sown in the warm soil come on rapidly, and with a little exertion tomato, cabbage, pepper, and other plants can be had and a pretty fair family garden yet be enjoyed.

**Asparagus**—The rule is to stop cutting when peas become plenty. If the bed has become weedy, hoe it over carefully, give a dressing of manure or compost, and let the plants grow.

**Beans**—Plant succession crops of bush beans. It is early enough in most places for limas.

**Beets and Carrots**—Thin and weed. The thinnings of beets are excellent to use as "greens."

**Cabbages**—The early sorts, in the best-managed gardens, are ready for use or sale this month, but in most family gardens there are no facilities for early plants, and those from an open-air seedbed are now transplanted. Keep the ground loose among young plants by the use of the rake. If the plants are troubled by cutworms, look for their holes (usually covered by a leaf) and dig them out.

**Celery**—The seedlings should be thinned and weeded. It is recommended that tops be sheared off young plants to make them grow stocky. The main crop is best set in July, but early plants may be set in well-manured trenches as soon as large enough.

**Corn**—Sow at intervals of two weeks, and have a good supply for drying for winter use.

E.A.WINHAM.

**Peppers**—Put out in a well-manured bed in a warm place, and give good cultivation. Set in rows 2 feet apart and 15 inches between.

**Cucumber**—Set out the plants, started under glass, and sow seeds in the open ground in well-manured hills, which should be about 4 feet apart. Keep off the striped bug.

**Eggplants**—These are warm weather fellows, and do but little until the soil has become well heated. Give a rich spot, hoe often, and each plant may yield six or eight large fruits, or only one.

**Endive**—Sow for a late supply, and transplant when large enough to a foot apart each way.

**Lettuce** for summer use does best in a somewhat shaded and moist place.

**Melons** are to be treated as directed for cucumbers.

**Onions**—Keep clear of weeds, and thin.

**Parsnips**—Thin and hoe, and keep the bed clear of weeds until the leaves meet between the rows.

**Peas** in field culture simply have the earth drawn towards the vines to form a ridge. Put brush early to the tall-growing sorts, and plant succession crops.

**Radishes**, if relished so late in the season, may be sown at intervals of a week in unoccupied spots.

**Rhubarb** should not be pulled so freely when fruits come; let the plants recover. Cut the flower stalks as soon as they appear.

**Rutabagas**, if sown in the garden, may be put in at the end of the month. Dust with plaster and ashes or lime as soon as the plants are up.

**Salsify**, a most excellent vegetable and often called "oyster plant," is grown in the same way as carrots. It is not too late to sow seed this month.

**Spinach**—A succession crop may now be sown.

**Squashes**—Treat the bush sorts as directed for cucumbers. Winter varieties must have room to run; give them plenty of manure; put in hills 8 feet apart each way; keep off striped bugs; hand-pick squash bugs; keep the ground clean until the plants take possession of the soil, after which do not disturb them.

**Sweet Potatoes**—Set out, if not already done. In field culture the plants get no support, but in gardens it conduces to neatness and fruitfulness to have some kind of trellis.

**Weeds** will need constant attention; they are easily managed when young, and are very stubborn when large. The free use of the rake or the pronged hoe will keep the garden in order with much less trouble than a periodical spell of hoeing.

*Flower Garden and Lawn*

The tender annuals sown the first of June will do quite as well, or better, than if put in the ground earlier. So with the majority of bedding plants, which are often seriously checked in their growth by chilly nights and are a long while in recovering.

**Greenhouse** and other plants in pots are often used with good effect in decorating the grounds. They may be turned out of their pots into the borders, or the pots may be plunged up to their rims. In the latter case, put some coal ashes under the pot to prevent worms from finding their way in.

**Oleanders, oranges, crape myrtles,** and such shrubs may be turned out with benefit, provided they are taken up and potted early enough in the fall.

**Fuschias** make good border plants if they have been grown sufficiently tall and are placed where they will have shade in the hotter portions of the day.

**Bulbs**—To have the best flowers of hyacinths and tulips, the bulbs should be taken up when the foliage begins to wither, dried, and kept until time to plant in fall; but in most gardens where special care is not given, they are left out for several years, the bloom decreasing in size and beauty each year.

**Annuals**—Transplant or thin out the seedlings. Many kinds will do well if planted now.

**Roses** of the perpetual sorts should have the faded flowers removed and their small branches shortened to induce a new crop of flowers. Train up some strong shoots of the climbing varieties to replace wood that will soon be old and need to be removed.

**Neatness** is much promoted by using proper supports for plants. Let the sticks and tying material be kept out of sight. Remove all faded flowers.

**Weeds**, of course, must be kept down. Use the rake freely. The bayonet hoe and a narrow, long-toothed rake are the best implements for working among the plants in the flower borders.

*Greenhouse and Window Plants*

Every thing that is to come out at all will be placed outside this month, and the sooner repairs are made, the better. The plants left in the house should not suffer from neglect. Those outside will need care in watering. Some must have shade during the greater part of the day, and all should be so placed that they will not be injured by high winds. Provide for potting soil, which, for general purposes, is best when made of decayed sods and well-decomposed manure.

# PROJECTS FOR
# JUNE

## The Art of Making Good Butter

**Milk** — First, you must have good, healthy young cows. They require good food and uniform feeding. They should be salted twice a week and have fresh running water daily. Second, the cow must be milked thoroughly and as rapidly as strength will permit; then, after standing 5 to 10 minutes, she must be stripped so that she will be left dry. *A pint of strippings will make far more butter than a gallon of the first drawn milk.* The milk should be strained immediately. A large two-gallon stone crock is best for setting and should remain standing for 48 hours in moderate temperature (about 60°) before skimming.

**Cream** — Churn every other morning in cool weather, but, when warm, churning should be done every morning and the cream kept in as cool a place as possible. Also, put a large lump of ice in the cream overnight, which will have no effect on the butter; but if the ice were put in the butter, it would spoil it. The milk should be skimmed every 24 or 36 hours. (Place the crock of milk in water from 8 to 10 inches deep when the cream rises in the above-stated time, and the milk will seldom get sour.)

**Washing and Cleansing the Utensils** — The best method of throughly cleansing milking vessels is to add to 10 gallons of water a half gallon of clean, strong wood ashes and let it come to a boil. Wash the stone crocks in warm water; then run them around in the boiling lye and wash in warm water. This process will do for the buckets, ladles, and churn, etc. No other mode will purify the rancidness that

will accumulate in a dairy. After washing and rinsing the crocks, expose them to the air and sun. They will be as sweet as when first bought from the store. Once a month will be sufficient for this cleansing. All good dairywomen know that the utensils should be washed in boiling water after using.

**Churning** — Never let the cream stand over 48 hours after it is skimmed and you will find no difficulty in churning. In midwinter, proceed as follows: Stand the cream near the fire, where it will become quite warm; then let it cool rapidly. Add more cream the next skimming, and so on until the fourth skimming. Let it stand all night, and in the morning scald out the churn before using. In case the cream is too cold, add a little boiling water. When the churning is finished, the butter should be drained and well worked, and on no account should the butter be washed, for this reason: if you wash butter, it will get strong in half the time it would by extracting the milk without washing. It must be worked out or the butter will soon become rancid.

**Salting** — To 12 pounds of butter use a pound and a half of salt, well worked in, and put in a cool place until the next morning. Then work again, working out the brine which will accumulate, which is almost equivalent to the amount of salt put in. If the butter is made for packing purposes, work it the third morning and make into rolls of convenient size.

**Keeping** — The best mode of keeping butter is to make each roll separate, wrapping a clean thick cloth around it tightly; then place in a tub as tight

and close together as you can. Cover with brine, which is made as follows: To 5 gallons of spring water, add 5 pounds of coarse salt, 2 ounces of salt-peter, 8 to 10 ounces of the best sugar, all well dissolved. This should cover 100 pounds of butter and preserve the same for six months or more.

**Coloring** — It is not necessary to use anything to color butter, but by observing the preceding rules in summer and winter, you can always have good golden butter.

### A Homemade Beehive

Make the four sides of a box (*b*) 12 inches inside each way. Make another box (*a*) 15 inches inside each way, and 1 inch deeper than the first one. A top board (*c*) is made, large enough for the larger box, and rabbeted back from the edge all around to receive the cap (*g*), made 13 inches inside. Nail this top to both boxes one within the other. The strips (*d*) are then nailed on the inside of the outer and on the lower end of the inner box. This closes up the space between the two and makes the hive warm in

winter and cool in summer. The bees will not come out of such a hive in winter unless the weather is warm enough to allow them to do so without harm.

To prevent millers depositing their eggs under the edge of the hive, take a strip of hoop iron (*e*), 1½ inches wide, and nail around the bottom, forming a band. This may be done easily by cutting it in four

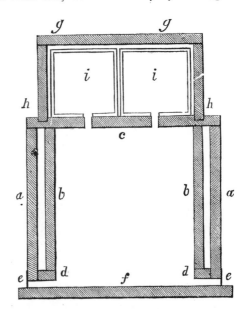

pieces, one to fit each side, and make close joints at the corners, punching holes and filing the edge straight. Nail them on the hive so that the iron will project about ½-inch below. The edge of iron will rest on the bottom board (*f*), leaving a ½-inch space between the bottom of the hive and the board, giving the bees a chance to operate on the board out to the iron. To give the bees an entrance, a notch is cut in the front piece of iron 3/8-inch deep and 3/4-inch long. Give them another entrance, 3½ inches above the alighting board, by inserting a plug which reaches through the two boxes with a ½-inch hole in the center.

## Transplanting Trees

Here is a way to transplant large trees that is not so difficult as such transplanting is by many supposed to be. The first move to make is to dig all around the tree, leaving a large ball of soil which is carefully wrapped in sacking or canvas to hold it on the roots and prevent drying. When this is well tied in place, a chain is passed round the ball two or three times and hooked, as shown in *fig. 1*. Then with a pair of

FIGURE 2—HOOK AND TRUCK

by the free use of blankets and bags. The secret of success in transplanting trees is to injure the roots as little as possible.

## A Wire Fence Corncrib

In the drawing is shown a handy, inexpensive corncrib which possesses several advantages not possessed by the ordinary slat corncrib. It is made on 4 x 4-

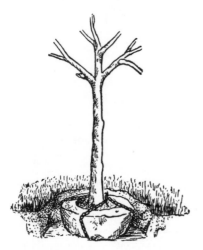

FIGURE I—BALLED

heavy wheels on a short axle and a strong pole laid across it, with a massive iron hook fastened to the pole, it is easy to back up to the tree. The sketch (*fig. 2*) shows the truck with its lever raised ready to hook into the chain. The rope at the end of the pole brings it down and the tree up, when the pole is fastened under a second pair of wheels. The young trunk must be kept from contact with the machinery

inch posts, with pans at their tops to prevent rats from climbing in. The sills are 4 x 4-inch, the scantlings 2 x 4, and 2 feet apart. The fencing is nailed to these on all sides, and the door frame is similarly covered. The roof is made wide, so as to shed all possible water. The height, length, and width may suit the farmer's convenience. A convenient width is about 5 feet at the floor, widening to 7 feet at the eaves. Owing to the very open nature of this crib, corn dries more quickly than in a slat crib, and as there is less chance for water to lodge in the cracks, the crib will be more durable than if built entirely of wood.

## Hay Making

The importance of the hay crop cannot be overestimated. Not only are grass and clover at the basis of our method of agriculture, but the hay as an article of fodder is our great dependence during the feeding season. It is therefore important that it should be gathered in such a condition that its nutritious properties should be retained in the highest degree. Generally our hay crop is gathered so late that it has lost much of its value. We may take it for granted that hay not in the barn by the end of June has lost one-fourth of its money value. This is the true light in which to view it. Clover, then, should be cut before a head has turned brown, and timothy, orchard grass, or redtop before fairly in blossom.

When cut in its best condition, still much of its value depends on its curing. Its greatest value is preserved when dried in the shade. It should therefore be cured in the cock and not allowed to be exposed to the hot sun for a longer time than to completely wilt it. If dried more than this, the leaves of clover will become crisp and break up readily, and a mass of dry, hard stalks will only be left. The practice should be to cut up to ten o'clock in the morning, leave until four in the afternoon, then gather into cocks before the dew falls, and by six have all raked up and cocked, and if there is probability of rain to cover with caps. As soon as ten o'clock the next day has arrived, open those cocks which were made on the previous day — or two days may elapse without any injury — and as soon as they are all opened by merely throwing over and loosening a little, commence to load and draw in until four o'clock. The exposure during loading and unloading removes all superabundant moisture, and it goes into the barn or stack without losing a leaf

and with many of the blossoms still opening. By providing ventilators, as in *fig. 3*, the moisture remaining and the heat of the fermentation pass off without any injury or doing any more than thoroughly curing the hay. With such hay, butter can be made the same high golden color in January or February as in June. The cocks should be made high and narrow. The moist hay soon commences to ferment, and if put up at four o'clock will be found quite warm at ten o'clock at night; but the heat easily passes off at the sides and carries the vapor from the hay with it.

Fig.1.—HAY-COCK AND CAP.

Fig. 2.
PEGS.

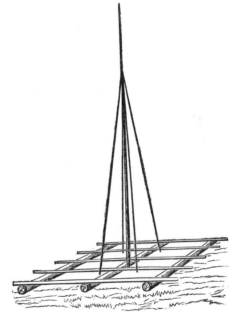

Fig. 3.—FOUNDATION FOR A STACK.

*Fig. 1* shows the form in which cocks should be built and the mode in which they should be covered. They may be made large enough to contain 200 pounds of hay. The cap is merely a square piece of sheeting, which may be procured of any width from a yard up to two yards, but a cap a yard square may be made to do good service. The ends are hemmed,

106

and at each corner an eyelet hole is worked in which a loop of small cord is fixed. Pegs are to be made either of a piece of shingle or of a twig, cut as in *fig. 2*. Hay thus protected may stay in the field for a week without injury, and in windy weather the tops of the cocks will not be blown off.

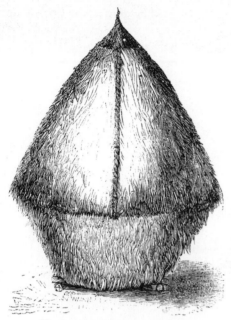

Fig. 4.—PROPER FORM OF STACK.

Fig. 5.—TWISTING STRAW-ROPE.

Stacking hay requires more care than is generally given to it. If stacks can be made rainproof, the expense of buildings is saved. They may be built in this way and so finished off that there will be no waste in using the hay. A stack-yard to which cattle or hogs cannot gain access, and near the barn or stables, is the best. Here foundations (*fig. 3*) should be provided to raise the hay from the ground on spots somewhat elevated so that water will not collect beneath them. The pole in the center should be set in the ground firmly; it will be a guide in building

the stack and will keep it from settling sideways and tipping over. The form shown in *fig. 4* will be found perfectly rainproof if the hay is well raked off from the sides as it is narrowed in, and the cap at the top neatly put on and kept tied closely to the post as the hay settles down. By making the stack quite steep, the rain gets no chance to enter and runs off freely at the eaves. In building, it is best to keep the hay well trodden down, and time is saved by having an extra hand on the stack for this express purpose. A ladder will be needed for the finishing off. A large sheet is very useful to have in readiness to cover the stack until it can be properly be finished off. A straw rope should be passed across the top in two directions to prevent the wind blowing the top loose, which would allow rain to enter, and should be tightly pegged down at the eaves. A straw rope may be twisted with a crank hooked at one end, as in *fig. 5*. This simple machine may be fastened to a fence post or the post of a shed or barn. Any kind of straw or coarse hay may be used, but it should be well wetted previous to using it. One man feeds the straw, walking backwards, and a boy or girl may turn the crank. Other contrivances for twisting a straw rope will readily suggest themselves.

## An Ingenious Hay Stacker

Set a stiff pole (*A*), 25 or 30 feet long, firmly in the ground, and about 8 feet from the top bolt on a block which has a socket made with a 2-inch auger. Fit to the socket one end of another light pole (*B*),

about 11 feet long, and shave the upper end so that it will go into a link of chain extending from the top of the main pole to the small one. Pins may be inserted in the main pole on which a man can ascend to the top to adjust the length of the chain. The tops of the poles should be about 5 to 8 feet apart. The upper end of the small pole should receive the end link of the chain, and a pulley can be hung on the hook. The main pole should bear a very little towards the stick so that the forkful of hay will swing clear over the stack as it rises. Guy ropes extend from the top of the pole to stakes driven firmly in the ground to keep it upright. These should be attached so as not to interfere with the swinging of the crane. It will be perceived that the draw-rope, to which the horse is attached, passes from the upper pulley beneath the lower one, thence over the upper one, and then through a block fastened at the base of the large pole. By this arrangement, the horse is required to travel about twice as fast as the fork rises.

PLATFORM AND SPOUT FOR WASHING SHEEP.

## The Art of Shearing Sheep

It is essential to good shearing to cut the wool but once, to shear smoothly and very close, to keep the fleeces whole, and to avoid cutting the sheep. When a shearer does not shear smoothly, but cuts a portion of the wool two or three times, there is not only a loss in the weight of the fleece and a loss in its value to the manufacturer, but much time is consumed in making the sheep look smooth. When the fleeces are torn to pieces by unskillful handling or the floundering of the sheep, it is impossible to do them up neatly and show the wool to advantage.

The chief difficulty in shearing sheep arises from their struggling. To prevent this, some tie their legs; but this practice is quite objectionable, and no good shearer will adopt it. Sheep will kick and flounder but little if they are managed gently and carefully. Every shearer should have a mattress of straw, at least 5 feet square, and so thick that his knees will not feel the floor while shearing a sheep. The object of the mattress is also to make it easier for the sheep. Laid on a hard floor, sheep will make desperate efforts to gain their natural position, and, if jammed down violently on the floor, or boxed, or held uncomfortably beneath the knees as they often are by unskillful shearers, instead of keeping quiet they flounder and kick worse and worse. Placed on a mattress, their position is comparatively easy; and if handled gently, the fleeces will be torn but little.

FOLDING FLEECES.

The sheep pen should be well littered with straw to prevent carrying much dirt on the shearing floor; and sheep always shear better if they are full and round than when empty. Even expert shearers are very likely to cut the skin of poor thin sheep. No man can shear a sheep well unless he has good shears and keeps them in good cutting order.

108

## Breeding Work Horses

The object with many breeders has been to secure style and speed, almost regardless of size and strength. The heavy work of the farm being done by oxen, and our farms in many of the horse-raising districts being small, the farmers themselves have not felt the need of heavier draft animals. However, it would be much better for us as farmers if we used heavier horses. Illustrated is a draft stallion which exhibits many of those points which the sire of a large-sized horse for heavy draft should possess. We do not undervalue blood on the side of the sire; but there are many reasons why thoroughbreds cannot be generally used for crossing on large mares, and why the cross would be undesirable. Horses by blood sires are very apt to inherit their temper, often none of the mildest, and a fractious great horse is a dangerous and unsafe piece of property.

Probably the best class of sires for heavy stock that would be available in this country would spring from crossing thoroughbred stallions on large handsome Norman or other large-sized mares. Such hor-

SIRE FOR HEAVY DRAUGHT HORSES. — *Engraved for the American Agriculturist.*

ses would be of good size, and in form and style combine the good points of the two races, and communicate probably many of their own excellences to their progeny. In selecting a mare, bear in mind that the qualities she chiefly imparts to the foal are size, constitution, form of body, and symmetry; while spirit and bottom, intelligence and action come more from the sire. The aim should be to obtain a mare of large size, having a large, roomy body, rather short legs, broad and deep in the chest, heavy behind, broad across the hips, wide in the pelvis, and carrying her hind feet well apart. The back should be short, the limbs clean and strong, the hoofs pointing forward, round and solid, rather than long or flat. She should have a small head, large nostrils, and a full quiet eye, a neck sufficiently long to allow her to graze on level ground without spreading her forefeet, and, more than all, she should possess high spirits and a tractable disposition.

In selecting mares, every one should be scrupulously rejected that has blemishes, bad points, or especially constitutional defects, for such things are almost sure to be transmitted to the offspring. These things are to be avoided with as much care in the selection of a stallion as a mare. A celebrated stallion in central New York, which had several spavins, got excellent colts; but before they were four years old most of them were badly spavined, and some of them had spavins on both hind legs.

The important points we should seek in a stallion for the purpose we are considering are: size, good form, muscle, bottom, vigorous health, quickness, and spirit. We cannot expect to raise large horses from undersized stallions. Every other good point may be developed in the most desirable manner, but if size is wanting, the stallion should not be used for raising horses for heavy work. The body of the stallion should be of as good proportions as the mare's. His back should be short, and his body round as a barrel, with well-ribbed back, and filled out in the flank, and not like the body of a greyhound. His head should be small and bony; his neck strong and of good length; his breast very broad from one shoulder point to the other; the withers high; the legs short, but very strong, having the hocks and knees low, and the legs below hard and smooth; the leg bones large and flat. Such a horse will not be likely to strain himself at a heavy draft; he will be an easy traveler, and his hind legs will not swing and twist out and in as he moves. The stallion should be solid and compact, kindly tempered and plucky; and, if possible, choice should be made of one which is known to impart with great uniformity his good points to his colts. It is neither necessary nor desirable to use a stallion as large as the mare.

## Farm Sleds for Winter and Summer

In some parts of the country, there is constant use made of sleds in summer, and very wisely, we think, as we always advocate the employment of animal labor to save hand labor when it can be done economically. But even if one does not intend to do any sledding upon bare ground, the sled pattern here presented is worthy of the attention of farmers now because they may take the leisure of rainy days of the present and coming season to have the stuff saved and put together before snow.

**Making the Sled** — It is so easily made that any farmer can make it, and we guarantee that after one week's using it, he will not be willing to be without one on his premises.

The runners are sawed out of sound hickory, the crooks coming out of the butt of the log and being, say, 6 inches in a length of 10 or 12 feet. Their width is 5½ or 6 inches, and their thickness 2 or 2½ inches. The beams are made of 6 x 6 oak scantling. The first beam is set 20 inches from the crook, pinned to the runners with inch pins, set diagonally and drawing a little, and wedged on the underside of the runner. The roller-gudgeons enter 3-inch blocks, bolted to the tops of the runners with two bolts each. No raves are needed. The stake holes are bored slanting through the beams so as to miss the inside of the runners; otherwise they will fill with dirt.

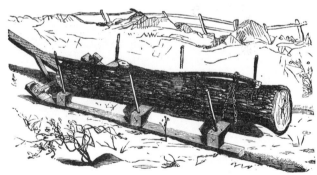

Fig. 1.—STARK CO. SLED.

**Advantages** — It is so low, a man using skids 8 feet long can roll on an ordinary saw-log with a handspike, thus saving unhitching and hitching his team. It is not likely to upset when loaded and will not cut in in crossing soft places. When there is but little snow, not enough to run an ordinary sled, a team can draw a heavy log with ease. It is not so likely to break in crossing uneven places, and passes over obstructions easily. In short, its superiority is so manifest that it needs but a day's trial to establish it.

**Summer Sleds**—There are a multitude of uses to which a light sled can be applied throughout the year, and the additional labor imposed upon the horses is very little. The following is a sketch for a tool-sled or drag. It is 8 feet long and 3 wide. The runners are two 4 x 4 scantling or other pieces of hardwood, though red cedar will do. There is a floor of inch boards, and 1½ x 3-inch raves nailed upon these. One-inch oak pins are used to fasten the parts together, and three or four carriage bolts on each side are an additional security. These should pass through runners, boards, and raves, the heads being well sunk in the runners, and the nuts on the top should be provided with washers.

Fig. 2.—TOOL-SLED OR TOOL-BOAT.

The sled is drawn by hitching the team to a clevis in the front, or, better still, to a sort of bale—an iron rod, bent at a right angle, and attached to both runners. *Fig. 3* shows a box which fits upon the top of

Fig. 3.—BOX FOR TOOL-SLED.

the rave, and is held in place by strong cleats which enter the stake staples. This addition converts the tool-sled into a very different affair. It is a handy thing with which to gather up the stones in a mowing lot, to haul compost or manure upon plowed ground, for manuring in the hill or drill, and to distribute drain tiles along by the drains. Without the box, and simply with the poles, it may be used for moving fencing stuff, bean poles, bog hay, brush, and many other bulky things. This tool-boat will be found especially useful (when men and horses are to be

gone all day) to carry food and fodder besides the tools, and almost any farmer having one will make one or two of different sizes.

## Cheesemaking

Nearly every farm home contains, or may easily be supplied with, the necessary appliances to make cheese, and it is not a difficult task when one is once familiar with the process. For a small batch of about 12 gallons of milk the following method is a good one: Take about 6 gallons of the evening's milk and leave it covered with a cloth in a temperature of 65 to 70 degrees until morning and then mix 6 gallons of morning's milk with it in a large tub or boiler. All milk may then be heated together to 80 or 90 degrees. Care must be used not to get it too hot or to expose it to a draft so that it will cool quickly.

Another good method preferred by some is to use 11 gallons of perfectly sweet morning's milk and to this add 1 gallon of milk that has soured and thickened. The sour milk should be stirred well to get out all the lumps and then left for about 15 minutes before the rennet is put in. The easiest way to heat the milk is to place it in a wash boiler right on the stove until it gets up to 86 or 90 degrees and then raise it from the stove by placing it on two bricks. The stove must not be too hot.

Rennet in the form of tablets is most convenient and useful for home cheese making. Dissolve one tablet in half a glass of cold water. Add to the milk after it has been heated and stir well for two minutes. Some cheesemakers use two or three tablets, as it saves time, but for beginners two are usually enough. If you have liquid rennet extract, use about two tablespoonfuls.

**Cutting the Curd**—The rennet will curdle the milk and the curd will be ready to cut in 20 to 40 minutes. This can be determined by noting if the curd breaks clean like jelly when raised on a knife blade. The cutting can be done with a wire toaster, a long knife, or a heavy wire. Cut lengthwise of the vessel and then crosswise until the curd is in nearly uniform pieces of ½-inch squares. After cutting, leave the curd on for five minutes, then heat slowly to 100 degrees, stirring all the time. Cook for about 40 minutes at as near 90 degrees as possible, stirring occasionally to prevent the curd from sticking together. Keep the heat up and do not allow the mass to cool.

To determine when the curd is ready, take a handful and squeeze it in the hand firmly, and if it feels elastic and does not stick together, it has been cooked long enough. If the milk is good, the curd should have a pleasant, slightly acid odor. As soon as the curd is cooked, draw off the whey or dip off the curd with a sieve and place in another vessel. After the curd is well drained and before it sticks together, add ¼ pound of fine salt and mix well. After salting, let it cool for 15 minutes, stirring occasionally, when it is ready for the hoop.

**Pressing and Curing** — For a cheese hoop, one can use a tin hoop 7 inches in diameter and 12 inches deep, or an old peck measure without a bottom if holes are punched in the sides for drainage. For a press a device shown in the sketch will serve well, the pail at the end of the lever being filled with stones. Before the curd is placed in the hoop, line it with cheesecloth, one piece the size of the bottom and another around the side. Turn the upper edge of the cloth over the edge of the hoop and fasten it tight. When the curd is packed firmly, put a piece of cloth on the upper end and fold it over tight. Make the pressure slight at first, but after an hour rearrange the cloth and make the pressure heavier. The pressing should be finished by the next day. Do not press in too cool a place, but keep the temperature about 50 degrees.

CHEESE PRESS

For curing, set the cheese in a damp room or cellar which has an even temperature. Turn it around daily, and if it shows signs of molding, rub occasionally with butter. It should be ready to eat in three or four weeks. Cheese will cure at 40 degrees, but it takes longer than when warmer. Twelve gallons of milk should make about 10 pounds of cheese, according to the richness of the milk. After one or two attempts, any housekeeper should be able to make good cheese by this method. It is necessary to keep all utensils very clean, and the liberal use of boiling water with a little soda will accomplish this purpose.

GUERNSEY COW "COTTIE," 14 YEARS OLD.

# FARM AND GARDEN WORK FOR

# July

Farmers naturally feel greater solicitude in regard to the results which this month will effect than about those of any other similar period. And well they may. It is not farmers alone who are interested; every man, woman, and child in the length and breadth of the land has a personal interest in abundant crops, well gathered. Upon no other thing does the prosperity of the whole country so much depend. The great bulk of the grass crop, which is more valuable than any other, the most of the wheat crop, and of all winter grains are harvested in July. The character of the season settles the amount which will be realized from spring-sowed grains, and, in fact, most summer crops. Where droughts prevail this month, they may almost, if not entirely, destroy the corn, potatoes, pastures, and aftermath. Protracted rains will cause great damage to grain hay not harvested; standing grass will become tough and wiry, losing much of its nutrituve value, and will fill up with new growth, chiefly of clover, which is not really healthy when cured for hay.

One of the most important things for us to do is to provide forage crops to take the place of short pasturage in the fall. The corn sown in May will help out the feed this month. Every one ought to have a set of hay and grain caps as a defense against showers and storms. We should arrange good plans for quick work. When the weather is favorable, keep the soil among hoed crops always mellow, not working it so deep, however, in dry weather as to cause the crops to wilt. The progress of the age is shown more in the application of machinery and horsepower to save the labor of human hands than in any other way, and it is essential to profitable farming that, so far as possible, we avail ourselves of the most valuable help. Smooth land is essential, if we would make the best use of haying and harvesting machinery. Clean land, that having a comparative freedom from weeds, is indispensable to the most advantageous use of horsepower in tillage. Freedom from water standing within a few feet of the surface, accomplished by means of thorough drainage, is, perhaps, the most important means of making the tiller of the soil in a measure independent of both wet and dry seasons. For the ease and comfort of the farmer and his teams and the durability of his implements, a removal of the stones, so far as possible, is most important.

## HINTS ABOUT FARM WORK

This is a month of hard work; haying presses upon hoeing, and this has to be neglected too often for the grain harvest. Then turnip and buckwheat sowing, cabbage setting, and a score of other necessary or desirable things fill every moment of the long days and may cause sore perplexity if the plans are not well thought over for each day and for several days ahead.

**Weather**—We expect hot weather, with some two or three weeks very hot and dry. We must be prepared to take advantage of a few rainy days early in the month to transplant cabbages and fill out tobacco or vacant spots in the rows of rutabagas.

**Grain**, caps of cloth are often very useful. Cut when nearly ripe, and, if the straw is short or dry, it saves time and labor to take to the field dampened, long rye straw for bands.

**Pastures** must be well looked to, and, if they begin to get short, the cattle should be fed daily with green corn fodder, or other green feed. Top-dress with guano, ashes, plaster, or any fine compost.

**Root Crops** — Rutabagas sown last month should be well hoed and thinned. Hoe other roots. Sow turnips any time during the month. A full crop of rutabagas cannot be expected, but a very good one may be excellent for the table. Sow late varieties of turnips only after the 25th. They will do well sown among corn at the last hoeing.

**Potatoes** — Keep weeds pulled; scatter turnip seed or set cabbage plants when hills are wanting.

**Corn** — Keep down the weeds with the plow and cultivator until the corn is too large; do as little hand-hoeing as possible, but pull the weeds close in by the hills and work the rest of the ground by horsepower. Sweet corn will mature "roasting ears" if sown as late as the 4th of July, and corn may be sown for green or dry fodder up to the 20th.

**Stacks** for hay, grain, and corn fodder, are best made long and narrow. For such, the horse fork attached to a pair of large shears may be used.

**Cabbages** — Set on rich land, where early potatoes, peas, etc., were taken off. Top-dress with lime, and water freely when first put out; when well established and beginning to grow, a few waterings at evening with liquid manure (barnyard) will give them a grand start and do much towards securing a large crop. Hoe very frequently.

**Buckwheat** may be sown any time during the month. It is one of the most profitable crops we raise, occupying the ground but a very short time, doing fairly on land not in the best heart, and well on any land not enriched with rank manure and not too wet. It makes so dense a covering as to choke down all common weeds and yields a very good return for the labor it requires, in grain and straw, which latter is a valuable addition to the manure heap. An old practice, rarely followed of late years, so far as we know, yet not to be overlooked, is the sowing of buckwheat as late as the last of this month or first week of August with wheat. This crop matures before frost, or not at all, and when it is removed, the wheat has the ground the rest of the season and is not perceptibly injured.

**Orchards**—It is often a problem to determine the crops to put in an orchard that should be tilled for the benefit of the trees. Potatoes seldom do well on a sod, and weeds will grow badly under the trees. Corn or grain should be out of the question because they make their strong growth just when the trees do theirs and are, therefore, a serious damage. "No white crop in an orchard" is the old English rule. Potatoes, roots, cabbages, and clover are beneficial. On rather light loams, the sward turned over flat, rolled, and harrowed so as not to tear the sod, buckwheat will make a fair crop. The sod will rot, the grass be kept under, and if the stubble be manured and plowed after the crop is off, the land will be in good condition for potatoes or root crops the next year if not too much shaded.

**Manure Making**—If the weather is dry, employ every spare hour in ditching and draining swamp holes and mucky places to get out a good supply of material for composts. All peaty material, bog grasses, ferns and rushes, sods, wherever found, (and, in the absence of these, good surface soil or even sand) ought to be freely used to compost with stable and yard manure. This is more important during the warm weather than at any other time. It is best to lay up the materials in compact rectangular heaps, having drainage secured under the whole bottom. The hog pens should be well supplied with weeds and green vegetable matters of all kinds, which they rapidly convert into manure. It is the saying of an old farmer: "Anything that grows in the summer will rot in the winter." This may not be exactly true, but it sufficiently well indicates the kind of material to put into hog pens.

**Animals**—All kinds of animals do better for being well fed. Young stock grows much more rapidly for a little meal; oil-cake porridge is grand feed for hogs, and they need but little to keep them well growing. Beeves ought to get grain in addition to the best grass; they do much better for it, and it costs less to fit them for market. Be sure that there is no lack of water, and it is best to keep salt where all the stock can always get at it.

**Weeds**—Maintain constant warfare; cut those in blossom, whenever seen, and throw them into the hog pen. Any that go to seed should be burned.

**Irrigation**—This subject is constantly exciting more interest. It is especially valuable for the production of grass, though its application is by no means limited to forage plants. The great value of the hay crop naturally leads us to wish to double it. Wherever an opportunity occurs, turn a gentle stream of water upon fresh-mown grass land, and so distribute it that it shall trickle over as wide a surface as possible. Let it stay on a day or two at a time, and report the result.

**Drainage**—The importance of drainage is only imperfectly understood. It is the best agency we can employ as a protection against protracted droughts.

## HINTS ABOUT HORTICULTURAL WORK

Our text this month is "weeds." It is a peculiar satisfaction to use the weeding implements in these scorching days. There are now no spring showers to make the weeds start all the better for a transplanting, but once uproot them—whether with the cultivator, hoe, or rake—and they immediately perish. It cannot be too frequently repeated that it is easier to destroy weeds when they are mere seedlings than after they become well established.

### Orchard and Nursery

**Thinning** is so much neglected, and yet so important, that we must, at the risk of repetition, often insist upon it. If one has any doubts upon the subject, let him take two trees of the same variety of peach or pear, and from one remove half or three-fourths of the crop, and upon the other let all the fruit grow. When the fruit is ripe, market the crop of each tree, keeping a correct account of all the expenses, and see which tree has *paid* the most. One bushel of good fruit will bring more than three bushels of poor.

**Peaches** should be handled with care; pick just before they soften, so that they will reach market in good order. Crates are better than baskets.

**Budding** will commence with the plum and cherry, according to the season.

**Pruning** is to be continued, and on young trees superfluous growths are to be rubbed off.

**Insects** are always to be fought. Sufficient directions for fighting them were given last month.

**Black Knot** on cherry and plum is to be cut out on its first appearance.

**Cultivate** young orchards as directed last month.

**Mulch** around young trees if this treatment is preferred to cultivation.

**Cherry Stones** are to be collected and mixed with plenty of sand before they dry up.

### Fruit Garden

Fruit sent to market must be picked in a "firmer" condition than that intended for home use. That which is to be used in the family may get "dead ripe" before it is gathered, and then it is improved by being cooled in the icebox before it is eaten.

**Blackberries** are to be kept in check; pinch back the side shoots to 18 inches, and keep the whole growth compact and within control. The pinching should be attended to at least every two weeks.

**Raspberries**—In garden culture it is best to prune out the old canes as soon as the fruit is off. Treat all suckers not needed for new plants like weeds.

**Currants**—If a late brood of the worm appears, give a dusting of white hellebore. By shading a number of bushes, the season of this excellent but much neglected fruit may be much prolonged.

**Strawberries** — These may be transplanted now, and the plants become sufficiently well established to give a crop next season.

**Dwarf Trees** in the fruit garden will need all the care with regard to insects mentioned for those in the orchard. Thinning is particularly recommended, especially with those pears that bear fruit in clusters. If the red spider appears upon pear trees, drench them with strong soapsuds.

**Grape Vines** will now need constant care.

### Kitchen Garden

**Asparagus** — Give a dressing of manure and let it grow. Fertilizing will do now better than at any other time. If the beetle appears, cut and burn. It is a quite small black beetle and a black grub. There is no natural help short of extermination.

**Beans** — Plant bush sorts for succession and pinch the limas when they are 6 or 7 feet high.

**Beets** — Thin, and use the thinnings for "greens." A crop may be sown even at this late day.

**Cabbages, Cauliflowers**, and the related plants which have been sown in an open ground seedbed are to be transplanted. Keep well cultivated.

**Celery** — Set the plants for the main crop in rows 3 feet apart, and the plants 6 inches distant. Plants set in trenches are to be gradually earthed up.

**Carrots** — Work between the rows until the size of the leaves prevents it.

**Corn** — Put in plenty for late use and to dry.

**Eggplant** — Manure, hoe, and coax in every possible manner. Do not let the fruit remain long in contact with the ground, or it will rot. A little straw or a shingle may be put under it.

**Endive** — Sow and treat just like lettuce — only, before it can be eaten, it must be blanched either by tying up each plant separately or placing a board over a whole row to exclude the light.

**Herbs** — Transplant from seedbed to ground vacated by other plants, and keep well cultivated. Our market growers make two or three cuttings.

**Melons** — Remove all the fruit that will not ripen.

**Onions** — Keep free from weeds.

**Peas** — Late sorts are sure to mildew. If a late sowing is tried, it is only as a venture.

**Seeds** — If you have not had the courage to save the best and earliest peas, cucumbers, tomatoes, etc., for seed, don't save seed at all. But if you would get better vegetables every year, save the earliest.

**Sweet Potatoes** — In the North it is not advisable to allow the vines to root. Keep free from weeds.

**Squashes** — Hand-picking is the only remedy we know of for the squash bug. Let the vines of the running sorts take root at the joints.

**Tomatoes** in some gardens are trained to trellises, but brush or anything that will keep the fruit from the ground is used in ordinary culture.

**Weeds** are always to be fought, and there is nothing better than a sharp steel rake with long teeth and a good man at the end of the handle.

### Flower Garden and Lawn

**Lawns** need frequent cutting and rolling. Whenever perennial weeds appear, such as thistles, plantains, dandelions, etc., take them out while young.

**Annuals**—Quick-growing ones may still be sown for a late bloom. Transplant the earlier sown ones.

**Dahlias** should now be making a good growth; keep well tied up, and water in dry weather.

**Roses**—Give the new growth of climbing roses care in training.

**Perennials**—Sow in a reserve bed as soon as they ripen, and they will make plants for next year.

*Greenhouse and Window Plants*

Keep the margins neatly cut, whether along a walk or those of a bed cut in the lawn. What a carpet is to a parlor, a well-kept turf is to a place, large or small; it sets off everything else.

**Neatness** in all parts of the grounds is to be preserved by constant attention. Daily care is needed.

**Climbers** will need attention; those upon buildings should not be allowed to twine around water conductors. See that they are properly supported so that a heavy wind will not bring them down.

**Bulbs**—The early blooming sorts, such as hyacinths and tulips, will now begin to ripen. As soon as the foliage begins to show by its wilting that the bulbs are maturing, take them up and lay them on their sides in a shady place until the foliage dries up; then store the bulbs until time to plant.

**Foliage Plants**, like coleus, should be made to grow bushy by cutting back. Where there are two or more colors, keep them from running together.

Plants out-of-doors should not be neglected. They often suffer for water, and some make a rapid growth that should be controlled. Camellias and other evergreens need shade from the hot sun. A lattice-work answers the purpose. Plants in the house will also need shading, either by a muslin screen or by whitewashing the glass. The sooner the greenhouse and heating apparatus are put in order and all needed repairs made, the better.

# PROJECTS FOR JULY

### Directions for Budding

Budding consists of removing a bud from one tree and planting it, so to speak, in the stem of another. The things required are: buds, stocks (as the tree to be budded is called), a knife, and some tying material.

**Buds** — Look at a shoot which has grown this year upon any fruit tree. When it ceases to grow in length, it commences to form buds which are to be developed and continue the growth next year. There will be a *terminal* bud at the end of the shoot, and others along the side, at the base of each leaf, called *axillary* buds. These last are the kind used in budding, and there will be a difference in these. Those nearest the end of the shoot will be the largest, while those farthest down will be very small and sometimes hardly perceptible. The shoots are cut when the buds are well formed, the time varying with the kind and somewhat with the season, just below the last plump bud. If the buds on the upper end of the shoot appear unripened, cut them off; then cut away the leaves, but let the leaf stalk remain, and we then have what nurserymen call a "stick of buds" (*Fig. 1*), which may be used at once or kept from drying in damp moss or other material, and be preserved a week or two in a cool place.

**Stocks** — Budding is usually performed on young stocks. Peaches are worked the first year from the seed. Pear, apple, and other stocks are grown one year from the seed, taken up and heeled-in for the winter, and set out in the spring in nursery rows, and are usually ready to bud the following summer or autumn.

**Knife** — Any sharp thin-bladed knife will answer

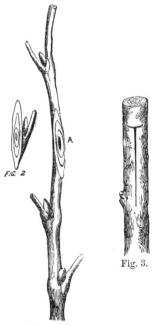

Fig. 2.

A

Fig. 3.

Fig. 1.

where there is but little budding to be done, but for continuous work, as in nurseries where buds are put in by thousands, a proper budding knife is used, the form of which depends much upon the fancy of the operator. Sharp and round-pointed knives are made for the purpose with a thin piece of ivory or bone at the end of the handle for lifting the bark. Some rapid operators lift the bark with the knife blade.

**Tying Material** — Bass bark or matting is the best material, though, in absence of this, woolen yarn, cotton wicking, or even a narrow strip of cotton cloth may serve as a substitute.

**Time for Budding** — Stocks can only be budded while they are growing and the bark "runs" or parts easily from the wood. Plums usually stop growing the soonest and are the first to be budded. The season for budding extends from July, with the plum, to September, with the peach, the time for each variety being modified by the season and location. When the buds are well ripened and the bark lifts easily is the proper time.

Fig. 4.  Fig. 5.

**Operating** — Remove a bud (*fig. 2*) from the stick by cutting from below, inserting the knife about three-quarters of an inch below the bud, and coming out half an inch above, taking as little wood as possible. The bud is usually held between the lips while an incision is made in the stock. Select a smooth place on the north side of the stock, as near the ground as possible, especially if budding on the quince or other dwarfing stock. Make a crosscut quite through the bark down to the wood, and then a longitudinal one extending from this down, as shown in *fig. 3*. Lift the corners of the cut portion without wounding the bark, and insert the bud, holding it by means of the leaf stalk (*fig. 4*), and crowd it well down into place. A portion of the bark of the bud will project above the horizontal cut. This must be cut off even with the crosscut so that the bark of the bud and that of the stock will fit nicely together, as in *fig. 4*. The bud is now to be securely tied. Commence winding below the bud and bind securely to exclude air and rain, finishing the winding above the bud, as in *fig. 5*. In a fortnight, if the buds appear plump and sound, the union has taken place. If they have shriveled, the operation may be repeated, if not too late in the season. In about a month, the tying may be removed, but the buds shoud be looked to before this, and if from the growth of the stocks the string is so tight as to cut into the bark, it must be loosened. Some propagators always remove the portion of wood beneath the bud, while others leave it in. Where it parts readily

from the bud, it may be removed; but where it adheres firmly, it is best to leave it as there is great risk of injuring the bud in trying to remove it.

### Keeping Pastures in Good Condition

Many an acre grazed will not maintain a sheep. Other acres will give full feed to a cow all through the summer and still be pretty good mowing when the frost comes. The difference is not in the original character of the land, for it is found on adjoining farms with the same formation and with the surface and subsoil looking just alike.

On one side of the road there is a big pasture of fifty acres, where fifty sheep would lose rather than gain flesh during the summer. The oldest inhabitant does not remember when it was last plowed, seeded, or top-dressed. It has always been pastured — generally by cows — until it ceased to yield feed enough to support them. There is some grass upon it now, but far more mulleins, five-fingers, and moss. The grass is nearly choked out. But the soil was originally good. The trees that still stand on the borders are heavy oaks and chestnuts that do not thrive on poor, thin soils.

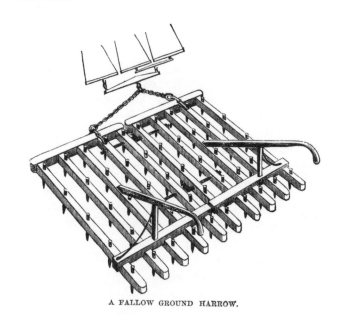

A FALLOW GROUND HARROW.

Yonder, on the other side of the road, is a field of five acres that pastures five cows and has done it for several years. The grass is luxuriant and grows much faster than the cattle can consume it. It was stocked down years ago, after several years of heavy cropping with vegetables and tobacco. Of course it was manured heavily and was very thoroughly cultivated. The land will feel that treatment and make grateful returns for a whole generation to come. It is far within the limits of truth to say that one acre of this five is worth the whole fifty of the other for the purpose of sustaining animal life and making salable products.

There is no royal road to thrift with these run-down pastures. Top-dressing will not answer, for the grass seed is not there to vegetate. Seeding will do little good, for the grass already is growing small by degrees. If the soil is fair, arable land, plow, plant, manure, and cultivate, and you give it a new start. That old sod of dead grass roots and moss rots becomes plant food and sends up joyful harvests. But this will cost money spent in manure, seeds, and labor. This investment usually gives full interest the first year and pays dividends for years to come.

In examining the condition of your pastures, remember this rule: It is with a pasture as with a man. The income must be greater than the expenses or it grows poor. Crops are the expenses. It is, therefore, quite possible to make the surface of any soil unproductive and unprofitable by carrying off more than is put on!

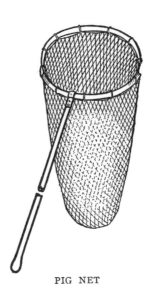

PIG NET

caught in the net will not squeal and struggle as when chased around the pen and caught by one leg. The element of excitement is greatly reduced by the use of the net, and some would find less fun in the net method. On the whole, however, we recommend it.

### Making a Handy Pig Catcher

Here is a homemade device for catching small pigs which saves much time and annoyance. The net may be made from a discarded lawn tennis net, the rim from a bicycle wheel, and the handle is a heavy rake handle. The net is securely fastened to the rim with some copper wire, while the rim is fastened to the handle with two pieces of band iron. Small pigs

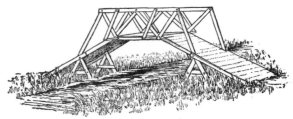

A BRIDGE OF TRIANGLES

### A Bridge for a Small Stream

For crossing a small creek or deep ditch a cheap bridge can be built as shown in the illustration. The lumber used is 6 inches wide and 2 inches thick, except for the floor and four side braces. Saw 11 pieces the length required for each of the two sides, then bore bolt holes 1½ inches from each end. Use 5/8-inch bolts, 8½ inches long where four pieces come together and 6½ inch bolts where three pieces meet. The A-shaped supports and the pieces for the approaches are bolted on at once, and then the side braces are put on. The sides of the bridge are made entirely of triangles. The first triangle is made of pieces *a*, *b*, and *c*, and the second triangle of the pieces *b*, *d*, and *e*. The piers may be posts, stone, or concrete.

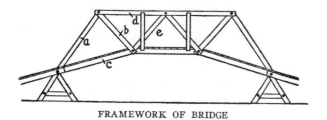

FRAMEWORK OF BRIDGE

## Tying Useful Knots

A sailor judges knots for their holding qualities and also their ability to be quickly unfastened without regard to the strain they have been subjected to. A knot's main office is to hold without working loose or slipping, yet they do occasionally fail absolutely to accomplish this when made by inexperienced hands. The accompanying diagrams show some of the simpler knots that may be of everyday use. In these, the mode of formation can be readily discerned because the rope's position is shown before tightening. The overhand knot (*fig. 1*) is probably the simplest of all. It is used only for making a knot at the end of a rope to keep it from fraying or to prevent another knot from slipping. If a slight change in formation is made, as in *fig. 5*, it develops into a slipknot or, as it is sometimes called, a single sling, and its purposes are obvious. A double sling is represented in *fig. 6*, and, though it is slightly more complicated, it is considerably more useful for any purpose where a rope is to be attached to a bar or beam and stand a steady strain.

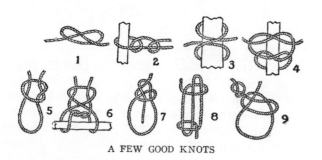

A FEW GOOD KNOTS

Probably for convenience and emergencies no knots equal the bow line (*fig. 7*) because it will not slip or give no matter how great the tension; in fact, the rope itself is no stronger, and the instant the strain ceases, it can be untied as easily as a bow. When the end of a rope is to be secured, the two half hitches or clove hitch (*figs. 2 and 3*) are of great importance, for either of these bends can be attached instantly to almost anything, and their holding powers are exceeded by none. The square knot (*fig. 4*) can be used for infinite purposes—from reefing a sail to tying a bundle, the advantage being, if made properly, of resisting any separating strain on either cord—and yet can be untied immediately by pulling one of the short ends.

One of the best and safest slip knots is shown in *fig. 9*, made with the overhand at the end, which, until loosened by the hand, maintains its grip. When a rope requires shortening temporarily the sheepshank (*Fig. 8*) affords a means of so doing. This knot can be applied to any part of the rope without reducing its strength of rectilineal tension.

## Building a Barn

This barn is arranged to meet the needs of a small farm. It can be built in most localities rather inexpensively, and, if a farmer has his own timber, it will cost even less. The outside dimensions are 36 x 48 feet, and it is 16 feet to the eaves, with a curb roof. The stables should be about 8 feet high, which allows plenty of loft room above for hay.

In the floor plan the cow stalls (*A*) can be made of any width desired, 3½ feet being best for general purposes. At *B* are two large box stalls for cows with young calves. The mangers (*C*) are 18 inches wide, with a rack for hay or fodder above. At *D* is the feed room and alley, which is 8 feet wide. At *E* are the mangers for the horses, with a feed box at the right side. At *F* are three horse stalls 4 feet wide, in which horses can be tied. At *G* is a large box stall for mares and colts.

At *H* is provided the granary, which can be subdivided into bins as necessary. The portion *I* is the driveway, which affords ample storage space for tools, wagons, etc., and is used as a driveway when hay is being elevated into the loft above.

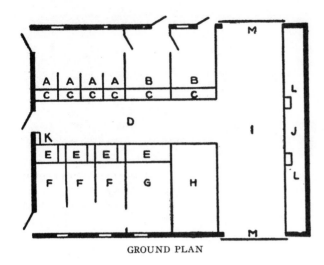

GROUND PLAN

There is a large corncrib (*J*) at the end, which can be filled from the outside and emptied from the inside. It is narrow and so arranged that the corn will dry out quickly. Chutes from this bin should be provided at *L*. A ladder to the hay loft at *K* is a convenience which should not be omitted.

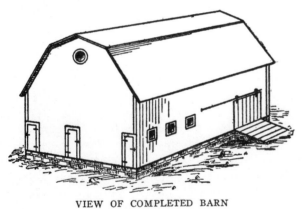

VIEW OF COMPLETED BARN

### Breaking and Training Colts

In breaking a colt the first lesson should be to turn him loose, either in a box stall or carriage house and, with the whip in the right hand, slowly approach him and crack the whip. The colt will run away from you and generally go into the corner. Follow him up, however, and keep cracking the whip until he turns his head towards you. The moment he does this, step right up to him and caress him on the point of the shoulder. If he should, as you approach him, whirl around and kick at you, keep your eyes open and quickly give him a sharp cut on the hind legs with the whip. By following this up carefully, in a very short time he will learn to his sorrow that when he turns away from you and attempts to let his heels fly, he receives punishment, and that when he looks you in the face, he is treated well and rewarded.

The intelligence of any colt is always sufficient to perceive this treatment, and in fifteen to thirty minutes he will follow you around like a dog. As he will feel that you are his superior and master, he will show no desire to kick. What the fingers are to a man, the nostrils are to a horse; and any object that seems to occasion a feeling of fear in the horse, you should slowly either take him to or bring up to him, and permit him to nose around it and smell it until he is satisfied it is harmless. For instance, before making any attempt to put on the halter, take it into your left hand and let him smell it; then buckle it on over his neck. Always be very calm and quiet in your manner, and talk softly to the horse, which goes a great ways towards getting him accustomed to your presence.

If the colt endeavors to pull away after the halter is on, this problem can be circumvented by a little strategy. Take a common clothesline rope and make a large slip-loop knot around the body, drawing it moderately tight, and pass the end up between the front legs through the halter. The reason for doing this is very apparent. He cannot understand how anything can pull the hind part of his body and his head at the same time; and on feeling the strain behind, he will go forward. Thus you will accomplish your object without being compelled to use force. Taking this rope in the right hand and standing directly in front of the colt, say, in a decided manner, "Come here!" and at the same time pull the rope sharply. The colt will invariably move forward, and, when he does, caress him. Repeat this two or three times until he will quickly move forward; then say "Come here!"

Next, with the rope hitch him to the manger or to a post, and, standing in front of him, open and close umbrellas, beat pans—in fact, make as much noise and commotion as possible without touching him. Of course he cannot think of two things at once, and the rope tied around him behind catches him by surprise, and he will end by giving up trying to get away when he finds that he is freer from pain when he is quiet and still than when jerking his head. For a very nervous horse put the rope as far forward as possible around the body. This treatment can be applied until he is thoroughly halter broken. The same arrangement is the most successful one in existence for halter pullers and is also a most valuable

124

TRAINING HORSE IN ENCLOSURE.

FIRST LESSON IN COLT TRAINING.

assistant in leading a horse behind a wagon. How many people are at their wits' ends continually when on a long ride with a horse tied to the carriage behind—and yet this simple invention would prevent it all, and they would not be obliged to even give the horse a thought.

The next lesson to be given the colt should be the harnessing. First, put on the open bridle with the straight bar bit, and run the lines back through the thill straps. Then teach the colt to turn to the right and to the left and to stop at the word "whoa." These lessons should never be longer than an hour each, and generally only two a day.

A colt should first be broken when about a year

old, but never worked in a vehicle until he is about five years of age. A great many of our horses are almost ruined, or at least greatly decreased in value, by being broken too young. Any good, practical man with good judgment can break a colt. Yet, he must never get impatient, but bear in mind that a colt is like a child just learning his A,B,C,. All colts, of course, cannot be handled alike and, as perhaps one has already inferred from the preceding, should each be handled according to his nature, while the common sense of the trainer should indicate the most advisable course to pursue.

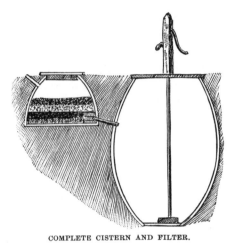

COMPLETE CISTERN AND FILTER.

## Building a Cistern and Filter

Rain water standing for months in impurities and filth cannot be purified by simply soaking through a brick wall, but should be filtered as soon as it falls. The main cistern illustrated here is made egg-shaped and will hold one hundred barrels. The filter is flat-bottomed. The end of the pipe from the filter to the cistern is built solid around the end with brick. All water has to pass through the brick. The filter is filled half full with charcoal, sand, and gravel in layers—one layer of each—the charcoal covering the bricks, then sand, and gravel on top. The water, as soon as it falls, begins to filter and passes into the cistern where it stands free of all impurities and as sweet as spring water. The filter is built to hold twenty-five barrels of water, but is half full of the filtering material.

## A House for Drying Fruit

However superior canned or preserved fruit may be, there is always a large demand for the dried article, and, when well prepared, it meets with a ready sale. The more rapidly the fruit is dried, and the more it is excluded from light and flies, the better it will be. To this end we recommend the following fruit-drying house to be made ready for the coming autumn harvest.

The house (*fig. 1*) is 8 feet, 6 inches long by 4 feet, 2 inches wide (outside measurement) and 7 feet high to the eaves. There is no frame except the sills and plates, which are 2 x 4 scantling, to which the boards on the sides are nailed; and the cracks are battened as shown in the engraving. The roof is shingles or boards, and it would be much better if it projected some feet over the sides and front end to afford protection to those preparing the fruit.

The ends of the house are enclosed by a series of doors, marked *A* in *fig. 1*. Each of these doors moves independently of the others and is hung by means of pivots near its upper edge, which pivots drop into sockets like that shown in *fig. 2*. Each door may be readily lifted from its place by lifting the pivots from the sockets. Both ends of the house are exactly alike. The fruit is spread upon shallow drawers, which are 4 feet square and 1½ inches deep (*fig. 3*). The sides and bottom are of common laths, placing the laths that form the bottom just close enough to prevent the fruit from falling through. The ends of the bottom pieces project half an inch beyond the sides to rest on slats nailed to the walls of the house, and the bottom of the drawer is strengthened by having a lath nailed across it, as shown in *fig. 3*. To support the drawers, laths are nailed to the sides of the house, 2 inches apart from center to center. The drawers rest upon these by means of their projecting ends. A set of these drawers is introduced at each end of the house, and they rest very close together, as seen at *B, fig. 1*.

The house is set on a brick foundation, level with the ground, of which a plan is given in *fig. 4*. The furnace (*A*) is sunk 2 feet deep; it is covered with heavy sheet iron, which to better regulate the heat may have a covering of sand. The pipe (*B*) is 6 or 8 inches in diameter, carefully riveted at the joints to prevent the escape of smoke, except at *C, C*, where the joints are put together in the usual manner, so as to allow the pipe to be taken apart and removed to a dry place when not in use. The chimney (*D*) is made high enough to insure a good draft. The covering of the furnace is 10 or 12 inches below the top of the wall, and the pipe rises gradually until it reaches the chimney in order to increase the draft and bring the cooler portion of the pipe nearer the fruit. It may be necessary to regulate the heat by covering the joints of the pipe that are nearest to the chimney with a strip of sheet iron.

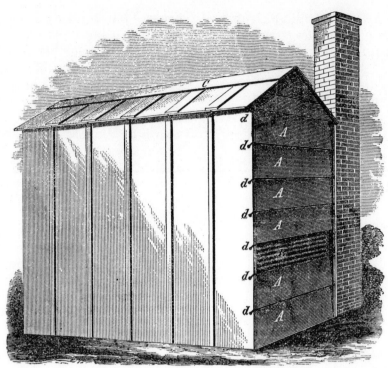

Fig. 1.—FRUIT DRYING HOUSE.

A pit (*E*) is in front of the furnace to allow for firing and should be sheltered from the rain. The heat rises through the successive layers of fruit and passes off at the ventilator *C (fig. 1)* at the apex of the roof. The ventilator consists of two boards nailed together and placed over an opening 4 inches wide, which runs the whole length of the roof. It may be raised or lowered to decrease or increase the temperature. The drawers should be made all alike, to fit in any part of the house, so that they may be moved up as the fruit in them becomes dry and that others containing green fruit may be placed near the fire. As the fruit dries, the contents of several drawers may be thrown together. By arranging one side of the cellar to receive the drawers, they may be made very useful in storing away green fruit for the winter. For this purpose, the slats to support them should be placed far enough apart to accommodate the different sizes of fruit. Fruit thus stored keeps well, and this use alone pays for the cost of the drawers. This dry house demands a simple machine to halve peaches rapidly, and it is hoped that Yankee ingenuity will soon supply one!

For those who wish maximum efficiency, we would suggest building the foundation higher and adding air holes to admit cold air below the pipe. This would keep up a constant flow of dry air through the house and dry the fruit all the more rapidly.

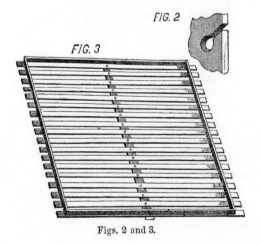

FIG. 3

FIG. 2

Figs. 2 and 3.

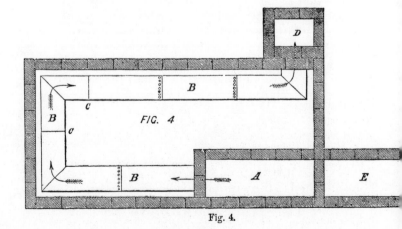

FIG. 4

Fig. 4.

## Hanging and Curing Tobacco

There is a simple and very handy contrivance for hanging and curing tobacco by which may be saved much labor and time and from one-half to two-thirds the usual space. The engraving shows how the tobacco is hung.

The stick at the top, from which the two cords depend, is 12 or 14 inches long, and extends between two joists upon which it rests. The joists are laid as for a floor in the uppermost part of the tobacco house. The tobacco is cut, wilted, and brought to house as usual. The plants are unloaded upon a convenient table. A boy goes aloft where there is a small moveable windlass. This is set over the place where the tobacco is to be hung.

A stick with the cords upon it is lowered upon a hook attached to the windlass to two men who stand at the table below. These men, handling the tobacco plants as fast as they can pick them up one after another, hang them upon the cord which meanwhile is being drawn up by the boy at the windlass. By a double-spooled windlass one pair of cords may be let down while another is being wound up—and thus no time lost. In this way the tobacco is hung very nearly, if not actually, as fast as the plants can be handled. The sticks are suspended upon cleats between the joists, and the windlass may be shoved about upon the top of the joists. Each plant is hung by a simple turn in the cord—as a sailor would say, "By a half hitch, the running part to jam." The plants lap more or less, according to the judgment of the hanger. The distance apart of these strings is the least possible so that the plants will touch, but not crowd each other.

When the plants first taken in have dried somewhat, they are easily moved closer together by simply slipping the sticks on the cleats. Thus fully one-third of the room can be regained if one's tobacco does not ripen all at once. The cord is 3-strand cotton, twisted very hard and is capable of sustaining a much greater weight than the 6 or 7 plants hung upon it.

## Device for Extracting Beeswax

Wax, as produced by the bees and worked into comb, is almost pure white, but, on being melted and cooked, is yellow. A man who knows advises every beekeeper to use a solar wax extractor. All that is necessary is to have a box with glass to fit over it, as shown in the drawing. To melt combs, put in the box an old dripping pan, having a hole at one corner, and that corner the lowest, with some kind of a dish set under to catch the wax. Set in the sun. To get the most out, break up the combs into fine pieces and then soak in water for a day or two longer before rendering.

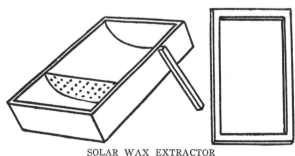

SOLAR WAX EXTRACTOR

FARM
AND GARDEN WORK FOR

# August

The meteorological character of this month varies greatly in different years, and the farmer's labors depend much upon the weather. In times of drought, when pastures are low and when the brooks and watering places fail, the stock need constant attention and no little labor. Summer fodder crops will come in use and are of great value, not only in maintaining a flow of milk, but in keeping dry stock in good condition. Summer fruits may be ready for marketing; spring grains will occupy the farmer's attention. Nevertheless, on the whole, August brings relief to the farmer; his labor is not so hard, and usually he can make a few leisure days, if he will, to visit friends or take a trip with his wife to some mountain or seaside resort, or one of inspection into some interesting agricultural section. It is very agreeable to blend business with pleasure when the business is the most important thing, and this is the only way some men can ever take any recreation—that is, by making believe it is in the way of business. But it is a great deal better for health and true recreation to drop business, cast loose, and give oneself up to having a real good time, hunting, fishing, sightseeing, visiting, etc., if not in this month, then in September, or during the agricultural fairs if attending fairs is not too much like business for most farmers.

## HINTS ABOUT FARM WORK

**Harvesting Spring Grains** takes place according to the character of the early part of the season and time of sowing, earlier or later by two or three weeks.

It is best to cut wheat, oats, and barley, and especially the last two, while the grain is doughy and soft; the straw in the case of oats is much more valuable to feed, and the grain loses nothing. Barley needs especially rapid curing and protection against rain, for its price depends upon its bright, clean look, and its adhering chaff is very sensitive to moisture and will quickly take a mildewy or rusty look. Cut oats when the field appears pretty well yellowed, but before it whitens too much. Always bind oats, if possible, for they take much less room in the barn or stack, and the straw cures and keeps brighter and is probably better feed.

**Buckwheat** may be sown south of the latitude of New York City up to the 10th of August with a reasonable hope that the frosts will hold off long enough to enable seed to form. Still, the longer sowing is deferred, the more hazardous it is.

**Turnips** may also be sown early in the month. It is too late to get a crop from any but the common white, although on good soil rutabagas or French turnips will produce a crop of nice, little table roots as large as a man's fist or larger, which are excellent for winter use. Fill spaces existing in rows of all root crops, and all spots not otherwise occupied, with turnips, either by sowing the seed or transplanting. Tuck in the seed freely.

**Root crops** generally will need hoeing and thinning. As a rule, don't spare thrifty plants if crowded, but thin them thoroughly so that when mature the leaves will barely touch. Where spaces are very wide from any cause, two roots may be left nearer than would otherwise be admissible, but it is a poor plan

BROWN. S C.

to let them crowd one another. Carrots make their principal growth after the first of August and need thorough weeding and thinning at this time. If the ground is stirred frequently, they will be much benefitted, and it is long before the tops interfere

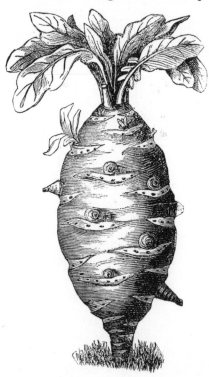

with cultivation or make so dense a shade as not to allow weeds to grow.

**Hoed crops**, other than roots, which include corn, potatoes, sorghum, etc., are or should be beyond tillage with plows, hoes, or cultivators. Weeds, however, should be thoroughly pulled and the ground kept clean, or one great advantage of these crops, namely ridding the land of weeds, will be in a great measure, if not entirely, lost.

**Weeds** are plants growing out of place, it is said—and, if this is true, an oak tree may be as much a weed as a mullein in a clover field. If we have hot, dry weather, make use of it to cut up weeds, to mow brush, to clear up fence rows, and to clear up pastures and such land. All herbaceous plants that have not matured their seed are peculiarly sensitive at this season, and shrubs and trees hardly less so though their roots go deeper. Should these sprout again from the stumps, sheep will browse the shoots, or they may be trodden upon and rubbed off with ease if not too numerous.

**Pastures**—Harrow lightly, sow, and bush in white clover, blue grass, and red top seed on upland pastures at this season, accompanied by a dressing of plaster and ashes. If the pasture is an old one, put on two to twenty barrels of bone meal. An old pasture treated thus will be rejuvenated, if not fed off too close the rest of the season.

**Swamps and Bogs** — If the season is favorable for ditching in low grounds, lay out the drains and have the men at work every spare half day; get out as much muck and peat as possible as you progress, throwing it out on one side only of the ditch. Even if the weather is wet, the ditch will most likely dry the ground in the immediate vicinity so that the muck can be hauled out as soon as dry. The drying of peaty land may be sometimes facilitated by thrusting smooth poles obliquely into the peaty mass on either side as far as possible, and at a level not much above the bottom of the ditch. Roots, brush, and tussocks of grass or brakes may be laid up in piles to dry for burning by and by. The ashes will be an excellent dressing for the soil.

**Draining** of uplands may proceed at this season if there is opportunity, and it often enables farmers to provide profitable work for their hands during a lull in the pressure of regular farm work.

**Grass Seed** may often be saved in sufficient quantity for one's own use by observing where any variety grows unmixed and allowing such to become ripe, cutting with a sickle, binding in bundles to be thrashed or rubbed out at leisure. Seeds of many of our best pasture and meadow grasses can only be bought at very high prices, while a little care taken in gathering them would afford an abundant supply for home use, if not for sale.

**Manure** — Compost heaps rapidly ferment and become homogeneous in character in hot weather. All sorts of vegetation in its green state is adapted to be used in this way. Swamp grass and brakes, sods, potato tops, and similar substances are valuable ingredients. Lay them in alternate layers with animal manure, or, putting them in thin layers, sprinkle each thoroughly with lime or ashes. If liquid manure can be pumped over the heaps, the advantage will be marked. Muck and peat should be got out and laid up to dry before carting.

**Manuring Grasslands** at this season or as soon as sown is productive of more good (both to the succeeding crop and to the land) than at any other season. The clover and grass roots are vigorous and strike deep at the time the hay is cut off. A little encouragement at this time keeps them active, the sod will be close, the aftermath strong, and the grass crop next year much improved. Even a dressing of common loam from an adjoining field will often make the difference on half a ton of hay to the acre on grassland beginning to fail if it is applied in July or August.

**Working Stock** — If the working cattle have been properly handled during the early summer, they will be capable of doing much hard labor in August without sensibly feeling it. It is best, however, to do the severest work in the early morning — heavy plowing or hauling stones, for instance.

**Cows** should have occasional change of pasture, not only for the good of the grass, but on their own account. If the pastures are short, give a liberal feed of green corn fodder regularly, once, twice, or three times during the day. It is best if wilted.

**Calves and Colts** — It is usually best to wean calves and colts in August, that is, at four or five months old, if they have been allowed to run with their dams. This must be done gradually or there will be marked falling off in flesh. Make up by feeding a pint or two of oil meal, beginning gradually with it on cut feed and as gradually withholding it if you do not desire to continue the feed.

**Sheep** — Wean lambs this month, or next, in time at least to allow the ewes to get in good condition for wintering. Have a care that the ewes do not suffer from caked bag when the lambs are removed, and examine and milk them if need be for a few days.

**Swine** — Where manure is an object, it is hardly worthwhile to begin seriously to fatten hogs before corn is nearly ripe. They may be employed to work over all sorts of manurial substances to excellent advantage. Feed them well; they will work the better and be in good condition to fatten.

## HINTS ABOUT HORTICULTURAL WORK

Two things will claim special attention of the horticulturist — pacing and forwarding his products to market, and insects. Look over what has been said in previous months.

## Orchard and Nursery

The harvest is already going on with our Southern neighbors, who should recollect that the more distant the market, the more care is required in shipping the fruit. Let them recollect that the fruit in large cities is sold almost entirely by its looks. An important point, is

**Assorting**—We wish we could impress upon fruit growers the importance and profit of assorting their fruit. Fruit will not only bring better prices if assorted, but depreciation of prices will be prevented. Too few shippers assort their fruit. Such as do so get from one-third to one-half more than those who do not do so. Full one-third of the fruit found in packages had better have been given to the pigs. If one-third of the fruit sent to market were left at home, the other two-thirds would bring more than the whole does now.

**Thinning** is a way of assorting on the tree, and we have in earlier months advocated this. What is the use of allowing fruit that can never be good for home use or market to exhaust the energies of the tree?

**Packing** does not receive sufficient attention. Fruit should be subjected to sufficient pressure to prevent bruising in transportation. One who sees how fruit packages are handled by shippers will not need to be told of this.

**Picking** should always be done by hand. For this purpose various kinds of ladders should be in readiness to reach all the fruit. A common ladder may be so stayed with ropes as to answer in the absence of better.

**Insects** are still to be fought vigorously. Pick up fallen fruit every day and give to the pigs. Later in the season the apples may be used to make vinegar. Red spider is not now rare on pear trees, and must be fought with soap and water. This insect only revels in hot and dry weather. Plant lice are to be treated to the same preparation or to tobacco water. Late broods of tent and other caterpillars are to be exterminated.

**Budding** is in order with all stocks upon which the bark will run and where well-developed buds can be obtained. If buds are slow in maturing, pinch off the ends of the twigs intended to be used to supply them. The cherry and plum are the earliest budded; then follow the pear, apple, cherry, peach, and quince. If the tyings on stocks budded earlier are too tight, loosen them.

**Weeds**—Keep clear of them. If the ground is not occupied by some crop that will benefit the trees, allow nothing to grow, but keep the soil nice and mellow by frequent use of the cultivator.

**Fire Blight**—The best treatment is to cut away the diseased parts as soon as discovered.

**Black Knot** is to be treated in the same way.

## Fruit Garden

The general treatment of trees in the fruit garden is hinted at under "Orchard." Market or preserve all fruit not consumed by the family.

**Strawberries** will have made good runners. Spring and autumn planting each have their advocates. Autumn planting succeeds well in all except Northern localities. We saw a fine plantation this spring that was made in the last week in November from plants started in pots. This plan is gaining favor among cultivators and nurserymen; the principal outlay is for small pots in which to strike the runners. One has only to turn the plants out of the pot and is thus almost independent of the season. This plan is of easy execution and commended to small cultivators.

**Strawberries for forcing** should be started in small pots and, when well established, are to be later in the season transferred to the larger pots in which they are to fruit.

**Blackberries** are to be kept within bounds and made to throw out more bearing shoots by pinching as heretofore directed.

**Raspberries**—The best cultivators take out the old canes as soon as the fruit is off, though many leave the pruning until the time for laying down or even until spring. Keep the ground clean by means of the cultivator and hoe, and remove all suckers not needed for canes or for making new plants.

**Experiments**—All of our cultivated blackberries, and many of our raspberries, have been found as wild plants and transferred to the garden. Those who wish to experiment with these, or with the almost uncultivated huckleberry, should mark the wild specimens of which the fruit is of fine quality and transfer them to the garden in autumn. A bit of white rag tied to the stem is not observable while the leaves are on, but readily seen at a distance when the stem is naked.

**Grapes**—One should be among his vines daily and give them such tying, pinching, and other treatment as they need. Do not pass by a caterpillar or other injurious insect without destroying it. Hand-picking is the surest way of disposing of many insects.

**Dwarf Trees** will need to have their fruit thinned, if not already done. Early fruit is to be picked as soon as well developed, and ripened indoors.

**Weeds** are to be kept entirely out of the fruit garden. Let the soil be clean and mellow wherever there is no mulch. Some hand-pulling of weeds will be needed among the strawberry and other plants.

**Mulch and Water** are the two helps for newly planted trees which suffer from drought. Either cover the ground all around the tree with a thick coat of litter, or draw away the earth, give the roots a good soaking, and replace the earth.

### Kitchen Garden

The garden should now be quite clear of weeds, and many of the crops have so taken possession of the soil that the labor is very much reduced.

**Asparagus**—Keep seedling plants free from weeds, and thin them to get strong, well-developed roots.

**Beans** of the bush kinds may still be put in to furnish a late crop for eating or to salt for winter.

134

**Cabbages**—Plants may still be set in the Southern states. If slugs appear, dust lime over the ground.

**Carrots** and all other root crops are to be thinned if needed, and the soil kept loose between the rows as long as convenient to work them.

**Celery** may be set out early this month to make a late crop. Keep the plantings well cultivated.

**Corn**—Save the earliest and finest ears for seed.

**Cucumbers** come on rapidly, and the vines should be picked over every day or two for pickles.

**Eggplants**—Forward them by the use of liquid manure; mulch to keep the soil moist, and prevent the fruit from resting on the ground. Look out for caterpillars, which are very fond of the plants.

**Endive**—Transplant a foot apart each way. When the plants are a foot in diameter blanch for use by gathering up the outside leaves and tying them by their tips over the center of the plant, or by laying a board over them. Darkness is what is required. The tying or covering should be done when the plants are dry. Sow seed for a late crop.

**Melons**—Removing a portion of the later—set fruit will improve with quality of that remaining. Save seed from fine and early specimens which have grown at a good distance from other varieties.

**Onions** are to be pulled as soon as the tops of a majority of the plants fall over. Dry thoroughly those that are to be stored for winter. They should not be put in large heaps, but spread thinly in a cool and dry place. Take up onion sets and store in a similar place, spread in layers about 4 inches thick.

**Radishes**—The early sorts may be sown in vacant places. Winter varieties are to be treated like turnips.

**Spinach** may be sown for fall cutting; the crop to winter over should be deferred until next month.

**Squashes**—Look for insects' eggs on the undersides of the leaves and crush them. Several ways of destroying insects are given in this and previous "hints." Hand-picking is a great help. If the runners root at the joints, do not disturb them.

**Sweet Potatoes**—Keep the soil clean and mellow. In the North the vines should not be allowed to take root at the joints; move them occasionally.

**Tomatoes**—If training of any kind is done, keep the vines tied up and in good order. If any worm droppings are seen upon the leaves or on the ground, search for the worm. It is the green worm that infests potatoes and tobacco and will not only eat leaves

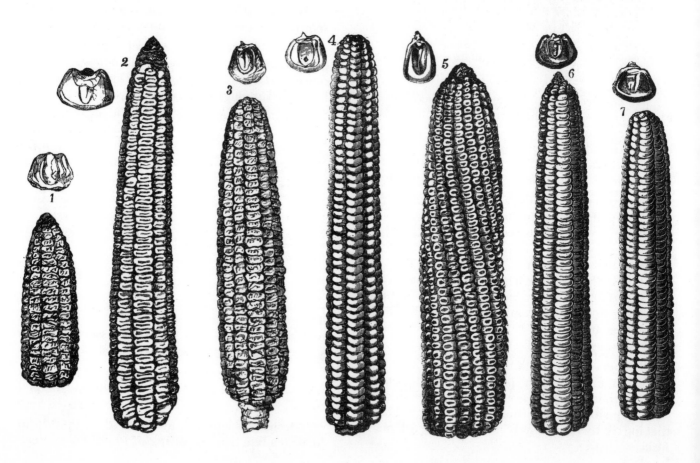

and stems, but green fruit. Catch and crush. Save seed only from the earliest and best formed if it is desired to keep the variety in its purity. If often happens that a vine will be more prolific or bear a better fruit than the rest. Save seed of such specimens for trial.

**Turnips** — Sow rutabagas early in the month and the flat kinds later. Give a dusting of lime as soon as the plants are up to keep off insects.

**Water** only when the plants are absolutely suffering; with thorough working of the soil, there is seldom need of it. If liquid manure is used, do not apply it during a time of drought, but only in a growing time.

*Flower Garden and Lawn*

The condition in which the grounds are kept in the month of August is a good indication of the gardener's industry. Some enthusiasts work well while they are rewarded by an abundance of spring flowers, but their zeal abates under the August heat. In this interregnum between the early and late — blooming flowers, the few that show themselves should be made to look at their best, and neatness and care make up for the lack of floral display.

**Beds in the Lawn** ought always to present a well-defined margin, and no grass or clover should be allowed to run into them. These beds are generally planted in masses and should be kept well weeded and the soil loose until the plants have covered it. When foliage plants are employed, they produce a much better effect if trimmed occasionally so as to keep the center of the mass the highest.

**Lawns,** to be velvety, need mowing every week. The clipped grass, if short, may remain since it serves as mulch and manure.

**Grass Edgings** are cut with the sickle or grass hook. Trim the margins neatly and remove all weeds.

**Dahlias** — Keep tied to stakes, pick off insects, and in time of drought give copious waterings.

**Chrysanthemums** are much liked by caterpillars which will destroy the foliage in a short time if not watched. The plants should be grown bushy by pinching, but not be allowed to become crowded.

**Roses** — If a late bloom is looked for, the plants must not be left to the depredations of insects of various kinds. Use the various insect destroyers heretofore mentioned, and hand-pick caterpillars. As soon as a flower on the constant-blooming sorts is past its prime, remove it, cutting back to a good bud to keep up a new growth to produce flowers.

**Fuchsias** need partial shade and frequent showerings. Cuttings of the new growth root very readily.

**Gladioluses** — Stake their flower stems. Remove the lower flowers of a spike as soon as they fade.

**Lilies** — Keep the tall-growing sorts tied to stakes, as they are top-heavy when in flower. If a whitish spot appears on the leaves, a caterpillar will be found on the underside. Remove faded flowers.

**Propagation** from cuttings is easily done in a close-shaded frame placed on sandy soil. A frame covered with cloth will answer if one has no hotbed frame and sash. Many shrubs, taken just as the wood is hardening, and most soft-wooded plants, will strike readily in a frame like this. Unless one has the means for keeping the tender kinds of plants over the winter in good condition, it is better to buy bedding plants each spring.

**Seeds** — Save always from the best flowers. Sow perennials and biennials as soon as ripe. Cut away all spent flower clusters if seeds are not wanted.

*Greenhouse and Window Plants*

There is little to add to last month's directions. They may be briefly summed up thus: Repair the greenhouse and heating apparatus, lay in potting soil, procure pots, see that the stock out-of-doors is kept in good condition as to water and insects. New wood of most things will propagate readily now.

# PROJECTS FOR
# AUGUST

## Rough Measurement of Land

SIMPLE LAND MEASURER.

Farmers are apt to pace off plots of ground by counting fence panels or in other "offhand" ways attempt to estimate the extent of plots of lands whose size or area they may wish to know something about. It is, of course, better to have a tape and measure accurately, but the simple instrument illustrated here will be found to give results closely approaching accuracy. It consists of two plastering laths (or light, stiff sticks of the same size) fastened together at one end and braced apart by a crosspiece, the whole forming a figure like the letter *A*. The free ends are each pointed bluntly and are fixed accurately 4 feet and 1½ inches apart, which is just one-fourth of a rod. In measuring, the implement is simply revolved, keeping the upper end in the hand and one foot constantly on the ground. The straddles should be made as nearly as possible in a straight line. The number of rods can be derived by counting the straddles and dividing by four.

## Making Cheap Sheds of Straw

It would pay every farmer to put up in the pastures some kind of protection for his sheep, hogs, and cattle. Where labor is scarce and hay and straw are plentiful and cheap, a condition which prevails in many large sections, straw sheds and barns are very profitable. Put up a framework of posts 8 feet high, 16 feet wide, and as long as needed; 30 feet is a good length.

STRAW SHED FOR STOCK WITH AN L.

The posts are hewed evenly on two sides and set so that a bale of straw will fit snugly between them. They are cut off at a uniform height and a 2 x 6 spiked securely on top. Rafters are nailed to this and covered loosely with poles. Baled straw is used for the sides. After the sides are up the roof is covered 2 feet deep with loose straw held in place with a few poles that are tied together in pairs and placed over the ridge. Several of these sheds have stood for five years and have not needed any attention.

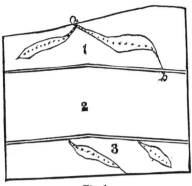

Fig. 1.

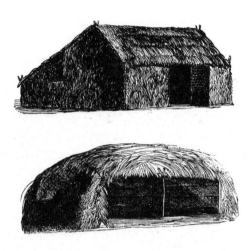

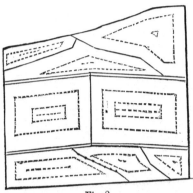

Fig. 2.

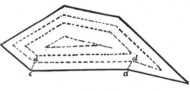

Fig. 3.

## Draining Land with a Plow

The present is a good time for farmers who have lowlands on which pools of water stand to arrange for keeping the water off in the best and cheapest manner. Standing water is even better for farmers than a spirit level as after a heavy rain you can get the trend of the land in every direction with the best outlets for the different pools. If the farmer will provide himself with a supply of light stakes and ride through the centers of the pools and down the outlets as the water flows out from them, placing the stakes as he goes, he will be prepared to drain his land when the water is off. This may be done mainly with the plow and without making uncrossable ditches.

When the land is dry enough, take a one-horse plow and run a furrow, following the stakes to the natural outlet as shown in *fig. 1*, starting at *a* and running to *b*, and so with the other lands, as indicated by the solid lines in *fig. 2*. Then plow all these lands, turning the soil always to the center of the plot, and finishing in the center of the ditches or drains. This can be accurately done, as shown in *fig. 3*, by laying the plot off as if for sowing grain, commencing at any corner and stepping twenty or any number of

steps towards the center of the plot, as at *c*. Put a man with a small plow at this point and let him wait until you get to *d*, which is the same number of steps from the next corner and towards the center. Then let him run a straight line to you. Repeat this until you have a furrow all around the inside of the plot, and continue to make these furrows, one inside of the other, as shown by the dotted lines in the different figures, until you come to the center of each plot. Now commence with your turning plow and plow out the center plot, as as it so small it does not make much difference which way the soil is turned, but afterwards turn all the soil to the center and see to it that no marking furrow is crossed until all inside of that lot is plowed. It is much easier to keep a small land in shape than a large one, and any good plowman will soon learn to keep his furrows parallel to the marking furrows.

Trying to plow to the center without laying the land off usually ends by having large slices in some places unfinished while in others you are running in the drains. In this way finish the whole field and you will find the land shaped so as to gradually slope from the centers to the drains, and every successive planting will make it better if this system is persevered in. If these drains are not found deep enough in places, plow a strip on each side of them, turning from them, and finishing in the bottom of these drains; repeat this until the drains are deep enough. We have frequently plowed the whole of a plot several times in one season when it was in bad shape. Such drains offer no obstruction to wagon, reaper, or plow, and corn rows may run straight across them and can be worked as if they were not there if you will take a one-horse turning plow and throw the soil out of the drain after each plowing.

## Steaming Food for Cattle and Pigs

Many a farmer raises magnificent crops of hay, which he stores in barns, only to feed it out either on the ground or in racks in his yards and fields.

The *profit* of farming by no means ends with the raising of large crops. The disposition of what is raised is quite as important to success as is the raising itself; and every ounce of nutritious matter which is allowed to find its way to the dung heap, if it might have been converted into meat, milk, or wool, is a throwing away of just so much of the result of the year's work. Ample practical experience has proven that the action of the digestive organs of farm animals is not of itself sufficient to extract from hay or corn fodder or grain nearly all of the nutritious matter

that they contain, and has shown that by the aid of cooking much of this wasted matter may be saved.

The easiest means by which cooking may be done is with the aid of steam. If it were attempted by boiling in iron vessels immediately in contact with the fire, great care would be required to prevent scorching, and enormous caldrons would be needed. By the aid of steam, the cooking may be safely, conveniently, and economically done, and scorching avoided.

It has been demonstrated by carefully conducted trials that if all of the hay and other coarse fodder and all of the grain and roots fed to livestock of any description is thoroughly steamed, quite one-third of the raw material is saved. That is to say, if the month's feeding on a large farm requires 10 tons of hay, 100 bushels of grain, and 500 bushels of roots, the same feeding with the aid of a steamer will be accomplished by the use of about 7 tons of hay, 70 bushels of grain, and 350 bushels of roots. Here, then, is a profit of 3 tons of hay, 30 bushels of grain, and 150 of roots to pay for the use of an inexpensive steaming apparatus, for a small amout of fuel, and a trifling amount of labor. Nor is this all. While successful feeding by the non-cooking process requires the use of the best grain and fodder, steaming enables us to substitute for these coarser herbage (which may even have become slightly musty) and musty or unsound corn. This is in part due to the freshening influence of the steam and in part to the fact that the flavor of the roots or bran, or whatever other fine food may be mixed with the cut forage before steaming, is imparted to the mass, and causes that to be eaten which otherwise would necessarily have been rejected.

## How to Build a Rowboat

Rivers and lakes being so plentifully interspersed over the country, boats become articles of great convenience or absolute necessity, and the ability to construct one, however rude it may be, is a useful accomplishment.

Here are directions for constructing a boat capacious enough to carry two good-sized men and a fat buck, if they should ever be so lucky as to be compelled to carry one home, and at the same time sufficiently light to enable it to be carried about easily when required to be removed overland from one piece of water to another.

Fig. 1.—THE BOAT IN USE.

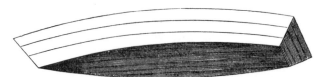

Fig. 3.—THE STEM.

Fig. 4.—BOAT TURNED TO SHOW BOTTOM AND STERN.

The boat is flat-bottomed, and the keel or bottom is of board 3/4-inch thick of white pine or other light wood that will not readily split. The length of the boat represented is 9 feet, width 2 to 3 feet, depth 18 inches. These proportions may be varied to suit circumstances.

To shape the bottom or keel, take two boards of the character before mentioned, and 12 inches wide; join them together by a tongue-and-groove joint; make the joint watertight by means of pitch, and fasten a cleat across with clinch nails or screws to prevent its spreading. Mark out with a pencil the shape represented in *fig. 2*. Cut this out very accurately, and plane very smoothly to line, with a slight bevel upwards. The more carefully this is done, the closer the joint and the dryer the boat will be.

The stem is made, preferably, of a tamarack "knee"; if this can not be readily procured, cut out of soft maple a "knee" 1-inch thick as a substitute. This should represent an angle of something over 90 degrees, so as to give a forward rake, as in *fig. 3*. The front of the upright portion should be beveled to a fine edge, the bottom dressed square and fitted to the keel in its place with screws or wrought nails riveted over burrs. The stern (*fig. 4*) is of similar stuff to the keel, cut 6 inches wider at the top than at the bottom. The side boards should be of well-seasoned ¼-inch spruce stuff dressed (at least on the outside) to present the least resistance to the water.

To give the boat the proper shape, cut out patterns representing the cross section of it at those parts crossed by the dotted lines. The sides should spread a little, that is, should be wider at the gunwale that at the keel, say 6 to 12 inches. The patterns should be cut accordingly, and then tacked lightly to the keel-board to hold them in their place until done with. The dotted lines which cross the boat are drawn at equal distances and show the width at those places which is greatest a little back of the center (*fig. 2*). It is a great point in hunting to have a boat that will make no ripple, and this gradual decrease of width towards the stern avoids all noise as the boat passes along. A boat of this pattern will do this perfectly, and will be found easier to row or paddle.

When the molds are properly placed, take the boards—which should have been previously soaked at the ends in water—and fit them to their places, holding them with a clamp until securely nailed to the stem and stern. All nails which pass through the boards where they lap should be clinched on the inside; boat nails should be used. When the first board, which is the bottom one, is put on, fit the next, allowing three quarters of an inch to lap. Between the boards, at the lap, place a piece of thick cotton cloth, dipped in tar, which will make the joint watertight, or nearly so, and calking will be unnecessary. Then fit on the top board, taking care the upper edge has a proper sweep. When the boards are fastened, put in two ribs, which should be of white oak ½-inch thick and 1½ wide. Soak them thoroughly until they are pliable enough to bend into their places, and secure them by nails clinched on the inside. These should be placed midway between the molds, and not only strengthen the frame, but give a bearing for the feet of the rower. A piece of tin should be bent over the stem and nailed from bottom to top for a cut-water. Before putting this piece of tin on, fill in well with pitch and tallow.

Fig. 2.—THE BOTTOM OF THE BOAT.

The molds may now be removed. A strip 2 inches wide and ½-inch thick should then be nailed all around on the inside. Cleats are to be nailed on for the thwarts (or seats), which should be placed 6 inches below the gunwale or edge. The hinder seat may be made of the lid of a locker or box in which tools, nails, lines, a supply of putty, tallow, and pieces of tarred canvas and tin should be stowed away as resources in case of damage or leaking. The bow of the boat should have a similar place made to hold a supply of eatables when necessary. A baling dipper should be stowed away in one of these lockers. The bottoms of these lockers must be elevated 2 or 3 inches above the keel to keep the contents dry. *Fig. 5* shows the arrangement of the lockers and seat.

Fig. 5.—BOAT, SHOWING RIBS, LOCKERS, AND SEAT.

A ring-bolt and cord, sufficiently long, should be attached to the bow for the purpose of tying up. To finish up the job, the seams must be gone over carefully, and putty and white lead must be applied to every crack. Then two coats of paint ought to be laid on, the name painted on the stern, and she is ready for the launch.

A pair of oars may be made of ash, or, what is preferable, a pair of paddles like the one shown in *fig. 6*. When properly made and used, paddles are much more convenient and efficient than oars. In using a paddle, one has his face to the front and can see all ahead of him; in rowing, it is necessarily the opposite to this. If oars are used, row-locks must be fitted on to the sides. To make a paddle, take a piece of inch board (cedar is the lightest and best, but an oak paddle is very durable), 6 inches wide; dress out the blade ¼-inch thick at the edge and ½-inch at the center, gradually increasing the thickness towards the handle. The handle may be whittled down until it fits the hand comfortably. Then dress it with sandpaper perfectly smooth, and rub with oil; a smooth handle will not blister the hands. A boat thus made will look very nicely, but if means

and time are wanting to finish it as here described, a rough one may be put together very quickly and cheaply by using the same or lighter materials in a rougher fashion. In place of three side boards, one wide board (12 inches) may be used, and the seats laid across flush with the top.

### Keeping Food Cool in Summer

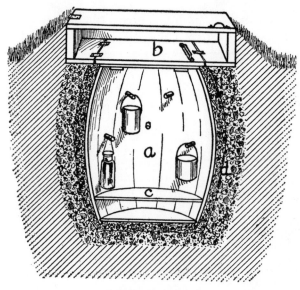

FOOD COOLER

A very convenient and serviceable place to keep dairy products may be formed by sinking a large barrel in the ground. A shady spot should be chosen, or the heat of the sun will affect the temperature. Fill in around the barrel with small stones, gravel, and sand, dampened in order to maintain coolness. Construct a box around and above the top of the barrel, and bank up with solid earth, preferably clay. This drains off the water when it rains. It also makes the bottom of the barrel farther down from the top of the opening, which further promotes coolness. Next shape a light, inner lid to place on top of the barrel, and then make a strong, hinged lid for the box, and arrange it so it may be fastened down tightly. Sprinkle a little dampened sand on the bottom of the barrel, and your little barrel cellar is ready for use. By being careful, several vessels may be arranged one above the other in this handy little receptacle. Air out occasionally to prevent mold and odors from collecting.

## How to Build a Cheap Greenhouse

The plans here given are intended for a small greenhouse suitable for an ordinary country residence where no regular gardener is kept and where the care of such an appendage to the house would devolve upon the family. Such a greenhouse can be built separate from the dwelling, and a shed attached to the northerly end for the purposes of a potting shed, the storage of tools, etc., but as drawn, it is intended to be attached to the dwelling and entered therefrom by means of a door from one of the rooms. This we consider preferable to having it detached as it is accessible and enjoyable in all weathers, and if the entrance door from the house is glazed it renders the room to which it adjoins remarkably cheerful and elegant. We prefer a double-pitched roof for such a greenhouse to a lean-to or single pitch as it gets the benefit of the early morning and latest evening sun, an item of much importance in growing plants, and escapes the intenser heat of the noonday sun (which in March and April is very great), as the end is perpendicular, the side of the roof being at an angle of forty-five degrees. Besides these benefits, plants grow better in such houses because they have more light on every side and, consequently, are not likely to become so drawn and one-sided as they are in a lean-to.

The proper exposure is southerly—that is, with the end facing any of the southerly points of the compass, from W.S.W. to S.E. If any preference can be given in locating it, it should be given to the easterly points, as it enables it to receive more of the early sun during the shortest days of winter.

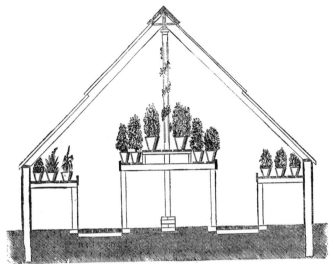

Fig. 2.—SECTION OF GREENHOUSE.

Our drawings, with the descriptions which are given, will enable any carpenter of ordinary intelligence to construct it. Many of them will no doubt object to the dimensions of the rafters, thickness of the sashes, etc., as it is a besetting fault with these men generally to make the rafters and other woodwork of such structures entirely too heavy. A plant structure cannot be made too light, provided due strength is maintained. It will be noticed that we do away entirely with all plates and sills and also tenoned and mortised joints, as these are only so many places for the admission of water and subsequent decay and also involve much outlay for material and labor.

The sashes measure 6 feet 3 inches long, by 3 feet 1 inch wide, and 1½ inches thick, made of the best quality of white pine. The side rails should be 2½ inches wide, the top rail 3 inches, and the bottom rail 4 inches wide. The sash bars should be 1 1/8 inches wide, rabbeted out 5/8-inch deep, and 5/16-inch wide, leaving the parting strip ½-inch wide. This should overlap the bottom rail 2½ inches. The top rail should not be grooved out to receive the upper edge of the upper pane of glass since, in case of leakage, it is almost impossible to clean it out. It should, therefore, be rabbeted to correspond with the sash bars. A crossbar of iron, ¼-inch thick by ½-inch wide, should be put across the middle of each sash, only lapping 1 inch on each side rail, or a crossbar of ash or some similar wood may be used: it should be about 5/8-inch thick and 3/4-inch wide and notched out half its depth to receive the sash bars. These last should not be notched out on any account since it weakens the sash very materially. The screws used in putting on these crossbars should

Fig. 1.—END VIEW OF GREENHOUSE.

be dipped in boiled linseed oil to prevent them rusting in the sash bars, which would weaken them. The joints should all be put together with strong glue and not with white or red lead and oil. The glue makes a much stronger joint and, when the sash is kept well painted, will hold as long as the wood lasts since it does not evaporate or dry out as the oil does.

The glass should be 6 by 8 French seconds, each pane to overlap the other about 3/8-inch. The lower panes should overlap the bottom rail at least ½-inch. They should not be bedded in putty when put in, as they cannot be so evenly laid when that is done. After being puttied on the face, they should be back-puttied—that is, the angular spaces formed by the overlaps should be filled up with putty. This makes a much neater job than any other way. Each pane should be fastened down at the overlap with a ½-inch copper or zinc sparable on each side.

The outside measure of the house is 18 feet 9 inches wide (from east to west) and 19 feet long (from north to south); overall, from the ground level to the top of the ridge pole is 14 feet. In constructing it, locust posts 7 or 8 feet long, squared on

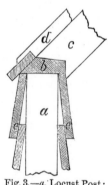

Fig. 3.—*a*, Locust Post; *b*, Plate; *c*, Rafter; *d*, Sash; *e*, Weatherboarding.

two sides to 4 inches thick, are set in the ground 3 feet 1 inch apart from center to center, leaving 4 feet above the ground level. These are weatherboarded inside and outside. On the top of these posts, after being sawed off level and square, a strip of white pine 2 inches thick and 6 inches wide is nailed down, which answers the purpose of a plate. It is leveled on the front to the angle of the rafters (45 degrees); and, from where the upper edge of the lower rail of the sash touches it, it is beveled back to the thickness of an inch, the object of this being to prevent the water-drip lying on it and rotting it. The space between the weatherboarding is left vacant because

the enclosed air is a better nonconductor of cold than any filling would be.

The rafters are 6 inches deep by 3 inches wide, 1½ inches of thickness being cut away for the lower sash, so that for the lower half of their length they are only 4½ inches deep. They may be made of uniform depth through their whole length, and a thickness strip planted on under the upper sash. The toe of the lower end of each rafter rests upon the plate strip, and is nailed through it to the head of the post immediately beneath it.

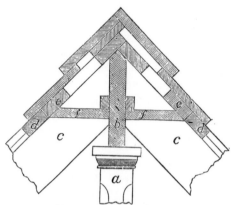

Fig. 4.—DETAILS OF ROOF.
*i*, Pillar; *b*, Ridge-pole; *c*, Rafters; *d*, Sash; *e*, Stop-piece; *f*, Ceiling.

A ridge pole, 2 inches by 12 inches, is carried the whole length of the house. The edge next to the dwelling is supported by a bracket. Two intermediate posts to carry it are placed one at each end of the center plant stage, and the outer end is supported by a small strip carried up from the door head. We sometimes see houses constructed without a ridge pole, but the roof in such cases is always weak and continually spreading, sometimes causing them to fall in. The upper end of the rafters is nailed to this ridge pole. No parting strip is necessary between the sashes, nor is it necessary to have the rafter grooved out under each sash, as is sometimes done to carry off the water. Such channels soon become choked up by dust and dirt and are the favorite resort of all sorts of insects; they are, indeed, worse than useless.

A stop piece, 1½ by 4 inches, is nailed along the rafters at the head of the upper sashes, and a similar strip is carried along the peak of the rafters. These two strips carry the weatherboarding of the cap. This weatherboarding should cover the upper rail of the sash about 2 inches. Inside, a narrow ceiling is carried across. This gives a neater appearance to the inside than if the peak above the sashes is left open.

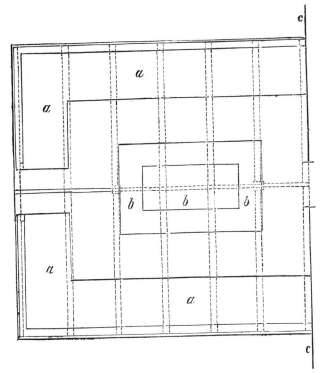

Fig. 5.—GROUND PLAN OF GREENHOUSE.
*a, a.* Front Platform for Plants; *b, b,* Center Platform; *c, c,* Side of Dwelling.
The dotted lines show the position of the Rafters and Ridge-pole.

## A Homemade Water Cooler

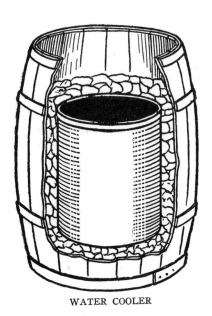

WATER COOLER

It's a mighty nice thing to have a good supply of cold water at the barn when threshers, corn huskers, or hay harvesters are at work. A simple and effective arrangement can be made by using a flour barrel and a 10-gallon stone jar. Place the jar inside the barrel and surround it with charcoal, sawdust, or even chaff if nothing else is available. With a tight lid and a wet cloth spread over the top, water will keep ice-cold in this arrangement. The uses of such a cooler may be multiplied to include keeping many things cool in the house.

### Raising Huckleberries (Blueberries)

When Bartholomew Gosnold in 1602 discovered wild grapes growing in abundance in the swamps and low grounds on a little islet near the New England coast, he gave to it the name of Martha's Vineyard, no doubt believing that he had found the home of the wild grapes of the New World. But that little islet (now known as No-man's Land) and the larger island (which bears the name of Martha's Vineyard) are not now considered favorable locations for vineyards, although the wild grapes do grow all along the New England coast and in swamps and low grounds thoughout these United States. While it is true that the wild grapes of North America are found more abundantly in swamps and low grounds than on high and dry soils, still no vineyardist would think of planing a vineyard in a swamp, because long experience has shown that high, dry, and well-drained soils are far preferable for such purposes than those that are low and wet.

There is another very valuable native fruit about which the same erroneous ideas exist that were for a long time held in regard to the indigenous grapes: it is our swamp high-bush huckleberry or blueberry (*Vaccinium corymbosum*). It is found growing wild in the same localities and under the same conditions as the wild grape, not only in swamps but also on high and dry soils. Because the plants are more abundant in swamps does not prove that under cultivation, low, wet soils would be the best. Experience has shown that sandy, well-drained soil is best. The plants thrive best in peat and the almost pure vegetable deposits of the swamps, in the light sandy soils, and even high up on the hills of New Jersey and adjoining in states in light, sandy soils in which the running blackberries and five-finger plant have to struggle to obtain nutriment from the sterile soil. A plant that will grow and

144

THE SWAMP HUCKLEBERRY (*Vaccinium corymbosum*).

In cultivating any of the huckleberries on sandy soils, it is advantageous to keep them well mulched, thereby insuring an abundance of moisture at the roots as well as preventing any baking and overheating of the surface soil. Under proper care and in rich soils, the plants will grow far more rapidly and yield larger crops of fruit than when left to grow uncared for as in their native habitats.

## How to Splice a Rope

Farmers are proverbially awkward in their use of ropes. Few can make a knot, or a tie, or a hitch that will hold and that they can undo in a hurry after it has been subjected to a heavy strain. We have to use ropes a great deal and should know how to manage them better, especially in connection with block-tackle and shears. Here, then, is described and illustrated the most useful and effective rope splice that homesteaders everywhere should master.

If one wishes to lengthen a rope for permanent use, as a well rope for instance, it looks very awkward if it is tied in the usual way, and it is much better to splice it neatly. Ropes in common use are composed of three strands, and each strand is itself composed of two or more strands or rope yarns. *Fig. 1* shows how two pieces of such a rope are united by

thrive in such soils—bearing a heavy crop of fruit in moderately favorable seasons—will certainly thrive under good cultivation, provided the soil is not a heavy, unctuous clay.

As there are several distinct natural varieties of the high-bush species, as well as of other species, it is as well to mark the plants to be taken up when in leaf or fruit. The genuine or true *Vaccinium corymbosum* bears quite large, round berries covered with a blue bloom; but there is a variety with oval fruit, jet-black without bloom, and another with globular berries and also destitute of bloom. Of the dwarf, early blueberry *(V. Pennsylvanicum)* common to high, dry, and rather sterile soils, there are also several distinct natural varieties, one of which is an albino, the fruit being pure white and fully as transparent as the white grape currant.

Fig. 1. SHORT SPLICE.

what is termed the "short splice." The strands of each end are first untwisted and placed together, each strand being placed between two strands of the other rope. Each strand in succession (first of one rope and then of the other) is then passed over the one it lies in contact with on the left, and is tucked under the next strand. To accomplish this tucking easily, the rope is untwisted a little and a sharp pin is inserted, and a place made through which the end of the strand may be passed. The course of strands may easily be traced by referring to the numbering of the dark strands in *fig. 1*. When all the ends are thus tucked once, we have already a perfectly strong splice which will bear any strain the rope will, but the ends must be left on, for if the rope is subject to an untwisting operation it might part. If a handsomer finish is desirable, the ends of the strands may be opened, and one of the two yarns of which each is composed may be tucked again. After this both yarns may be cut off. This splice is twice as large as the original rope, but not nearly so large as the knots commonly tied in ropes, and it will go through most pulleys in which the rope runs loosely.

### Growing Currants

Those who live in the country can have the very best currants as long as the season lasts by a little expense in getting a start and a little trouble thereafter. A most wholesome fruit is the currant, and

VERSAILLES.

its sharp acid is very grateful in the hot days in which it comes. The currant belongs to the genus *Ribes*, which furnishes us both the gooseberry and currant.

As currants will grow and bear something in spite of total neglect, many people are not aware of the benefit it is to any variety to give it the best possible chance for development. Manuring, pruning, and mulching will work wonders with the currant. An annual manuring is essential to successful culture, and if large fruit is desired, the bushes should be properly pruned, and during the fruiting season, heavily mulched. Plants one or more years old can be procured from the nurseries, or they may be raised with the greatest ease from cuttings. Portions of wood of this year's growth, set this fall, will give good plants next year. Having obtained cuttings, about a foot long, from a reliable source, remove with a sharp knife all but the three upper buds and set them in good soil with the buds above the surface, Take particular care to press the soil closely in contact with the lower end of the cutting.

The next year the object should be to get one good and strong upright shoot. Select the shoot from the bud that pushes strongest, and train it to a stake, pinching back the others. In this way plants with a strong single stem will be obtained, which are to be planted out 5 feet distant each way in autumn. The next spring the treatment will depend upon the mode of training adopted, which may be the tree, pyramid, or vase method. To train a bush in the bush style, remove all buds so as to leave a clean stem from 6 inches to a foot above the surface of the ground, and then cut the top back so as to leave three strong buds. These will form three branches which are allowed to grow during the season, and the next year are cut back to two buds each, which will give a round-headed tree of six branches. The six branches are then to be cut back one half and have all superfluous shoots trimmed out.

The vase-form of training consists in having several main branches with fruit-bearing side shoots and is preferred by many good cultivators. To practice this, cut back a one-year-old plant of a single stem to four or six buds. Encourage the growth from these, and, if necessary, train them to a hoop to ensure an equal spreading of these main branches. These upright stems may throw out side branches the first year, or not until the second. In either case, they should be pinched back to 4 inches when they get to be 6 or 8 inches long. If any shoot afterwards pushes from a side branch, pinch back to a single leaf. By training bushes in this form with the center kept open, fine fruit can be raised.

# FARM AND GARDEN WORK FOR

# September

Work will vary with the weather. If we have a moist time, the opportunity should not be neglected to have the plowing done early and then to kill several crops of seedling weeds with the harrow. If the weather is hot and dry, no better time can be found for burning weeds along stone walls, or cutting and drying those in the field or in the meadow that are in seed. If the fall work that can be done at this season is finished, look to the swamps and to the draining of boggy ground where too much water stands in ordinary seasons. Rainy-day work is plenty. There is grain to thrash and prepare for market — peas and beans also. The corn silo should be put in order as well as the apparatus for grinding and cooking pig feed. Nevertheless, save time to attend the fairs, and by all means exhibit something.

## HINTS ABOUT FARM WORK

**Apples** — Windfalls are full of worms, usually. Pick them up regularly, and feed to the pigs all not fit for cider or at least for vinegar.

**Field Crops** — Beans should be pulled as soon as the pods seem well matured. They will cure in a loft better than in the field, and a few may be cured on a barn floor. In the field, stack them between stakes to keep off the ground and thrash when dry.

**Potatoes** — The death of the tops indicates the maturity of the tubers. If the rot is amongst them, it is better to let them rot in the ground than in the cellar or pit. Many, however, dig and market at once. If consumed before the disease makes progress, a larger portion of the crop may be thus utilized. When other work does not press, early potatoes should be dug and put in cool cellars or in pits in perfectly dry soil.

**Corn** — Pulling corn fodder is a Southern practice which we do not approve of. If it seems best to pull leaves this year, do not do it until the grain is glazed. Topping is much less objectionable — in fact, we do not object to it in the case of large, coarse-stalked varieties. This, too, should never be done until the glazing of the kernel shows that the grain has its full size. No doubt it is a damage to the corn, but there is proportionate gain in the feed, which is very valuable. Cutting up at the ground has much in its favor. The field is as good as cleared at one operation, and may be plowed and sown at once if desired — provided the stooks are made on as few lines as possible, standing very close. Taking 25 rows the longest way through the field, it is no very great labor to close on the middle row, taking 12 hills on each side, and so make a stook to every hill on this row — leaving plowlands of 100 feet or thereabouts in width, which should be plowed "inward," or "right about." The grain must be well glazed before the stalks are cut. It loses scarcely perceptibly in weight, while the stalks and leaves are saved. One day's or half a day's drying after being cut up will save the fodder from injury from severe frosts, which would otherwise render it flavorless and of little value as fodder.

**Corn Fodder**—Cattle and horses will eat corn leaves and husks well; they will eat almost the whole of the toppings, but unless it is cooked they will not eat all the butt stalks. However, if cut up and soaked, they will eat a good portion of them, especially if dusted with a little meal or oil cake. What they refuse is worth, we presume, half as much as green manure as it would be if eaten. The immense waste of feeding corn fodder on the ground is that but a comparatively small part is eaten, and the rest is utilized as manure to but a small extent. Corn fodder, sown for the purpose, should be cut as close as possible, bound in small bundles with new rye straw, and set up against rails laid on crossed stakes, or in crotches against a fence, or in open shooks, to dry. It will not mould enough to hurt it unless it lies long flat upon the ground.

**Roots**—Beets, carrots, parsnips, and turnips make astonishing growth this month. Keep them clear of weeds, which sap the very life of the soil. It is an excellent plan to run a subsoil plow between the rows. If crowded, roots of all kinds may be thinned to advantage and the surplus sent to market or fed to stock. Hogs will grow fast on the diet, though it is not very fattening.

**Grass**—If the aftermath is to be cut, do it in this month, and, if you can, manure with fine compost or some "hand manure" afterwards. This gives a chance for a good covering to grow, to protect the roots of the grasses from the winter. If the second growth is to be fed off, it is good economy to tether the cows.

**Seeding Down**—Grass may be sown alone at this season, or a little earlier perhaps, better than at any other. Prepare the ground well, giving thorough harrowing and top-dressing, picking off the stones; sow the seed, and roll. A bushel of oats harrowed in before the grass seed is sown will afford the young plants the protection of a fine mulch during the winter, and unless the season is very mild will be thoroughly dead and out of the way when spring comes, making good manure.

**Saving Seed**—Seed corn should be marked before it is cut up by selecting the best ear where two or more are on a stalk and tying strings tightly around them. They will thus be found and thrown one side at husking. Seed potatoes should be selected from those that have healthy stalks and ripen first. It is very well to go through and dig from hills before the general digging. If the whole crop is to be saved for seed, or if it is desirable to keep it pure, go through carefully and dig any suspicious or peculiar-looking hill. Seed of all kinds should be kept where it is dry, in nets, baskets, loosely covered pails, or in net bags, or tied together suspended. Close vessels are often fatal to seeds, causing them to mould or heat.

**Winter Grain**—*Wheat*: The land should be put in order, well manured on the surface, harrowed to a fine tilth, and the seed sown as early as possible this month. Use any fine, rich, well-rotted compost. Fine bonemeal and almost any good fertilizer combining both ammonia and phosphoric acid will pay. Soaking the seed in a strong brine and drying with dry slaked lime prevents smut to a great degree. Pickling enables one also to skim off and separate many of the light grains which the mill leaves. *Rye*: This grain may be sown the latter part of the month, but is usually sown in October, as sometimes it makes

too rank a growth and is smothered thereby in the course of the winter. Much depends on the land.

**Buckwheat** is greatly injured by even a light frost. Be prepared to cut and put in little cocks or gavels (piles or divisions) as soon as frost threatens. The tops should be gathered and bound at the top, more to prolong the drying and to prevent the wind scattering the grain than to make the little gavels shed rain. Many kernels, half formed when cut, will fill out at the expense of the juices of the haulm (stems).

**Sorghum** should be topped, cut up, stripped, and stacked before frost, to be hauled to the mill and worked up before hard freezing weather.

**Livestock** of all kinds require good feeding, for they lay on flesh and fat much more readily in mildly warm weather than when it is colder and in cool weather better than in cold. When severe weather comes, it is almost impossible to make cattle and hogs hold their own unless warmly sheltered. Ani-mals in good condition are easily maintained so, unless exposed to great cold, for they are already as if well blanketed. Horses and sheep bear vicissitudes of weather better than other stock if they have enough to eat, but if either is allowed to run down, it is hard to get them up again.

**Hogs**—Feed old corn (ground) if you have it—it gives them a splendid start. Grind and cook all grain fed to swine if you would get the full benefit of it. There is a difference of 25 percent in favor of grinding alone, and we doubt not nearly or quite as much more in favor of cooking. However, there is probably little loss in feeding nubbins and soft corn whole, if fed early, and it makes a relishable variety. A few handfuls of charcoal mixes with some ashes and a little sulphur make an excellent tonic and regulator for almost any kind of stock, and especially for swine. It will be eaten readily if a little grain is thrown upon it.

**Beeves** that are to be ripened off and marketed this fall should be early in condition to sell and held ready for shipment at the shortest notice.

## Hints About Horticultural Work

Ripeness is the characteristic of the month; not only do fruits mature, but the new wood ripens. Autumnal flowers bloom in the borders, and the cool nights and warm days are particularly congenial to the growth of the later crops of the kitchen garden. It is the month of fairs. Go to your nearest fair, as a matter of duty, and take such fruits, flowers, and vegetables as you have. Let prize-taking be the second thing in your thoughts—helping make a creditable display, the first. The home fair being attended to, visit as many others as possible. One is always sure to learn something, if not from examples, at least from warnings.

### Orchard and Nursery

**Autumn Planting** of trees is best where there is likely to be a long, mild autumn, but, where the winter shuts down suddenly, it is better to plant in spring. Next month the trees will be ready to remove from the nursery, and the ground should be prepared for their reception. A deep, well-drained, but not overrich soil is best. Plow and subsoil, and if possible make the whole place intended for the orchard so well prepared that a tree will grow in one place as well as in another.

**Selecting and Ordering** — Order early, but make a well-considered selection first. Selections of best varieties for states are not always safe guides. Experience of those in the neighborhood is best, and its value decreases as the distance from which it is derived increases. Visit fruit growers, go to fairs, talk with everyone who has any knowledge of the subject, and follow that advice which seems most reliable. Do not aim at too many varieties, unless you have time and means for carrying on an experimental collection. Twelve kinds of apples or pears are enough for family use, and six are plenty for market purposes.

**Picking and Packing** of autumn fruits require considerable judgment. They must be taken from the tree when fully matured, and yet before they have begun to mellow. This is especially the case with autumn pears, which ought always to reach the retailer before they are in eating condition. The fruit will give better satisfaction to the consumer, and the shipper will be saved much loss. In packing apples use new barrels; open the bottom of the barrel and place in a layer of good fruit with the stems towards the head, or downwards; then fill in with fruit properly packed, and put the bottom head on with pressure so that there will be no shaking.

**Fallen Fruit** is of as much importance, in one respect, as that which is picked; it usually contains insects, but should be gathered regularly. The best use to make of fallen apples is to grind, press, and make vinegar of them. If sufficient care can be given, the sound part of such apples and pears may be cut out and dried or preserved.

**Drying and Canning** fruit for winter use must be attended to. Much of the drying is done in the open air by sun heat. Where this is the case, it will be found to be a good help to have a room, which can be readily heated by a stove, to which the fruit can be removed on a damp day or during a rainy spell.

**Budding** may continue as long as the bark of the stock will lift or "run," which it will do with peach and quince stocks this month. Examine previous buddings and loosen the bandages if need be. Where buds failed, put in others, if not too late.

**Seeds,** especially of the stone fruits, must not be allowed to get too dry. They are best preserved in sand or sandy earth, just perceptibly moist, which should be mixed in sufficient quantity to preclude drying or heating. A box in a cool and dry cellar or shed will answer as well as to follow the European plan of burying or stratifying.

**Manuring** — Nurserymen who raise the best trees pass between the nursery rows with a plow and turn a shallow furrow in which a well-decomposed compost is distributed and the earth thrown back. In this way the land is kept in excellent condition.

**Prune** young trees to form a proper head.

**Weeds** — Let none of them ripen their seeds.

### Fruit Garden

Prepare the soil for fall planting. A rich, fine, deeply-worked soil is needed for successful fruit culture. The hints under "Orchard" apply to such trees as are grown in the fruit garden.

**Pears** are to be picked as fast as they mature. When fully developed, the stem will part readily from the tree. Ripen them in the house.

**Blackberries** — Remove the old stems as soon as the fruit is off. Pinch the side shoots of the new growth to about 18 inches. This will induce the wood to ripen and prevent injury by winter-killing.

**Raspberries** in garden culture are best if kept in place by some kind of trellis or support. Keep the ground clear of weeds and allow no suckers to grow, except such as are wanted for new plants.

**Grapes** — Full maturity is shown by the stem assuming a ripe appearance and losing its stiffness, allowing the bunches to hang directly down from the vine. Use scissors in gathering, and handle the fruit as little as possible.

**Strawberries** — New beds are to be kept clean and no runners allowed to grow. Beds may be set now, taking the plants up carefully and removing all the large leaves to prevent evaporation. Where plants have been struck in pots, this precaution is unnecessary as the roots of the plants are scarcely disturbed by turning them out of the pots.

152

*Kitchen Garden*

Clear away all old stuff, such as spent crops of beans and whatever may be encumbering the ground without profit. Plow in manure and prepare for the winter crops.

**Beans**—If the limas set more than can be used in the green state before frost, shell and dry for winter. Soaked overnight before cooking, they are nearly as good as when fresh. Salt string beans.

**Cabbages and Cauliflower**—The time for sowing seed for winter plants in the Middle Atlantic States is from the 10th to the 20th of the present month. Sow the seeds in the open ground in a well-prepared bed. Keep the seed beds well weeded, and sprinkle lime upon the plants if insects appear.

**Kale** for spring greens is sown this month in drills a foot apart.

**Corn** should now be dried for winter use. Some prefer to salt it. It is cut from the cob without boiling and packed in a jar with salt.

**Cucumbers**—Go over the vines at least every two days and gather for pickles; remove the overgrown.

**Celery**—Continue to earth up for blanching. That grown in flat culture, i.e., not in trenches, requires to be earthed up about ten days before it is blanched sufficiently for use. The main winter crop is not earthed up until later in the season.

**Endive**—Blanch as directed last month.

**Manure**—The compost heaps should now grow rapidly from the addition of garden refuse. All but very young weeds should be dried and burned.

**Melons**—Young fruit that will not ripen is to be picked and used for pickles.

**Onions**—See that those stored are so thinkly spread that they will not become heated. Take up sets, if not already done, and spread in thin layers in a cool, dry loft.

**Radishes**—Winter sorts may be sown early in the month with a prospect of a fair crop.

**Shallots**—These are set this month, placing the little bulbs 6 inches distant, in rows a foot apart. Keep clear of weeds as long as the ground can be worked.

**Spinach**—Sow for the winter crop before the middle of the month in rows 12 or 15 inches apart. Thin and weed the young plants when large enough.

**Sweet Potatoes**—Some of the larger roots may be taken by carefully removing the earth from the ridges, and the smaller ones left to grow as long as frost will let them. Dig with the first frost.

**Tomatoes**—Make catsup and can while the fruit is at its best. Later, it is poor and watery stuff.

**Turnips**—No plant better repays good culture than the rutabaga. It should be thinned so as to have room to grow, and then be encouraged by frequent hoeings. A little good phosphate helps it wonderfully. Round turnips may still be sown and still make a crop.

**Winter Cherry or Physalis**—The fruit of this, preserved, makes a strawberry-flavored sweetmeat much liked by many. The fruit, left in its hulls, will keep for some months if spread in a dry place.

*Flower Garden and Lawn*

**Bulbs**—The hardy bulbs, such as hyacinths, tulips, crocuses, etc., that were taken up, may be planted the last of this month or early in October. Purchase as soon as the dealers receive their stock.

**Perennials**—Those which complete their growth early, such as dicentra, may be divided and reset if the plants are large enough to require it. The seeds of many perennials, if sown now, will make plants large enough to pass the winter.

**House Plants** that have been turned out should be taken up and repotted before there is danger of frost. Keep them shaded until they recover, but do not take them into the house until cool weather.

**Chrysanthemums**—Have them properly staked. The bloom of the tall-growing kinds is so heavy, especially when wet by the rains, that they are apt to be broken down. Those intended for blooming indoors are to be potted when the buds are well-developed. They will wilt at first, but with a few days' shading and watering will recover.

**Dahlias**—Autumn storms will prostrate these just as they are at their best if they are not carefully staked and tied. Pick off flowers that have passed their prime as well as misshapen buds.

**Violets**—Prepare for forcing by setting the plants in fine rich soil in a cold frame which is not to be covered until frosty weather.

*Greenhouse and Window Plants*

Greenhouses and their heating apparatus should be put in thorough repair as it is very poor economy to have work going on after the plants are taken in.

**Plants in Pots,** whether they are to go into the greenhouse or the window, should be looked to. They must not be allowed to suffer from dryness.

**Hanging Baskets,** so pleasing in winter, may be planted now to get a good start. Use plenty of ivy, which bears transplanting at any season.

**Bulbs** for winter blooming may be potted if they are at hand or can be obtained. After the bulbs are in, plunge them in dry earth, or cover with coal ashes until time to start them.

**Cuttings** of bedding plants may be made for a winter stock.

**Annuals,** which are desirable for winter blooming, may be sown.

# PROJECTS FOR
# SEPTEMBER

## Digging, Stoning, and Curbing Wells

The annual waste of manure, and of flesh and fat, caused by driving animals to the brook or spring for water, and by the lack of an abundance of it, will on many farms equal the expense of making a good well once a year. In the summer, all the stock, and the teams in particular, suffer for want of good water, while during the foddering season, when storms prevail, cattle often will not go to drink for a whole day or even longer because the water is at a distance from the barn. Then, when thirst compels them to leave the yard and break their own path through snow drifts to obtain water, they drink too much. On their way to and from the water, they drop much manure, which is wasted. The importance of a good well at every barn where water cannot be obtained from some other source less expensive than digging wells need not be argued.

The best time to dig wells is in September before hard autumnal rains have raised the streams. At this season of the year, those veins of water only a few feet below the surface are dried up, so that permanent water can be found only by digging deep. If a good vein of water can be reached in a dry time, a well will not be likely to fail. But, if dug when most springs flow abundantly, the water is likely to fail at a period when it is most scarce—at the very time when it should be supplied by a never-failing spring.

The next consideration is where to dig a well. Our advice is to dig it where it will be most convenient for watering stock. If it is to be dug in the field, the most suitable place would appear to be near the intersection of the lines dividing four fields, so that animals in each lot could be watered from one well without leaving their respective enclosures. When dug near the barn, a location convenient to two or more yards should be chosen. Sometimes it is necessary to sink a well far below the surface, while in other instances living water may be reached by digging only a few feet.

For wells of ordinary size, 5 feet in diameter is sufficiently large; and they cannot be much smaller than this, as a man will not have sufficient room to swing his pick and handle the shovel. If the well is, without doubt, to be 30 or 50 feet deep and to be stoned from the bottom to the top, and if the stones are boulders of irregular form and size, it would be more advisable to dig 6 feet in diameter on account of making a thicker and more substantial wall than is required in shallow wells. If a large number of animals are to be watered, or much water required for any other purpose, the diameter should be increased to 8 or 10 feet for the purpose of forming a large reservoir in which the water can accumulate.

If the well is to be stoned many feet deep, the stone should be hauled to the spot before it has been sunk. If the inside is to be lined with brick or wood, everything should likewise be ready for immediate use. The location of the well being determined upon, strike a circle of what diameter is needed, and mark it deeply and accurately with a shovel or pickax, leaving the outer edge firm and well defined.

The first 12 or 14 feet of earth may best be thrown out with shovels, by making a platform 5 or 6 feet below the surface from which a man shovels the earth to the surface as fast as it is thrown up to him. When a well is to be sunk to a greater depth, one man with a horse can haul up the dirt with great ease by erecting three poles over the well, as represented by *fig. 1*. A strong stake, having a large 2-inch pin through the bottom of it, horizontally, should be set firmly in the ground so that a horse cannot pull it up. Then he will need no one to lead him. This stake or post must not be placed beyond the

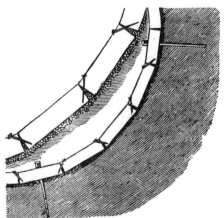

Fig. 2.—WOODEN CURBING.

Fig. 1.—DERRICK AND BUCKET.

foot of one of the poles, for the tendency would then be to draw the tripod over. At this stake a block or pulley is fixed, and a rope passes through it and over a pulley near the top of the poles, thence around another at the bail of the bucket, and the rope should be tied near the upper end of the poles. The upper pulley should be suspended at such a height that the dirt bucket may rise just high enough to be emptied into a wheelbarrow when the blocks come together. Thus the horse may continue to pull with all his might without being able to get away or to hinder the workman who manages the bucket. By having a wheelbarrow near, the earth may be turned quickly into it before the horse can back up. When a bucket is drawn up in this manner, it rises only half as fast as the horse travels, and he can with ease elevate three or four hundred pounds at a time.

**Digging and Curbing Wells in Soft Ground**—Whenever there is danger that the earth will cave in, it becomes necessary to curb the sides as fast as the well is sunk. To do this, dig out the earth in a true circle, plumbing accurately the sides of the well, and when it is 6 to 12 feet deep, set up pieces of 2-inch plank, 6 or 8 inches wide, as represented in

*fig. 2* which illustrates an end view of the staves. Set up one stave perpendicularly, and pin it fast to the earth with wooden pins, at top and bottom, as shown in the illustration. Then set up 3 or 4 more, nailing them together at the edges. Pin every fifth stave to keep the curb from settling down when it is undermined. After the last stave has been set up, drive in thin wedges between the staves in four places, if possible, to keep it tight. The staves will soon swell on the outside, and the chinks between them will fill up with sand and gravel, and thus they will form an arch that will resist a much greater pressure than will ever occur at any part of the curbing. Now dig 6 feet deeper, if it is safe to sink it so far, and set up another course of staves under the first, fastening them as previously directed. In this way, the well may be sunk and curbed with great dispatch and perfect safety to any desirable depth. No other curbing will be required until the staves have decayed. Still, the whole may better be stoned or bricked up at once on the inside of the curbing.

**Stoning and Plastering Wells**—When wells are sunk through sufficiently compact ground as will not cave in, the side may be plastered with two thick coats of water-lime cement from the bottom to within 4 or 5 feet of the top, when there should be an offset for a brick or stone wall to rest upon, extending to the surface of the ground. Sink such a well 4 feet deep, 7 or 9 feet in diameter; then dig it 6 feet deeper, 5 feet in diameter, and plaster the surface. After this, dig and plaster about 6 feet, and so finish successive sections until permanent water is found. This will be as good as stone if well done. If veins of water break through the green cement, drive a circular piece of tin or wood a few inches long into the plaster and earth, just below the issue of the water to

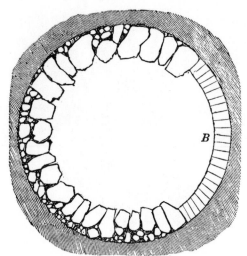

Fig. 3.—STONE AND BRICK WALLS TO WELLS.

keep it from running down and washing off the mortar. Where stone is abundant, it is economical to use it instead of cement. If bricks are used instead of stone, they should be well burned and made wider at one end than the other so as to fit the curve of the well as represented by *fig. 3*, at *B*. Water will find its way between the staves at the ends and between the bricks, which should not be laid in mortar.

There is a right way and a wrong way to stone a well. The object is to build a strong wall that will not fall inward instead of a wall having a smooth face, which is of little account. *Fig. 3* illustrates the manner of placing the stones. In laying up a common wall, the large ends and face sides are laid in front. But, when stoning a well, the large ends are placed in the opposite direction so that every course of stone on the face or inside will form an arch. The back side is leveled up with small stone, and much care should be exercised to place many small ones against the earth (instead of packing in large ones) to keep the dirt from washing down to the bottom of the well. If gravel can be obtained conveniently, it is a good practice to fill all the interstices between the stones with it. Place a wide board across the wall to stand on when laying the brick or stone. Marks on each edge of it will serve as guides for carrying up the face of the wall true. Brick and stone may be lowered by the horse and bucket in the same way as hauling up the dirt. There is no quicker way to draw the water from a well, when cleaning it out, than to make a valve over a large hole in the bottom of a barrel, and draw up a barrelful at once with a horse. If there is room for a barrel to dip, a valve is not necessary. The stone or brick should be laid in

cement for at least 3 feet down from the surface to exclude worms, reptiles, and mice.

## Propagating Plants from Cuttings

A large number of our plants are propagated from cuttings, and as this is the season at which many are started for winter blooming, a few hints upon the rationale of the process will be timely. A plant may be regarded as a sort of compound, being made up of a number of distinct parts, each of which is capable, under favorable circumstances, of becoming an independent plant. Every plant, at least all those in cultivation, will be found to be made up of a succession of joints, each consisting of a piece of stem of greater or less length and a leaf or pair of leaves as the case may be, each leaf having at its base a bud which may or may not be large enough to be noticed. The point at which the leaves are attached is called a *node* or knot, and not only do the leaves start from here, but when the stem is buried in the earth, the nodes are the points from which roots most readily start. Though in some plants they will spring from any part of the stem, in the majority of cases they are only successfully produced from the nodes.

We make two sorts of cuttings: those from the ripened wood after the leaves have fallen, and those in which the plant is still in a growing condition and retains its leaves. The last named is the kind made at the present season. With proper care and treatment each joint of a plant may be made to grow, but in the ordinary way of making cuttings, a shoot containing several joints is taken.

To make a cutting, a shoot is taken from the parent plant, its lower leaves are cut off, and it is set in the ground with one or more knots beneath the surface. In removing the shoot, we separate it from its natural source of nutriment, and it has to make new roots before it can begin on its own account as an independent individual. Plants differ very much as to the readiness with which the cuttings will strike root. Some are so difficult in this respect as to require all the skill of the professional propagator, while others will root by being merely placed in the soil.

The roots are formed from material contained in the stem and leaves, and they must be produced before any considerable growth can take place. Evaporation is constantly going on from the leaves, and, in most plants, it is necessary to cover the cuttings with a glass or other protection to prevent exhaustion by evaporation. Let us take for example

SMALL-LEAVED FUCHSIA—(*F. microphylla.*)

BRILLIANT FUCHSIA—(*F. fulgens.*)

HEART-LEAVED MANNETTIA.

GERANIUM CUTTING.

not having these appliances or the skill to use them are deterred from propagating, thinking that cuttings can only be grown by these means. The fact is that a large share of our shrubs and herbaceous plants can be readily propagated by means within reach of everyone. We have used with great success a common soapbox with the bottom knocked out and a piece of muslin (common cotton cloth) tacked in its place. The cuttings being placed in a sandy soil are covered with this box, which admits sufficient light and retains the moisture. If air is required, the box may be tilted and a brick or other support placed under one side. Where there are hotbeds in use, a frame with the glass coated with whiting or shaded by muslin will be found much more convenient. In this way we have rooted in large quantities and with very, very little trouble fuchsias, lantanas, petunias, verbenas, ageratums, and a host of other bedding plants, as well as weigelas, forsythias, roses, and numerous other shrubs. The soil should be made very sandy and kept well watered. In making the cuttings, strong and well-or partially-hardened shoots should be taken.

## Reclaiming Waste Land

There are scores of acres of as valuable land as can be found in the country overgrown with weeds and worthless bushes. Often seen are strips of uncultivated land along the highway and between farms, and even in the midst of a farm close to the fences where elder bushes, blackberry bushes, milkweeds, and other pernicious plants have rooted out almost the last spear of grass and are bearing undisputed sway. Such things are disfiguring blotches on the face of a nice farm as well as a reproach to any farmer. The land where such pests flourish from year to year is rich and would pay the expense of cultivation and produce at first more valuable crops than that on each side of it. It ought to be reclaimed, and the unsightly weeds and bushes should be exterminated—for the sake of appearances, if for nothing more. The job is best done in August or early in September rather than not at all.

Where it is not found convenient or practicable to plow such uncultivated strips of ground, mow everything as closely as possible, collect it in heaps, and burn it. If the bushes are small, they may be cut with a short, stiff grass scythe; but if they are large, use a bush scythe. Let everything be cut close to the ground. Then harrow thoroughly and stock down

a cutting of a common pelargonium or geranium, as it is commonly called. A shoot of tolerably mature wood is cut at a node or knot, the lower leaves removed, and it is set in the ground as far as the dotted line. In about two weeks, more or less, it will be found that a new growth has commenced between the bark and wood. It appears as a sort of excrescence or *callus* as it is called by the gardeners. This callus is material supplied by the stem and leaves and forms a sort of bed from which roots will start. It often attains a considerable size, as is shown in the illustration, and seems capable of performing the functions of the root, as cuttings that are well callused will often make considerable growth before any roots are pushed out. A cutting which makes a good callus is pretty sure to live. In a rich soil, cuttings are apt to decay before they root, and much better success is usually had if they are planted in a naturally poor soil or one made so by a large admixture of sand.

The professional gardener strikes his cuttings in pure sand and uses bottom heat. Many plants cannot be rooted except in this manner, and all are more certainly managed in this way. Many persons

with grass seed. Sow orchard and Kentucky blue grass seed so that the grass will be fit to mow for hay next season before weeds have attained a large growth.

If the ground can be plowed, remove the fence when it can be done with little labor. Put a sharp point and a sharp strong colter on a good plow, and attach a chain for hauling the weeds beneath the turning furrow slice. Hitch on a strong double team, and break it all up as deep as the plow will turn well and the team is able to draw it. Always plow around such plots instead of beginning in the middle, thus forming a ridge where the roots will not be disturbed. Harrow several times, and sow at the rate of half a bushel of buckwheat per acre. If the work is properly done, weeds and bushes will give little trouble next season if the ground is occupied with some hoed crop. If, from some cause (such as wet weather after plowing or the abundance of rose briars or brambles) the weeds spring up very badly in spring, another application of the buckwheat after plowing will leave the land in good condition by midsummer.

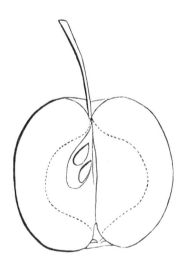

**Picking Apples**

There are three things essential to safe and rapid apple picking: an ordinary light stepladder, a couple of half-bushel handled baskets with a hook on the handles, and a smart boy who is not afraid to climb. The ladder is the least essential article of the three. If trees are properly trimmed, they will allow a man with a basket to enter the top. An ordinary iron hook will serve to hang the basket on a limb while it is being filled. Apple limbs are strong and they will hold a boy or man more safely

than is generally supposed. As a general thing, a boy is afraid to venture far, but a little training will enable him to climb well. Nor is it essential that the boy should be exceedingly young and light in order to reach most of the apples on a high tree. It is quickness and agility rather than lightness that makes a good apple picker.

When one basket is full, it is handed down and another one returned. A bag strapped on one's back, in the manner used for sowing grass seed, is usually a nuisance in a tree, although it may be handy on a stepladder. The more one practices, the more he will be surprised at his ability to reach apples on the ends of limbs. There will be some, however, which he cannot reach. If a fruit picker is to be used at all, here is the only place where it is necessary—in picking a few apples which have escaped reach or notice. For this purpose a cheap and simple picker may be made by bending a stiff wire into the form of a circle 6 inches in diameter, with one side of the circle prolonged 3 inches into a V-shaped projection. Upon this wire sew a cloth bag a foot or so deep, and fasten it on to a pole by the end opposite the V-shaped extremity. This V-shape projection will serve as a corner in which to catch the apple and pull it off, allowing it to fall into the bag.

Fig. 2.

An excellent picker, as shown in *fig. 2*, can be made from stiff wire by a tinner. The span across the top should be about 6 inches, and the depth from 8 to 10 inches. The wires should not be more than a ½-inch apart at their tips. The wires being more or less flexible, the apple is apt to draw through them if they are not close together. Care should also be taken to have the implement made as light as possible. A bungling mechanic will probably use too much solder.

Fig. 1.

Another good picker is pictured in *fig. 1.* It is light, durable, and pleasant to handle. When, however, an apple, being very short-stemmed lies close to a limb, it is much more easily removed by the former device than by this. A simple flattened hook with a thin, almost cutting edge, secured on a pole, *fig. 3,* is often handy for pulling off stray apples. This is the best implement for thinning apples. With this one can hook off the wormy and ill-formed apples every week in July and August. This practice of thinning fruit is a profitable one, especially in the instance of a heavy bearer.

Fig. 3.

## Save the Leaves

Many homesteaders do not understand the value of leaves. In their desire to keep the garden and grounds neat, they put the fallen leaves out of sight without a thought of the value of what they are throwing away. Leaves are useful in two ways—in their entire state as a mulch, and decomposed as a manure. Leaves are the natural mulch. Go into the woods in autumn and look under the leaves and you will find various seeds sprouting under them and getting a sufficient start to enable them to winter under this genial covering and break into vigorous growth with the return of spring. The beautiful wild flowers, which die out when taken to the garden, are in the woods nicely tucked up under a coverlet of leaves; they sleep warm and awake strong and refreshed. There is no better winter covering for a strawberry bed, and for herbaceous plants generally, than a good coating of leaves. The great difficulty is that they will blow away. This may be prevented by laying brush upon them or giving them a light sprinkling of soil. Plants protected in this way have a covering which will ward off the injurious effects of sudden changes of temperature, but will not pack so closely as to endanger the health of the plant.

Decomposed leaves are valuable and in the form of leaf mould are considered one of the chief fertilizers. Aside from the purely vegetable matter they contain, the leaves have also a great deal of mineral matter which is deposited in them during the constant evaporation that·is carried on during the grow-

ing season. This mineral matter is in just that finely divided and soluble state which makes it ready to be again taken up by other plants. The leaves of trees when burned give from ten to thirty percent more ashes than the wood of the same tree. It will be seen that leaves are of the highest value in the compost heap, the barnyard, and the pigsty, and he who neglects to save them disregards the sources of fertility which nature is kindly offering him. Even this early in autumn, many leaves will fall, and the collection should be begun and continued. Any place, large or small, will find a well-sheltered pile of leaves valuable to draw upon for mulch, for winter covering, and for use in equal proportion with manure in hotbeds. Those not needed for these purposes may add to the richness of the manure heap. By all means save the leaves!

## A Homemade Cabbage Cutter

A cheap and easily-made cabbage and root cutter is shown in the drawing. Take two 12-inch boards and nail them strongly together. With dividers mark around a circle, then saw out and mark in quarters. Cut four slots 7 inches long on a slant, as shown by dotted lines, so the cabbage will fall through easily. Next cut two circles 4 inches in diameter. Nail one to the large wheel on the back and leave the other loose on the shaft to act as a bearing. Make a frame to admit the wheel, leaving 2 inches clear and just wide enough so the knives do not strike the side. Make a top over the wheel and put a hopper on the opposite side from the

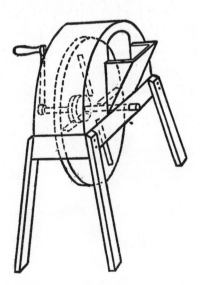

crank. The knives are 8 inches long and can be made from an old bucksaw and ground down sharp with a bevel on one side. Screw these on the wheel at a slant according to the thickness the cabbage is wanted. A square hole should be cut through the center of the wheel for the shaft.

## Saving Seed Corn

Here is a handy device for preserving select ears of seed corn. It consists of a wide board fastened between two supports nailed to the edges. The board stands upright on one end and may be as long as desired. Drive heavy spikes through it from the opposite side and stick an ear of corn upon each spike. This allows for the passage of air, and the ears can be examined without removing them from the rack. It is much to be preferred to expensive wire racks, as each nail may be numbered and a record kept of the ears in this way.

SEED CORN RACK

## Preventing Cows from Kicking

Cows will kick—some of them; and heifers with their first calves are expert at it. An unhandled, "ungentled" cow takes as naturally to kicking as Leghorn hens do to scratching. Of course, every heifer ought to have her udder handled before calving, when it is sensitive, and when a little manipulation is soothing and agreeable to the ani-

THE PRIZE JERSEY COW "AUGEREYS LASS."

mal. This breaks the ice, so to speak, and then if the calf if removed as soon as dropped, the novelty of the experience and the entire lack of knowledge of what she has lost leads the great majority of heifers—no doubt, nine out of ten—to submit to milking with pleasure and evident satisfaction. If, however, the calf is dropped in the pasture or at night, and is found with the cow in the morning, she may resent any attempts to milk her, even though her udder is full and hard. The calf should be placed at the cow's left side and encouraged to suck, but, whether it does so or not, let the milker at once begin to milk. Saving the milk is of no importance, so, if the heifer is nervous, keep the pail away, and milk on the ground. If she kicks, soothe her, and begin again. Do not let her think her kicking has any effect. A rail may be placed so that kicking may be a disagreeable performance, and sometimes a cow may be placed close to a rail fence, which defends the milker from the blows of a really vicious kicker and allows the milking to go on. The cow will ordi-narily yield to circumstances and stand still after a while; at least, the pressure of the milk in the udder, which may cause inflammation, can thus be relieved.

If the cow continues nervous and will not be pacified, the thing to do is to tie or strap her legs. This may be done with a light rope. It is passed once around the left leg below the hock, tied by a half hitch (half a knot), then twisted a few times, and another hitch turned in it, and finally passed around the right leg, and tied in a bowknot so that it can be quickly untied. A cow so tied cannot kick, but she is almost sure to take short steps backward. And when she gets to the end of her tie-strap or back as far as she can get in the stanchions, her hind legs may be strained far back, and as her position is very un-steady, she may fall down. To prevent this, a rope may be passed twice around the tie-rope, carried forward, and fastened to the manger. This will pre-vent the backing, and the cow will probably soon give up and stand quietly.

## Making Posts

There is quite an art in splitting logs into posts. Every post should have some heartwood, which lasts the longer for two reasons: that there may be durable wood into which to drive the nails, and that some of the posts may not rot off long before others, as they will be composed entirely of sapwood, making the most annoying of all repairing necessary. If the log is of a size to make twelve posts, split along the lines of *fig. 1*, which will give each post its share of heart-

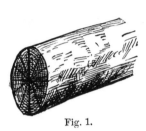

Fig. 1.

wood. This will make a cross section of the posts triangular, the curved base being somewhat more than half of either side. This is a fairly well-shaped post, and much better than a square one having little or no heartwood. Although the log may be large enough to make sixteen or eighteen posts, it is better to split it the same way. It should first be cut into halves, then quarters, and then twelfths. If you attempt to split one post off the side of a half, the wood will "draw out," making the post larger at one end than the other—not a good shape, for there will be little heartwood at the small end. When the log is too large to admit of its being split in that way, each post may nevertheless be given enough heartwood by splitting along the lines shown in *fig. 2*. First cut

Fig. 2.

the log into halves, then quarters, then eights. Then split off the edge of each eighth, enough for a post—about one-fourth only of the wood, as it is all heartwood, and then halve the balance. A good post can be taken off the edge, and yet enough heartwood for the remaining two posts will remain.

## How to Plow Wet Ground in Autumn

All wet ground ought to be underdrained; then it can be plowed and worked at any desirable time. Through lack of labor and means, it is seldom practicable to do in one season all the draining that should be done, and many fields must be plowed and cultivated where the soil is decidedly too wet. It is well to know in what manner to best plow such wet fields.

When the surface is nearly level, cut the furrows in the direction for carrying off the surface water most readily, or up and down the greatest descent. But when there is so much slope that the water will form gullies by its rapid flow, the furrows should always be made along the side of the slope, instead of up and down, in order to carry off the water slowly, and thus avoid washing away soil with it.

When wet ground is plowed, as it often is without reference to the points alluded to, and with wide lands, without opening the middle furrows, the soil often becomes so thoroughly saturated with water that it runs together before spring, like sand and lime in mortar, frequently settling firmer than before it was plowed. Thus all the efficacy of fall plowing is lost.

# FARM AND GARDEN WORK FOR

# October

Somber yet happy autumn is here. The landscape wears the sere and yellow hues, blended with red and green, the more brilliant for the contrast. But for the sighing winds and the chill that is in the air, and the drifts of leaves that are swept across the view, one might take October for the gayest month of the twelve. And it is gay. Why should the falling of the leaf inspire sad thoughts? All things grow old as do garments, and like them they are changed with the season, or in their appointed time. If we change with them, it should be as the buds mature on the trees, to burst into leaf in the spring, or as the fruits and seeds ripen for the Master's use, or as the bulbs wrap up the vital germ which will rise into a new and beautiful life when the springtime comes. This is the season of abundance, when man and beast prepare for the coming winter. The days are growing shorter, and long evenings invite to reading, study, and meditation. The experiences of the summer, the results of the harvest, the memorandums and recollections of what was seen at the fairs furnish topics of conversation and induce visiting among farmers. Fruits and nuts and sweet cider may well add to the sociability. Such visits will in many instances ripen into farmers' clubs with their meetings for discussion, for exchange of seeds, and for the exhibition of products of the soil or of skillful hands.

## HINTS ABOUT FARM WORK

Farm work at this time of the year is naturally classified in order of its importance; as 1st, necessary autumn work, that which must be done now, like the harvesting of the corn and root crops, gathering the fruits of the orchard, etc. 2nd, spring work which may be done now, as preparing the ground for spring crops. 3rd, winter work, that which may appropriately be done at any time during the winter, such as getting out timber or cutting firewood, work in the muck beds, etc. It is well to bear this in mind, so as to make all work tell to the best advantage.

**Animals**—Nature provides nuts for the squirrels, mast for the swine, the seeds of cereals (grasses and grains) for the cattle, both small and large, and innumerable insects for the feathered tribes. Thus they all fatten readily and prepare for severe weather not only by laying on a warm coat, but by storing fuel for maintaining internal warmth. The weather is not severe, yet shelter will be found to make quite a difference in the rapidity of fattening. Cook, if possible, all or most of the feed of fattening animals, except, perhaps, sheep, which are just as likely to remain healthy on uncooked and even whole grain. Keep beeves and sheep at pasture as

168

long as the feed is good, and give grain morning and night. Hogs must be kept growing and gaining by well-cooked food in more or less variety. Give them a few shovelfuls of wood ashes in which is a good deal of charcoal, and throw a few handfuls of corn into it.

**Milch cows** if well fed will give rich milk, if not a great deal of it; and as rich and beautiful butter may be made now as in any month. After sharp frosts the pasturage will be less nutritious. Feed pumpkins (remove the seeds, which are excellent for hogs), roots, turnip tops, cabbages that do not head, etc. Decaying leaves and rotten turnips will make the milk taste bad. Cows must have all the pure water they will drink, and salt is essential to thrift.

**Calves and Steers** will "get along" on coarse fare; they will not starve on wheat straw, or bog hay with some corn stalks; they will probably not if they stand out until next March on the north side of a barn; but they will be stunted in their growth and never have any thing like the form or size they should and would have had. One of the highest pleasures of a good farmer is to see his young stock grow. They need shelter quite as much as the older cattle, and if a pet heifer or pair of nice steers get a few ears of corn more than their share, the farmer had better wink at it unless it is carried too far. That the liberal hand shall be made rich is constantly demonstrated in the barnyards of this country. Don't attempt to carry over too much young stock. That kept should be well fed.

**Horses**—As pasturage begins to fail, commence regular feeding and grooming in comfortable quarters.

**Purchase of Stock for Wintering**—If the hay crop has been abundant, buy sheep and cattle to consume the surplus straw, hay, and grain, and to make manure. Buy so as to give them a good start on grass before winter sets in.

**Fall Plowing for Spring Crops**—There is great economy in plowing in the autumn. It must only be attempted on land not exposed to wash badly. It is well also to regard the direction of prevalent winds, and, if the lay of the land is such that the fine particles which the wind will move a distance of several rods will be blown off the farm, this will be an argument in favor of spring plowing. Plow deep if there is richness enough in the soil or manure enough applied to warrant it.

**Roots** usually make the best part of their growth after frost; yet they will not stand severe freezing without harm, and it is risky to leave them undug after the ground begins to stiffen mornings, for some fine day you will find them all frozen and solid. A good, well-ventilated barn cellar, which may be closed so as to keep the frost out, is the best place for storing roots; but they keep perfectly well in pits or outdoor cellars.

**Root Pits** may or may not be pits. If actually in part below the surface, the drainage must be perfect. If above the surface, first place the roots in uniform piles, say 6 feet wide, 3 feet high, and as long as convenient. Cover with a few inches of straw and a light covering of earth, and let them lie lightly covered for a few days. Provide ventilation by placing bundles of straw upright in the ridge of the heap. As the cold increases, add to the thickness of earth until the roots are covered about a foot deep at all points. Remove the earth for covering, so as to leave good ditches to carry off water.

**Potatoes**—Dig when the vines are dead and store. Potatoes are not roots, and require different

treatment. The tubers are fleshy underground stems. They are more sensitive to frost and do not require the same amount of ventilation.

**Sorghum** — It is best to make clean work as you go. Cut up, top, and strip at one operation; bind with two hands, and if possible have the stalks hauled at once to the mill. The seed makes good feed for sheep and other stock, and the dried leaves and suckers tolerable fodder.

**Corn** — Husk when the corn is hard and the husks dry. Bind the stalks and set them up in well-braced stooks or shocks, bound firmly at the tops so that they will stand through a gale of wind and the rain. Use as fodder.

**Soiling Crops** — Wheat and rye may both be sown for spring feeding.

**Winter Grain** — Wheat often does well sown as late as the early part of this month, but it is better, as a general rule, north of lat. 41° to sow earlier, and to put in rye if the time has passed by even though the land is prepared for wheat. Rye may be sown any time during the month on good land with assurance of a well-paying crop.

**Draining** — This is one of the most favorable seasons for pushing ahead this kind of work, for it interferes less with the work of the farm — either by disturbing the fields or taking hands away from other work. Make thorough work; halfway work never pays in the long run.

**Weeds** — On wet days cut weeds, put them in heaps, and burn them when dry. The ashes will be of some use; the seeds will be killed.

**Buildings** — Push forward all necessary repairs; tighten up barns and sheds, look out for loose clapboards and patch shingle roofs. It is not best to re-roof barns at this season when they are full of hay.

Many nails in hay are often fatal to cattle and horses, and a few are bad for their teeth and also for hay cutters of all kinds.

**Cooking Hay for Cattle** kills weed seeds, many of which would otherwise pass through the animals and grow when carried to the field in manure.

## HINTS ABOUT HORTICULTURAL WORK

The leaves have done their work! All summer long they have taken the sunlight and given off nothing but green, but now that their work is accomplished, they and the sun are having a gala time of it, and they throw this light back in crimson and gold. The fruit, too, which has hithertofore been green, now splashes itself with carmine and turns its ruddy cheek to the sun. The Great Artist puts the last touches to the fruit in the beautiful waxen bloom that betokens perfection. The harvest of the orchard and the great harvest of the forest are this month gathered. The ripe leaves lighten the scene with their transient glow and dutifully fall to the earth to give up what they have received. Did you ever look at the place from which a leaf has fallen? Just there is a bud all ready for the next spring's work. Is not there a lesson here, when even an inanimate leaf, as we are accustomed to call it, thus early makes provision for another year? We might dwell upon this point, but as one old philosopher says: "I have said enough for those who take me, and for those who do not, nothing would be enough."

### Orchard and Nursery

**Picking** of the late varieties of fruit is mainly done this month. Hand picking with every care to avoid bruises is the only method to be commended. Place the fruit carefully in bins or on shelves in the fruit cellar, or put in barrels at once.

**Barrelling** should be done in clean new barrels; take out the bottom head, place the fruit in regular layers, and fill to about an inch above the chine; bring the head into place by means of a screw or lever press. A few of the apples next to the head will be indented, but the rest will be held in place and will not bruise in transportation. Turn the barrel over and mark the top with the name of the variety. Never put more than one kind in a package and keep poor fruit out altogether. Keep the fruit, whether in barrels or not, at as low and uniform a temperature above freezing as possible.

**Late Pears** may be treated the same as apples. Autumn varieties should be placed on shelves where their progress in ripening may be watched.

**Cider Making** — The best cider is made from the best fruit. A rich saccharine juice is needed to make the finest article. Assort the fruit and convert the inferior lot into vinegar. Put the juice into clean casks and allow the fermentation to go on slowly in a cool cellar. When the fermentation has ceased, rack off into other clean casks and bung up.

**Vinegar** — A good batch if cider vinegar finds a ready sale.

**Pomace** (apple pulp) may go to the piggery or into the compost heap. If seeds are wanted, wash them out before the pomace ferments. In washing large quantities, a continuous stream of water is required. This is run into a box in which the pomace is placed. The pomace being stirred, the lighter portions are carried off by the flowing water, and the heavier seed remains. Collect and dry it.

**Planting** may be done if the land is in good order. Lay out the ground beforehand, either in regular rows or in the quincunx order. The last plan allows the land to be occupied to the best advantage.

**Labels** are attached to the trees at the nursery and often are wired on so firmly that the bark is strangulated. Look to every label and see that no injury can result from this cause. The position of every tree should be recorded, so that when the labels become lost, as they will sooner or later, there will be no doubt about the identity of the trees.

**Nursery Stock**—Look to that budded this autumn, and loosen the tyings if needed. Manure between the rows of the older stock, and cut back the growth to give a proper shape to the trees.

## Fruit Garden

**Planting** of shrubs and trees may be done whenever the autumns are usually mild, and it is better to do it now with the blackberry and raspberry than to wait until spring, as the buds start early.

**Raspberries and Blackberries** when set out should have the canes cut back to the ground. If left, a slight crop may be gathered next summer at the expense of the future welfare of the plants. Raspberries may be set from 4 to 6 feet apart and blackberries from 6 to 8 feet. If grown as a hedge, they may be placed much nearer, say half the distance.

**Gooseberries and Currants** may be pruned whenever the leaves have fallen. Cut out as much of the old wood as will leave the bush open, and shorten this year's growth one-half, more or less, according to its vigor, cutting back the weakest shoots most severely. Use the prunings of new wood for:

**Cuttings,** which are to be about 6 inches long and planted 4 inches apart in trenches, with only an inch above the surface. Ram the soil firmly against the base of the cuttings, and cover the bed with leaves or litter when freezing weather comes on.

**Grapes**—Full ripeness is desirable, whether they are to be used for the table or for wine. Grapes to be packed for winter should be allowed to stand a few days to "cure." They are then put in 5 or 10 pound boxes, which are to be packed full, the cover, or bottom, rather, crowded on with a slight pressure and nailed. The boxes are then to be kept in a cool, dry room at an uniformly low temperature, but the fruit must not be allowed to freeze.

**Strawberries** started in pots may still be planted.

## Kitchen Garden

**Prepare the Soil** for spring crops. Sod ground may be manured and plowed, as well as land from which

crops have been removed. Plowing is now much more easily performed than in spring. Stiff land should be thrown into ridges, to get the benefit of the ameliorating action of the winter's frosts.

**Protection** to those crops left out over winter ought not to be given too early. All of these plants are nearly hardy, and there is danger of smothering them if covered too soon. Many things make a good growth in the warm autumn days.

**Preserving Roots, etc.** — Only in very cold localities will roots need to be stored for winter as early as this month. It is best, however, to have everything ready to store and house the crops should heavy frosts make it necessary. If cellars are used for storing, have bins, barrels, etc., ready. Pits are better than cellars. They must be made 3 or 4 feet wide and 6 feet deep. A section 2 feet in length is packed with roots, then 6 inches from that another similar section, and so on. The spaces between are filled with earth, and later in the season all are covered with earth. This is only done when freezing weather is at hand.

**Asparagus** — When the tops turn yellow, cut and burn them. Do not put them in the compost heap, as the seeds retain their vitality, and if distributed in manure produce troublesome "weeds."

**Beets** — Let them grow until hard frosts are at hand; then dig and store in pits or in the cellar.

**Cabbages** — Prepare frames for wintering young plants, which should be a foot high at the rear and 8 inches in front, wide enough for the sash to be used, and as long as needed. They should be set on light soil and where water will drain off readily. The plants are to be set 2¼ inches apart each way, deep enough to cover all the stems. Do not cover with sash until the approach of freezing weather.

**Cauliflowers** — The young plants to be wintered are to be set as directed for cabbages. Gather the late crop as it is ready. There are often many plants that do not head. These, at the approach of frosty weather, should be set in a pit or light cellar, and many of them will form heads.

**Celery** — Finish earthing up. The earth is to be banked up against the stalks nearly to the top of the leaves. In most places, next month will be early enough to store it away for winter.

**Lettuce** — Young plants may be set in frames, as directed for cabbages. In warm localities young plants of the hardy kinds, covered with leaves or other light litter, will pass the winter safely.

**Horseradish** is to be left in the ground until frost, when it is to be dug and preserved like other roots.

**Rhubarb** — Where vegetation is at rest, new plantings may be made. Cut an old root so as to leave a bud to each piece, and plant in rich soil.

**Spinach** — Keep the late crop clean. In cutting for use, take it from those portions of the rows that are most crowded and need thinning.

**Squashes** — Cut before they are injured by frost, and leave for two days in the sun. Place them in a cool, dry place, where there will be no danger of freezing. In handling them, great care must be observed, as the least bruise leads to decay.

**Sweet Potatoes**, when the vines are first touched by the frost, are to be dug. In digging and handling, be careful not to bruise them. Those to be kept should dry for a day in the sun, and then be packed in sand, cut straw, or leaves. Whatever material is used must be perfectly dry. Keep in a warm and dry place, where the mercury will not fall below 60°.

## Flower Garden and Lawn

The weather is now more favorable than in spring for all work like grading, road and walk making, draining, laying out borders, and the like.

**Lawns** — In preparing for these, a deep and rich soil is necessary, and usually drainage is required.

**House Plants** that have been in borders during summer should not be left there too late. The overgrown ones should be well cut back. Shade them for a few days, until they recover, and then give them a good exposure until it is necessary to remove them to the house.

**Cannas** must be taken up before the frost has killed the foliage, otherwise the roots are apt to rot.

**Chrysanthemums** — When the buds are well formed, pot for blooming indoors. See that those left out are well supported by stakes.

**Perennials** of most kinds need to be taken up every few years, divided, and reset.

**Peonies** — These almost fail to flower if removed in spring. Take up the roots early this month, while they are dormant, divide so as to have a bud with each piece, and plant in deep, rich soil.

**Bulbs** — The hardy kinds, such as tulips, hyacinths, crocuses, crown imperials, etc., are to be planted as soon as they can be obtained. The tender varieties, like gladiolus, tiger lilies, etc., are to be taken up after the early frosts, dried off, and stored in a cool, dry place, where they will not freeze.

**Dahlias** are to be left awhile after the frost kills the stems. Take them up in the morning of a dry day and let the roots remain in the sun to dry off, label securely, and store them where they will not freeze or be too damp.

**Trees and Shrubs**—All the hardy deciduous ones may be transplanted now, and hedges of deciduous shrubs, such as buckthorn, privet, etc., may be set.

**Protection** to half-hardy things should not be applied until quite cool weather. The object is not so much to prevent freezing as to avoid frequent changes. Materials should be in readiness. Collect leaves from the lawn or wherever they can be found. One of the best materials is the boughs of the red cedar. Where these can be had in abundance, a good supply should be laid in. A coating of light peaty earth upon beds of seedlings of perennials serves as an excellent protection. Salt hay, readily procured near the coast, is a favorite material with gardeners living in those districts.

### Greenhouse and Window Plants

The more tender plants are to be taken in first. Have the pots in good order. Top-dress the plants by removing the surface soil and giving a supply of rich compost.

**Insects**—See that none are taken into the house with the plants.

**Bulbs**—Pot for winter blooming. Use rich, light soil, and when potted place in a cool, dark cellar for the roots to form; or the pots may be placed in a frame and covered with some inches of coal ashes or tanbark. In this case it is best to invert a small flowerpot over each pot, to avoid breaking the bud, should it start, in removing the pots.

**Forcing Plants**—Many of the perennial herbaceous plants and shrubs are used for forcing. In France the lilac is forced in large quantities. The most commonly treated in this way here are lily of the valley, dicentra, deutzia gracilis, wiegela, astilbe (spiraea), japonica, etc. The plants are to be potted and kept in a cool place until it is desired to bring them into flower.

**Cuttings** of bedding plants should be made at once, if it has not already been done.

**Annuals** may be sown in pots for winter blooming. Mignonette and candytuft are always in demand for making bouquets in winter.

**Ventilation**—Ventilate as much as the weather will allow, and make the transition from free air to the confinements of the house as gradual as possible.

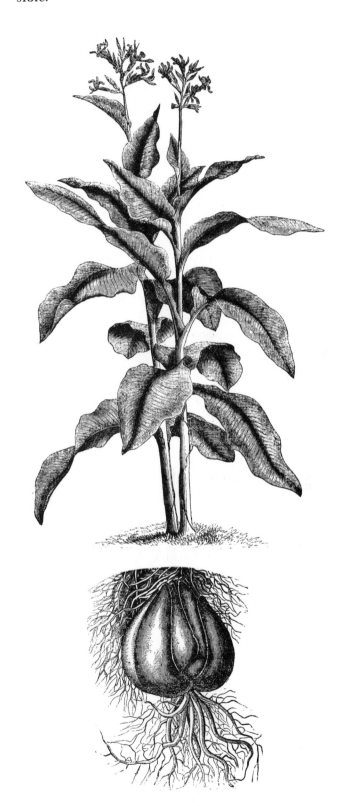

# PROJECTS FOR
# OCTOBER

## Sauerkraut

Our native Americans turn up their noses at this preparation of cabbage, and many do at the article itself no matter how it may be dressed for the table. Yet cabbage is a great institution and is growing in favor among all classes of laboring people. As an adjunct of the farmer's boiled dinner it is indispensable. Sauerkraut is a convenient preparation of the article, easily made, and easily preserved for use where the fresh article cannot be had. Our German fellow-citizens generally prefer it to coleslaw or to boiled cabbage.

To save the labor of cutting it by hand, various machines are employed, one of which—simple and easily made at home—is here described. Common corn knives are used for the cutting part of the machine and are fitted into a frame (*fig. 1*). This consists of a heavy oak plank with ledges (shown also in end view in *fig. 3*) and a hole beneath the knives to allow the cut cabbage to drop through. A suitable notch is cut in the ledges to allow fastening the knives, which are fixed at the desired angle by means of wooden plugs or wedges. The corn knives (*fig. 2*) are 3/8-inch thick on the back and are preferred to a piece of scythe as they do not bend. *Fig. 3* gives the complete machine in perspective. *A* is a box, upon each side of which are slats (*b, b*). It will be seen by the examination of the end view of *fig. 3* that the parts *b, b* belong to the box, and those marked *c, d* are attached the frame. This box enables one to hold the cabbage firmly, and should run freely

Fig. 1.--FRAME WITH KNIVES.

Fig. 2.—CORN-KNIFE.

Fig. 3.—MACHINE COMPLETE.

backward and forward. It would be well to have a wooden follower to fit the box to avoid all danger to the hands when the cabbage is pressed down. The box should be of the size to hold a large cabbage, and the frame long enough to go across a barrel or tub.

For making sauerkraut, select the most solid and perfect heads, and after splitting them, remove the stalks and green leaves. They are then passed over the knives and cut fine. A tight barrel, perfectly clean, is then lined with cabbage leaves at the bottom and a little way up the sides. A layer of about 3 inches of the slitted cabbage is then put in and pressed with the hand, and about 4 tablespoons of coarse salt are sprinkled over it. After four layers are put in and salted in this way, it is pressed down with a wooden rammer as closely as it can be packed. Then follow four more layers and a ramming, and so on until the barrel is nearly full. It should be pounded so hard that the juice of the cabbage and the melting salt will appear on top. Cover with cabbage leaves and with a board or follower, and press down with a heavy stone. Set the barrel away to ferment, and in about three weeks remove the top scum and brine and add enough water to keep the kraut covered. In four more weeks it will be fit for use. It needs a little looking to occasionally, and will keep good for a year or more. To the American palate the taste is a little peculiar at first, but it is much relished by people who have become accustomed to it.

## Breeding Trout and Other Fish

Here are two ways to breed game fish. Although the first sometimes achieves results, we prefer the second that follows. First, mature trout of both sexes are confined in ponds fed by springs. Shallow ditches with still pools and gravelly bottoms are provided. From the middle to the last of October, the male fish, adorned like a bridegroom in his most brilliant colors, prepares the gravelly nest for the eggs. He then coaxes the female upon it; and it is at the time that she begins to lay her eggs that she should be caught in a net and her eggs very gently pressed from her into an earthen basin containing water. The fish is saved alive, and the male fish is proceeded with in the same manner. The "milt" which flows from him is stirred, gently but thoroughly, among the eggs. These eggs, at first being of a dull orange color, rapidly change as soon as impregnated, becoming clearer and almost transparent. After this, the eggs are placed upon clean gravel in boxes in running water—if possible, in a brook or channel fed by living springs, and in which the water is entirely under control and not liable to floods. This should be more or less shaded, and the boxes ought to be covered—for in the natural way trout cover their eggs with gravel. Nine to twelve weeks elapse before hatching. They then appear like the magnified sketch in *fig. 2*, adjoining which are two small outlines showing the actual size of the egg and of the fish newly hatched. The

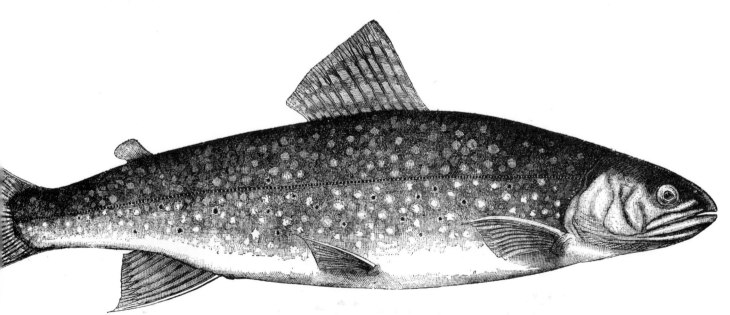

Fig. 1.—FEMALE TROUT, TWENTY MONTHS OLD.

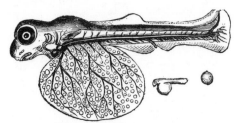

Fig. 2.—TROUT JUST HATCHED.

mass attached to its belly is the yolk of the egg. This is encased in a bladder-like sack, and furnishes the little fellow food for the first 30 days of his life. After this he begins to pick up animalcules which abound in shallow water and increase in numbers greatly after the warm weather of spring comes on.

This second method is in brief the process of fish breeding recommended by the authorities: Do not attempt the artificial impregnation of the eggs yourself, but provide suitable breeding ditches fed by perpetual springs. Allow the fish to have their own way, make their nests, lay their eggs, impregnate them, and cover over with the usual gravel. The ditches are watched, unfriendly fish, beetles, eels, etc., expelled and excluded as far as possible, sediment of decaying leaves, etc., removed from the nests, and every effort made to keep the eggs undisturbed.

The male trout, as the breeding season approaches, not only puts on the most brilliant colors, but the projection upon his under jaw increases very much, becoming a real shovel, and with it he moves the sand and gravel about and scoops out his nest as he likes. This appendage makes it very easy for the males to do great damage in rooting out the eggs from the nests. Young males should therefore be rigidly excluded from the breeding ditches. The eggs are usually deposited, as already stated, after the 20th of October and begin to hatch in January, the majority hatching in 9 to 12 weeks. The breeding ditches should have certain pools or

expansions in them where the water is very shallow. Into these the young fish soon find their way, and by the time they have absorbed their paunches, they may be seen very actively pursuing the animalcules which breed in such places. For this reason shallow basins in their breeding ditches or brooks are quite essential to success. Where the young fry are numerous, regular feeding should begin in March. Bullock's blood in small quantities has been successfully used. Lean scrap beef or mutton, thoroughly boiled to remove the grease and then mashed very fine, has been used, and any kind of fresh meat would doubtless do as well. When trout have plenty to eat, they grow astonishingly fast. *Fig. 1* shows a female trout, only 20 months old; *fig. 3* shows a male trout 7 or 8 months of age.

## Making Plank Drains

Stone suitable for forming a channel for the water in the bottom of a ditch is often scarce, and tiles cannot always be obtained within convenient distance, but planks are comparatively cheap and easily got almost everywhere. Where the subsoil is compact, planks may be used with the assurance that they will last in the drain for 30 or 40 years. And as long as they last, they will be fully equal to tile or stone.

The best way to use planks is to saw them all of a certain length and lay them crosswise of the ditch. When they are thus laid, planks of all widths may be used up very economically and make a much stronger drain than when they are placed lengthwise. Planks should always be well seasoned before they are put underground as they will last much longer than if green. If every piece is dipped in coal tar a few weeks previous to being laid in the ditch, they will, no doubt, last 100 years.

When laying dry planks in the ditch, leave

Fig. 3.—MALE TROUT, SEVEN OR EIGHT MONTHS OLD.

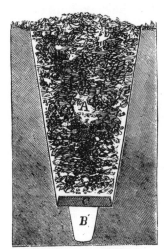

Fig. 1.—PLANK DRAIN.

pointed as shown in the figure to give a current when there is but little water, and also to prevent it washing the earth from under the side pieces.

The planks should always be sorted previous to being laid. All the best ones should be placed by themselves towards the lower end of the drain. If there are any poor pieces, better burn them for firewood, or lay them together at the upper end or in short branches. One poor piece of plank will render a good drain useless in few years.

Great care should be exercised in returning the first dirt into a ditch lest some of the planks be displaced. Before using a plow or scraper to cover with, shovel in enough of the hard earth to hold the planks in place. The earth that was thrown out last should be returned first, especially if it is cold and unfertile. Every ditch should be filled heaping full to keep surface water from washing open holes and filling the drain with earth.

them temporarily about one-fourth of an inch apart; they will soon swell and touch. If there is little danger that the earth will be washed away, excavate the bottom as represented in *fig. 1*, with offsets on each side, laying the planks on these shoulders or offsets.

If the earth where the draining is done is so shaky and loose that the water might wash it away, it is not wise to use planks unless the sides are protected with wood, as represented in *fig. 2*. After

### Cider Making

Good, sound, ripe apples, washed clean, are the first and indispensable requisite. Specked and wormy apples and those dropped from the trees before they are half ripe and have become tough and insipid or bitter can never make good cider. Indeed, a few apples of this description in a bushel of good ones will materially injure the good flavor of all the cider.

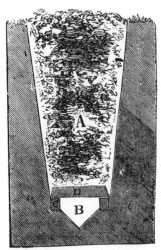

Fig. 2.—PLANK DRAIN.

the ditch is dug, say 10 inches wide on the bottom, the corners must be dressed out true so that a scantling will lie solidly and squarely. The size of the side strips should be somewhat in proportion to the amount of water to flow in the channel. We have used strips 1½ x 2 inches square, and 2 x 3, 2 x 4, an 2 x 6. The bottom of the ditch should be

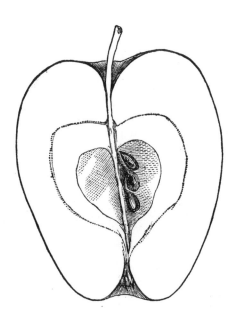

## Cider Vinegar, Quickly Made

Vinegar made from cider is unsurpassed for domestic use. It is quickly made in the following manner. Set up a cask of hard cider, four feet from the floor, in a clean, dry place. Arrange a set of sloping boards, grooved along the middle, so as to make a series of zigzag channels, as shown in the engraving. The cider is allowed to drip slowly from

ZIGZAG CHANNELS FOR VINEGAR.

the faucet, upon the upper board, and, guided by the groove, flows slowly down and falls on the next board, and so on over the whole series of boards, into the tub at the bottom. The cider is emptied from the tub back into the barrel, once a day, the drip being so arranged that the tub will not overflow in twelve hours. A gelatinous film, called "mother of vinegar," will form upon the board conductors. This is a vegetable organism, a form of a fungus, which has the effect of soon producing the acidification of the cider and its conversion into vinegar. It should be scraped off and put into the barrel. When the vinegar becomes strong enough for use, it should be strained from the tub into a clean barrel for keeping.

Grind the apples to a fine pulp, without crushing the seed, which will impart a bitter taste to the cider. The pomace should be kept in a large vat or tub for at least 24 hours before the juice is "expressed" or pressed. If the weather is so cool that fermentation will not start, it will be better to allow the pomace to remain four or five days. If the pomace is pressed soon after the apples are ground, the juice will often be very insipid and light colored, and always destitute of that excellent flavor and rich color which good cider possesses when the pomace has lain a few days.

In the usual way of fermenting, the cider after becoming perfect soon becomes hard and contains more or less vinegar. This can be avoided by taking the same care with cider as with wine. Procure a tin, glass, or rubber tube, and fit it closely in a hole bored through a bung which perfectly fits the barrel. The bung being placed in the bung hole, the other end of the tube is placed below the surface of water contained in a cup or other convenient vessel. If all is tight, the gas liberated in fermentation will pass through the tube and bubble up through the water, but no air can enter the barrel as long as the end of the tube is covered by the water. When bubbles cease to appear, the fermentation is complete, and the cider may then be racked off into clean barrels and bunged tight. The fermentation should go on slowly in a cool cellar.

## Growing Spring Bulbs

Those who would have their gardens bright with early spring flowers, as well as those who would enjoy their indoor blooming in winter, must look to it *now* as this is the month in which certain bulbs go into the ground, as well as the one in which others, such as the gladiolus and certain types of lily, come out of it.

It is much better to plant the bulbs in groups than to scatter them here and there. If set in ordinary garden soil they will flower tolerably well, but their much finer bloom in a properly prepared

THE LONG-FLOWERED LILY—*Lilium longiflorum.*

soil will well repay the trouble of fitting it for them. The soil should be light, warm, and rich, and though sufficiently retentive of moisture for the plants not to suffer in drought, it should not be wet. If the garden soil is stiff, add sand in sufficient quantity to make it light, and an abundance of well-decomposed cow manure—at least enough to have it form one-third of the soil to the depth of 18 inches. The spot being well spaded over to that depth, it is ready for the bulbs, and the sooner they are planted the better.

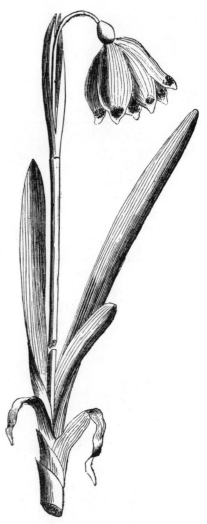

SPRING SNOW FLAKE.

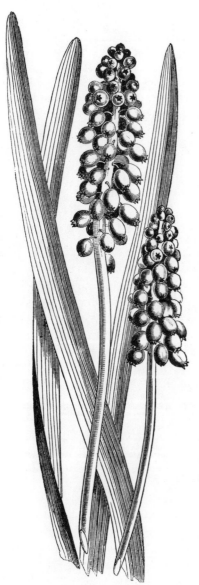

GRAPE HYACINTH.

Where there is a sufficient number of the bulbs, a very pleasing effect may be produced by planting them in circles one within another, each circle being formed of those with flowers of the same color, the colors alternating to suit the fancy.

The large bulbs require to be set deeper than the smaller ones; as a general rule the depth should be twice the length of the bulb. In spading up the earth and adding manure, the bulb bed will be raised above the general level; it is best to leave it so as it will prevent water from settling on it. When the weather becomes cold enough to freeze the ground, cover the bed with a good coat of manure, leaves with a little earth thrown on to hold them, or any other convenient litter which is to be carefully removed in spring.

Bulbs may be easily grown in pots, and they make most pleasing ornaments for the parlor, one to three of the larger bulbs, and more of the smaller kinds being planted per pot. The soil used for potting should be similar to that for garden culture—equal parts of sand, good garden mould, well-rotted cow dung, and, if the garden soil is not rich in vegetable matter, some leaf mould. Provide the pots with good drainage by putting in the bottom an inch or so of fragments of pots. Then fill them with the earth and plant the bulbs, leaving their crowns well above the surface of the soil. Water thoroughly and place the pots in a dark closet or other dark and warm place, where they are to remain with occasional watering until the earth is well filled with roots. With a little care the ball of earth may be turned out of the pot and the condition of the roots inspected. When the roots appear in abundance upon the outside of the ball of earth, remove the pots to a light window. If the leaves and flower spikes have pushed in the dark, they

will probably be very pale, but with a few days' exposure to the light they will take on a green color. Give plenty of water and remove the small offsets that spring up from the base of the bulb. After blooming, the plants need less water, and when the leaves fade, the bulb should be dried off altogether and removed from the earth and kept for planting in the open ground the next fall.

Bulbs may be flowered in pure sand or in moss, the treatment (as to keeping in the dark, etc.) being the same as in pots of earth. But in these cases the bulb (if wished for future use) needs to be planted in earth after blooming in order to mature it. Hyacinths and tulips are frequently bloomed in water in glasses sold for the purpose. The glasses are filled with rain water and the bulb placed so that the bottom just touches the water. Keep about two weeks in the dark, and then bring them to the light. The roots and the glass need washing and the water to be changed about once in two weeks. If it is desired to save bulbs grown in water, they must also be transferred to earth to ripen.

### Digging Potatoes

When potatoes grow several inches below the surface of a heavy soil, digging them with a hoe is fatiguing labor. It is more laborious to dig with hoes than with some other instruments, and, more than this, the edge of a hoe will wound potatoes more than others. We have dug with hoes, spading forks, spades, and shovels, and, for digging in heavy soil, we like a good fork better than anything else, particulary when the potatoes are unusually deep. The sharp corners of the tines of forks should be filed off smooth so that they will not break the skin of potatoes.

When digging with a fork, thrust the tines into the ground perpendicularly, as close to the hill as may be and yet outside the row of potatoes itself. Now grasp all the tops with one hand, and pull gently upwards as the other hand pries out the potatoes, tops and all. If they are not spread out much in the hill, nearly every one will come to the surface at the first thrust of the fork, when they may be shaken from the vines between two rows. A good spade, carefully handled, is almost equal to a fork for digging. When digging with hoes, instead of striking the blade directly in the top of a hill, as many do, haul off the dirt gently until the potatoes are almost laid bare; then bury the blade of the

VALLOTA PURPUREA.

hoe its whole length into the soil and draw them all out at once. When digging with hoes, it is better to pull the tops first.

## Fattening Turkeys

One great advantage of this kind of stock is that they mainly take care of themselves and do their own foraging. After the young broods are fairly started, say a month old, they shift for themselves until the cool nights of autumn come on, when the fattening process should begin. Those make a mistake who put off the feeding until later. At this time their feed of grasshoppers, crickets, and other insects, which has so largely supplied their wants, begins to fall off. There is no objection to their roaming still and gathering what they can; we do not approve of shutting them up. This will do very well for ducks and geese, but the turkey is a more enterprising bird, and it chafes his restless spirit to be confined in a pen, no matter how well he may be fed.

The flocks will gather a good deal from the woods and fields all through October and November, especially if mast is abundant. What is wanted is that they should go to their roosts every night with full crops. As the insects drop off, their other food should be increased. At first they need only be fed at night. This will not prevent their excursions in the morning. They will make for their familiar pastures as soon as they leave their perches. Regular feeding will encourage them to come home early and to roost near the farm buildings where they are safest. A ton or two of turkeys is too much property in these days to have lying round loose. Encourage them to come at call, and keep the flocks well in hand.

TOMMY'S HOUR OF TROUBLE.

TOMMY'S HOUR OF TRIUMPH.

As the weather grows colder, increase the feed and improve its quality. To promote thrift, nothing perhaps is better than boiled potatoes mashed up with oat or corn meal and given warm. To prevent wasting, these should be fed in troughs made for the purpose. The bird is a gross feeder and almost anything that ordinarily goes to the pigsty will be acceptable. He has, however, his decided tastes, and knows which side his bread is buttered as well as taller bipeds. He has an eagle-eye for grain, oats, barley, buckwheat, and corn, and all these may be given with decided advantage. His especial weakness is Indian corn, and his eye twinkles with delight at the sight of this golden grain. His flesh tells the story of his keeping. For the last six weeks of his life, he should be plied with corn as the standard diet. There is no cheating the consumer. Be honest, give him a plump corn-fed fowl, and sleep with a thriving pocket and a good conscience though the crib grows lean.

## Making a Good Barnyard

Several things are essential to render a barnyard a good one. It must be so constructed that water from any source will not accumulate in it. It must not be uncomfortably wet or disagreeably muddy for stock. The surface must also be firm so that coarse manure will not be pressed down into the soft earth and thus make hard pitching.

The first thing is to provide for carrying off any surplus water that will be likely to find its way among the manure. Cut a good ditch entirely around the yard, not less than 30 inches deep, and fill it with tiles, if they can be obtained, or with plank. Stones will be just as good to drain the soil and carry off the water, but the drains are more likely to be filled up by rats. This drain will keep the ground dry on each side of it and will not carry off the liquid manure. Conduct all the water by eave-troughs from the roof of the barn and sheds into this underdrain.

The next step is to grade the yard either by hauling earth away, leveling off the knolls, or by drawing in compact earth to fill up the depressions. The surface of the yard should always descend gradually from the barn and sheds. There ought also to be buildings or cheap sheds on every side of the yard. Excavate at the lowest part so that liquid from all parts of the yard will descend to that place, and there sink a barrel and cover it with plank so that nothing can fall into it. Then set a cheap pump in this barrel, pump up the liquid, and send it in board or bark troughs among the solid manure in any part of the yard. This will be a perfect security against its heating and becoming "fire-fanged."

The next job will be to pave the whole or a portion of the barnyard. Stones of various sizes and forms may be used. Flat stones 3 or 4 feet square are objectionable, for heavy cattle are likely to slip on large stones so as to injure themselves. Large stones and small ones may be placed side by side, by excavating a little for the large ones, so that the surfaces of each will be of equal height. Stretch a line across the yard and lay the top of each row of stones even with the line. In this way there will be little or no difficulty in making the surface of the pavement even. When laying the stones, the workman needs a trowel to place sand or fine gravel beneath thin or small stones to raise them up to the line, and a rammer made of a billet of hardwood with an iron ring like that of a beetle on the bottom of it to drive those stones that are too high down even with the line.

After the paving is finished, spread sand, gravel, or finely pulverized clay all over the pavement and work it into the interstices. This will make a barnyard that every good farmer will be proud of. On many farms there are loose stones enough lying in the fields to pave several yards. Where stones are scarce, the surface may be covered with gravel, clay, or compact earth instead of stones. Where timber is cheap, a yard can be paved with wood by sawing off logs, 5 or 6 inches long, with a drag saw, and placing them on the end. This would make a pavement that could not fail to please the most incorrigible faultfinder or grumbler. Hemlock, pine, oak of all kinds, and many other kinds of wood sawed into paving blocks and well tarred on the lower ends with coal tar would last many years, always making a very smooth and agreeable surface to work on, and not slippery for animals. It would also hold liquid manure well.

## A Corn-Husking Rack

Many who husk their corn by hand find it very tiresome to sit on the floor or ground in a cramped position. A rack made as shown in the drawing

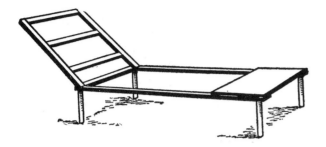

will hold two or three shocks and gives a better place for the husker to sit. Place the stalks crosswise of the bench in front of you.

### A Homemade Feed Cutter

An old lawnmower can be arranged to make a fairly satisfactory straw or feed cutter. One must rig up a hopper, as shown in the sketch, and attach the mower to the lower end of it so that the straw or grain will just strike the knives where the grass usually comes into the mower. A crank and a belt arrangement makes it easy for one man to feed and turn the cutter. This is a good use for a lawnmower in the wintertime when it is not working outdoors.

### How to Make Concrete Buildings

A very substantial and cheap building may be put up with concrete, which is a mixture of hydraulic lime, sand, and coarse gravel or broken stone. Common lime may be used for common farm buildings, or even for dwellings, but as common lime is not nearly so durable when exposed to the weather, hydraulic lime should be used for a good building. It has also been found that broken limestone is better than any other stone to use in concrete, a

MANNER OF CONSTRUCTING CONCRETE BUILDINGS.

more perfect adhesion being formed between the particles. The proper proportions to be mixed are 20 parts of hydraulic lime mixed to a paste with water, 30 parts of washed sand, and 50 parts of broken stone or gravel. The chips from limestone quarries make the very best material for concrete. No more should be mixed at once than can be used in a day since it hardens very rapidly.

To proceed to build, the foundation must be made and the courses laid on it in a box or a mold, shown in the engraving. This mold is laid in place; the cement already mixed is shoveled in and beaten down with a rammer even with the top of the mold, which is then moved into place for laying the next block. The mold, being open at one end, laps a few inches over the end of the first block which holds it in place and permits a close joint to be made. When the first round is laid, two small sticks are laid across the blocks, and the mold rests on them until filled. These sticks, when the building is completed, are sawn off close to the wall, and they will furnish a hold for the nails. As the walls are carried up, the door and window frames are laid in their places. This process is so simple that any intelligent mason is competent to carry it out. The important point is to get the materials of the right sort and mix them properly. The size of the blocks may be as desired, and as the material is very strong and acts very quickly, 8 to 12 inches is sufficient thickness for a wall of any ordinary dwelling house. When a common lime is used instead of hydraulic lime, more time must be given for the concrete to set.

# FARM AND GARDEN WORK FOR

# November

It is a bad plan to be in a hurry; even the farmer who has only one pair of hands to keep employed should have definite plans and work according to them. Of course it is vastly more important for those who give employment to several laborers to lay out their work well ahead. Winter will come among the mountain valleys and forests of the North, while others, perhaps, are enjoying the bland, bracing weather of the late autumn. Sleighbells will jingle and keep time to the pace of mettlesome horses, dashing over frozen roads with happy sleighloads of parents and children at Thanksgiving time in one state, while the children of another celebrate the same festival in summer clothing, playing upon the lawns or rambling in search of nuts in the grove. Nevertheless, irresistible winter slowly and surely marches onward, and we should all be ready when he comes.

The harvests are abundant; prices of farm produce rule high; there is no pressure of famine, no short stock of any of the necessities, and hardly of the luxuries of life. With these blessings come responsibilities and accountabilities which we cannot avoid. This month, closing as it does in the farmer's year of toil in the fields, and filling his heart with gladness, should remind us that we are not alone in the world, and that all are not prosperous, so that receiving freely we should remember the good Giver in bestowing freely of our surplus.

## HINTS ABOUT FARM WORK

The order of farm work in the North is, first, to secure crops still in the field before freezing weather; second, to protect those already in store, as well as houses, barns, and manure stores from damage from any source; third, to put the farm in order for a sudden freezing up. Early winters come now and then and shut down upon farm work just when a day or two more of outdoor labor would save the labors of months, perhaps, from loss.

**Root Crops** — These continue to grow as long as the ground is open, but it is a poor plan to trust too long to the weather. No date can be fixed applicable to different latitudes, but in the North it will be wise to lose no time after the first of November in harvesting roots of all sorts. *Parsnips* will not be injured by the severest freezing, though they may be frozen up and not be available before next spring. They are wintered thus as they grew and are ready for feeding or for market as soon as the ground opens. *Rutabagas* will bear more frost than white turnips, but neither should be subjected to severe freezing. *Mangels* and *sugar beets* bear, perhaps, an equal degree of cold without *apparent* damage. Yet, if they stand in the ground after they cease to grow, they become tough and woody, and roots exposed to freezing, if not used soon, decay at the crown. Growth ceases with beets after a few sharp frosts; hence they should be dug and housed early. *Carrots* are also liable to injury from freezing, and the first frost that stiffens the soil should be a signal to harvest beets and carrots with alacrity, if not already done.

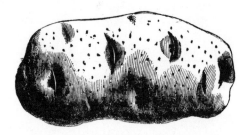

**Potatoes**—In parts of the country where the digging of potatoes has been delayed, or where it is safe to wait so long as November, digging should be postponed no longer. This valuable crop must be housed at once or placed in frost-proof pits.

**Winter Grain**—Top-dressings are sometimes recommended for application early this month. These are of two kinds. One acts chiefly as a mulch, and is often very useful. Poor composts of sods, peat, etc., made with but little manure, or with lime, ashes, guano, fish manure, castor pomace, or something of that kind, if they have lain until fine and uniform, may be spread on pretty liberally, and the ground

rolled. The second type, guano or some fine "hand manure," may be sown on to quicken the growth of late crops and to promote tillering when the stand is thin.

**Housing or Stacking Corn Fodder**—Corn stalks dry so slowly that if often takes all the fair weather of autumn to dry them. It is rarely safe to leave them in the field after the middle of the month, and they make much better fodder if housed as soon as they are dry enough. Whether in stacks or under "barracks," lay the bundles with the tops inward, and inclined slightly upward, so that rain and thawing snow will all be carried off.

**Buildings**—Look well to the roofs, eave gutters, and weatherboarding of all buildings. Where everything is not snug and tight, a few nails will add greatly to the durability of barns and sheds. If stables have only single outer walls, line them with bog hay or other litter, stuffed between an inner boarding or lathing and the weatherboards. This is a favorable season for outside painting, as the weather is seldom so dry as to be very dusty. New paint is not disfigured by small insects, flies, etc., sticking to it, as often happens at other seasons.

**Roads**—Employ spare time of men and teams in putting the farm roads in good repair and protecting them against washing during thaws or rains.

**Fences**—Tear away all fences not absolutely necessary. Small farmers who keep only four or five head of cows and heifers should keep them tethered while grazing, rather than be at the expense of putting up many interior fences. Grain fields must be securely enclosed, and fences between neighbors and along the highway should be looked to before the ground freezes. Weak posts must be strengthened by stakes or reset.

**Manure** may be carted out if it can be spread and plowed in, or put into compost heaps with sods or muck, or even put in heaps and covered with two or three inches of soil. The swamps and roadsides, old fence rows and the woods, should contribute to the supply of material for composts to be made now, or to be worked up during the winter by mingling the vegetable mold with manure as it accumulates. To get rich, fine manure for spring grains, flax, garden use, and many other purposes, build up heaps, consisting of alternate layers of strawy stuff, fresh manure, and litter from the stables, and wet the whole now and then by pumping barnyard liquor over it to saturation. It will all rot down before spring and become fine and uniform.

**Hogs** gain flesh and fatten very rapidly during most of this month. Feed regularly all they will eat, and only ground or cooked grain. Every few days it is well to mix a few handfuls of charcoal and ashes from a wood fire with their food, or to throw them a little charcoal dust and corn mixed and slightly moistened. It keeps them in good condition and sharpens their appetites. After hogs are fat enough to kill, it is easy to keep them so awhile, even in severe weather; but when it is very cold they must be in very warm quarters or they will eat a great deal and not gain a pound. This month is the time to prepare for a litter of pigs in March. These will be old enough to consume their share of milk when the cows come in.

**Sheep** should have dry sheds, sunny yards, and be fed from racks and troughs. Graining should commence as grass falls, and the flocks should be so divided that those placed together are of about equal strength. The high price of linseed cake and meal will prevent their use to a great extent. Corn is the natural substitute, and a good one, but it must be used with greater caution. Keep sheep constantly and gradually gaining. Ewes served in November will yean in April; that is, in 150 days.

**Horses** — It is a good plan to give farm horses the range of weedy stubble and other fields late in the season. They eat a great many weeds as other

forage fails. We keep our horses too warm, as a rule, for the sake of giving them smooth coats. Make it a rule never to give a horse feed or water until he has stood an hour after coming in off the road or from hard work. Rub him down as soon as he comes in, throw a warm blanket over him, and remove it when he is fed or within an hour. Never leave a warm horse to cool off in drafts of air or in the wind out-of-doors. A horse stable should be light, airy, and roomy. A horse that does nothing will do well on hay alone, watered twice a day, and groomed twice a week. If he is used, groom daily. Keep the stable always clean.

**Beef Cattle** — This season is the best in the year, perhaps, for putting flesh upon beeves. They must be fed at each meal all that they will eat with a relish and digest thoroughly, so as to be hungry when the time comes for feeding again. All success, we may say, depends upon appetite, and this upon health. It is promoted by an occasional change of diet, by the use of the card and curry comb, but above all by punctuality in giving stalled cattle their feed. Litter well and save every drop and particle of manurial value. These are the feeder's principal profits. Keep the stables warm, but the air pure. Quiet and darkness are important.

**Cows** — Keep them quiet. Feed corn stalks cut fine, soaked 12 hours, with meal upon them. If possible, keep water before cows all the time. It will pay those having good, warm milk rooms to make butter all winter. We are in the habit of drying our cows off very much too early. To make butter, however, will require liberal feeding with cornmeal, rye bran, or something of the kind.

## HINTS ABOUT HORTICULTURAL WORK

### Orchard and Nursery

Fruit is much accelerated or retarded in ripening by the temperature. That will keep best which is subjected to few alterations of temperature and has been as cool as may be without actually freezing.

**Ripening** is an interesting process; it is the first step towards decay. Changes go on in the fruit after it is picked quite as important as those which occur at any other time. Not only do the access of air and the temperature affect the fruit, but the fruit in ripening affects both air and temperature. Oxygen is absorbed, carbonic acid given off, and heat pro-

duced. Open the fruit cellar or room whenever the outside temperature will allow, provided it is not warmer without than within.

**Planting** may often be done this month, but on no account set trees in wet or partly frozen soil. It will be much better to heel-in the trees in a dry, sandy spot, unless the soil is in a condition perfectly well-suited to receive them.

**Cider** is still to be made. Good cider requires good apples. It is much better to assort carefully and work up all poor fruit by itself for vinegar. If the pulp is allowed to remain a few days before pressing, the cider will have a higher color and finer flavor. Use new or thoroughly clean barrels and observe the greatest cleanliness in every step of the process.

**Vinegar** — Convert all inferior fruit into vinegar; it will pay better than to turn it into pork.

**Stocks** for root grafting are to be taken up, assorted, and tied in bundles of convenient size, and either buried where they can be got at when needed, or, what is better, packed in boxes of sawdust of its natural dampness and placed in a cool cellar.

**Cions** may be cut at any time when the wood is not frozen. Store them in sawdust and see that it does not dry out and that the boxes are kept cool.

**Seedlings** will need protection, but this should not be applied too early. Nature uses leaves, and nothing better has yet been proposed. In the absence of these, use boughs of cedar or other evergreens.

### Fruit Garden

**Pears** of the choice kinds that have been well kept now bring a good price in market. It will pay to pack fine specimens in cheap boxes holding a single layer of fruit and wrap each pear in some very soft white paper. A good pear is such a royal thing that it cannot be treated with too much attention.

**Covering** of all plants, whether of raspberries and grape vines with earth, or strawberries with straw or other material, should not be done too soon nor delayed too late. Try to catch just that time when winter sets in and the ground is about to freeze.

**Root Cuttings** of blackberries, raspberries, and all plants propagated in this way are to be made. The whole story is: cut the roots in pieces 2 to 3 inches in length, and pack them with earth in a box.

If the box is at all tight, make holes to allow any moisture to drain off and bury it in a place deep enough to be safe from frost and where no water will accumulate. If the spot is not naturally dry, put in a drain of some kind.

**Cuttings** of currants, gooseberries, and quinces may be planted. One condition of success is that the soil must be closely pressed against the lower ends of the cuttings.

**Grape Vines** — It is better to prune these now, but they may be left until very early spring. We are often asked "How shall I prune my grape vine?" The question is as difficult to answer as it would be for a doctor to prescribe merely upon the information, "My wife is sick, what shall I do for her?" Each vine must be treated according to its individual needs, no matter what "system" of pruning is adopted. How to prune — the merely mechanical art — will depend on how much is to be done. Where there are many vines, pruning shears, will be found best, but a good knife will do. It is safer to leave one more bud than is needed on each cane; i.e., if two shoots are wanted in a place, leave three buds. When the severity of winter is over, say in late February, go over the vines and remove the extra bud. In all pruning, do not cut too close to a bud, but leave about an inch of cane above the last one.

**Grape Cuttings** — The wood resulting from pruning may be used for propagation. It should be kept cool and prevented from drying. There is a great difference in varieties as to the ease with which they may be propagated.

## Kitchen Garden

Follow the suggestions given last month concerning the preparation of the soil. Have every foot spaded or plowed that can be done. Sod land, intended to be used for garden crops next year, should be heavily manured and plowed. Put down drains, if needed.

**Asparagus Beds** are to be covered with coarse manure or with straw or other litter.

**Roots** placed in pits as directed last month are to be covered with earth only when the weather renders protection necessary. The hardier roots, such as parsnips and horseradish, may be dug as long as the ground is not too frozen.

**Manure** — Success in gardening depends in the main upon not only generous, but heavy manuring. There is an important item, night soil, usually neglected.

**Rhubarb** is better transplanted now than in spring. It may be done as long as the ground remains open. This plant needs an abundance of manure.

**Cold Frames** — Cabbages and other plants wintered in these are oftener killed by too much heat than by the cold. They will endure a moderate freezing without injury. The sashes should be put over the frames at night only, unless the weather becomes colder than usual this month.

**Celery** may be stored in trenches or left, still later, if it can be banked up with earth. The storing for winter is done in trenches a foot wide and as deep as necessary to admit the plants. Set the roots close together without any packing of earth, and, when cold weather comes on, cover with straw.

**Cabbages** — The best method yet devised for preserving these is to invert the heads and cover them with 4 to 6 inches of earth. This should be postponed as late as the earth can be worked.

**Spinach** will, in most places, need a slight covering, applied only when the ground begins to freeze.

**Soil** should be prepared for use in hotbeds next spring. It is often difficult to get it at the time it is needed, and it facilitates matters much to have a good heap in readiness. A light, rich loam is required, and, if the garden soil is heavy, use a portion of sand. Let well-rotted manure form one-third the bulk. Incorporate the whole thoroughly, and place in a heap and cover with boards or sods.

*Flower Garden and Lawn*

In this department there is little to add to our notes of last month, and many directions given then will prove quite timely now. In this, as in all other gardening, endeavor to do now everything that will save work next spring.

**Planting** of many things may yet be done, the rules governing the planting of deciduous ornamental trees and shrubs being much the same as already indicated under fruit trees and shrubs.

**Bulbs** should have been planted last month, but they may be put in now with good results. Bulbs of gladiolus, etc., are to be taken up. Lilies are quite hardy. Cover all bulb beds, new and old, with a good coat of coarse manure, applied when the ground begins to freeze.

**Chrysanthemums** will need stakes. Put those in pots, after their bloom is over, in a cool cellar.

**Dahlias** — If these are still in the ground, take them up and store as directed last month.

**Protect** half-hardy things as the weather gets cold by the use of litter and evergreen boughs.

*Greenhouses and Window Plants*

Give air whenever the temperature will allow, and in greenhouses use heat only when absolutely necessary. Plants that are only to be kept from frost, without regard to bloom, may have the house as cool as 40 degrees to 35 degrees, but flowering plants require a temperature of 60 degrees.

**Bulbs** — Bring those potted early into a warm place, provided the pots are well-filled with roots.

**Camellias** — Syringe frequently. If the red spider attacks them, remove the infested ones and use redoubled care in showering.

**Climbers** — Soft-wooded climbers grow rapidly from cuttings and may be useful in decorating the greenhouse.

**Hanging Baskets** — Those in dwellings are apt to suffer for want of proper watering. If the basket is of wire or other open work, the best way to water it is to set it in a pail or tub of water until the earth is thoroughly soaked through.

**Ivy** has its appearance, as well as its health, much improved by an occasional washing of the leaves.

**Annuals** — Where there is room, a stock of annuals should be sown. Sweet alyssum, candytuft, and mignonette are always useful to add to bouquets; and lobelias, nemophilas, etc., soon make fine specimens if well grown.

**Fumigate** — The greenhouse should be well smoked with tobacco once or twice a week to keep the green fly in check. It is best done at night. Window plants should be placed in a box or under a barrel and smoked if this insect molests them.

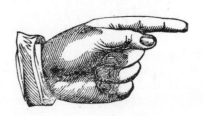

# PROJECTS FOR NOVEMBER

## Building an Icehouse

In a properly constructed icehouse, and when the ice is properly packed and cared for, no waste should take place from the inside of the pile of ice. The melting from the sides, bottom, and top is caused by insufficient insulation. The waste from the bottom is generally the greatest. The amount of ice melted in the bottom of the icehouse varies from 1 to 6 feet during the year, depending upon the construction of the floor. If the icehouse is provided with an airtight floor, with the ice laid on at least 18 inches of dry sawdust, the bottom waste rarely exceeds 12 inches during the year. On the other hand, if the ice is piled in the icehouse on the bare ground without any insulation under it, or any provision made for drainage, the meltage frequently is 6 feet. The side and top meltage is not so great, but it frequently ranges from 1 to 3 feet, depending upon the insulation.

**Location and Building** — The location should be where the ice can be removed and delivered with the least amount of labor; however, it is very important that the icehouse should be located in the coolest place, in as dry a place as possible, and always above ground. The lowest layer of ice should always be at least 6 inches above the outside level of ground.

The size of the building must be determined by the amount of ice used during the year. For instance, a dairy farm upon which 35 cows are kept and from which the milk is sold needs an icehouse 16 x 16 and 14 feet high. If the cream is to be sold and skim milk fed to the calves immediately from the separator, an icehouse 14 x 14 and 12 feet high is of sufficient size. In both cases we make allowance for the use of 25 pounds of ice per day during the summer months for household purposes. For a man who keeps about 20 cows and sells the milk, an icehouse 14 x 14 and 12 feet high is of sufficient size. However, in no case should an icehouse be smaller than 12 x 12 and 10 feet high, because the outside surface is too great compared with the volume, and, therefore, too much ice is wasted in proportion to the amount used.

The building should be as near the shape of a cube as possible, for the cube contains the greatest amount of volume with the least amount of surface exposed other than circular forms. It is not always practical to build as high as we build square, owing to the amount of labor and the inconvenience of storing the ice; therefore, the dimensions given are really the most practical.

If the icehouse is not built upon a sandy surface and where rapid drainage is natural, it is necessary to cut a space to a depth of 12 to 18 inches; where the icehouse is to be located, lay a tile drain and fill it with sand or finely crushed stone. Put a 6-inch foundation of concrete of the size you wish to build your icehouse in this pit, and fill around the outside.

**Framing the Icehouse** — The framework is made by laying a 2 x 4-inch sill on the concrete foundation. Fasten this to the foundation by cementing a few bolts into the concrete and allowing them to extend through the sill; 2 x 4 studding is then placed upon the sill, 16 inches apart from center to

194

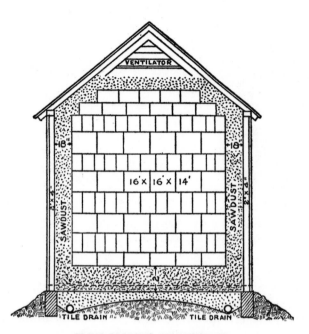

CROSS-SECTION OF ICEHOUSE

center. The rafters for the roof are likewise made of 2 x 4's, placed the same distance apart as the studding, but the purlin plate upon the studding should be at least 6 inches wide. The outside of studding may be boarded either with common sheeting and paper, upon which poplar siding is nailed, or with patent siding or shiplap siding, the latter being the cheapest and requiring only a single thickness of board.

The roof should be made with not less than one-half to one-third pitch and preferably covered with shingles, for shingles are better insulators than either slate or metal. Paper may sometimes be used to good advantage. A cupola or flue should be built upon the roof to allow for the removal of the warm air from the top of the ice. A ventilator may be placed in the gable end.

A continuous door should be cut in one end to allow the ice to be put in. This door may extend from the gable down to within 5 feet of the bottom. Before putting in the ice, place from 18 inches to 2 feet of sawdust or dry peat upon the floor. The ice should be harvested in regular shape—oblong rather than square, and not less than 18 inches in width and 30 inches in length.

## Thatching Roofs

In some countries thatching is a regular trade, but with care anyone may do it. It makes a beautiful finish for rustic houses, porters' lodges, well-houses, beehive shelters, etc., and is in addition the most excellent roofing for icehouses—so the subject has interest for almost everyone. For durability and imperviousness to water, and for warmth in winter and coolness in summer, a straw roof well put on is nearly all that can be desired. Its liability to take fire from sparks is by no means so great as would be supposed, especially after it has been laid a few months. There are many ways of making a straw roof. The mud roofs of the log cabins in the South and the West are not unfrequently thatched by laying light courses of straw and binding each with a layer of clay or sods upon the upper end, covered out of sight by the next course, and they look very well.

Roof frames are prepared for thatch much as for shingles, so far as the plates, purlines, rafters, and ridge poles are concerned. Upon the rafters are lashed (with well-tarred rope yarn) boughs of hazel or Scotch fir in England. In America, however, nothing could be better than hemlock, and in lack of such boughs, long sedge or reeds laid horizontally would perhaps be equally good as a basis upon which to lay the straw.

The straw is put in a heap, sprinkled with water, and turned till it becomes uniformly moist, then drawn out in even handfuls, laid in armfuls, and delivered to the man on the roof as he needs it. First, a single course is laid at one end, from eaves to ridge, the handfuls lying horizontally, butts out, and projecting over a little as a cornice. When a length of about 3 feet is laid (the straw being put down in even handfuls, each handful pressed close and firmly against the preceding), a strip of hooping stuff, 1 inch wide, half round, is laid on about the middle of the straw. This is tied down firmly to a rafter at several points with tarred rope yarn. An assistant standing beneath thrusts a long wooden needle up through the straw, close to a rafter; the thatcher returns it, and the cord is tied below and cut off.

When the end courses are finished, the horizontal courses are commenced at the eaves, the thatcher placing his ladder on the roof so as to give himself a convenient reach. The straw is laid in handfuls as described above, with the butts down. Where it covers the end course, it is not quite so thick as

elsewhere. The binding strips are placed about one-third the distance from the upper ends of the straw. The second course follows the first, lapping two-thirds at least, and is bound down in the same way. And so the thatcher proceeds until the ridge pole is reached, over which the upper course is allowed to project one-half.

Thus one side of the roof is done, breadth by breadth, and then the other side in the same way. When the second side is brought up to the ridge, the top course of the other side is bent down, and a course laid upon the ends. It is very important that the straw should be compressed as solidly as possible when the strips are tied—hence the thatcher with a mallet beats the course of straw down very solid by striking upon the strips, the assistant being ready to tie at the point of greatest compression.

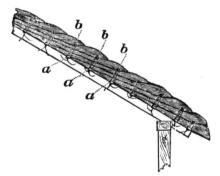

SECTION OF THATCH-ROOF.

There are several methods of finishing off the ridge. The simplest, and perhaps the best, is to lay a course lapping equally on both sides and held by three binding strips on each side, fastened not by tying in the usual way, but by pins made of the same half-round stuff which forms the strips, notching in the middle so that they may be bent in a U-form (like a hair pin). The ends are sharpened and notched by single cuts of a knife or hatchet so that, when driven into the straw, they will hold. These strips are exposed; hence, it is a thatcher's pride to have them small and neat so as to look workman-like. Finials or end pieces made of straw bound tight and hard, of any appropriate shape, give a picturesque finish. The corners of the roof at the eaves, and wherever the wind lifts the thatch, may be pinned down in the same way as described for the top course.

The roof when thus far done is combed down by a tool made like a hay rake, with the head about 4 feet long—one end being without teeth—and with a handle 18 inches long. Finally the eaves and ends are trimmed. This is done with a sharp hay knife or a scythe blade set straight in a handle so that it can be used with a saw-like motion. The eaves are cut off evely at right angles to the slant of the roof.

## A Farm Slaughterhouse

If one butchers his own stock on the farm he would do well to fix up a small building for a slaughterhouse. This can be done so easily and at such small expense that almost any farmer can afford one. It is generally most convenient to have it near the hog yard, for then the refuse can be easily conveyed to the hogs. Indeed, it would not be a half-bad idea to have it in some instances a part of the hog house.

The room in which to kill cattle and hogs should not be less than 15 feet square. This will give plenty of space for the work. As much of the room should be kept clear from fixtures as possible. The floor should be made of concrete graded so that it will all drain to a central opening. A pipe should carry the liquid from this opening to a trough in the hog yard. The ideal way would be to make the walls of concrete for about 3 feet from the ground. This will make it much easier to keep the place clean. It is quite necessary that a good supply of water be close at hand. If possible, a water pipe with hose attached should be in the house. This will enable one to flood the floor at any time.

Pictured is a very good device for handling the carcasses. It is made of a heavy roller (*c*), 5 to 6 inches thick and long enough to reach across the width of the room. It is supported in the middle by a bracket (*d*), a detail of which is shown in the drawing. This makes it possible to lift a carcass of any weight. A drum (*b*) is attached to the roller at one end, over which is run the rope that communicates with the crank (*a*) at the floor. Any man handy with tools can make this derrick.

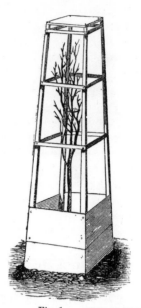

Fig. 1.　TREE PROTECTOR.

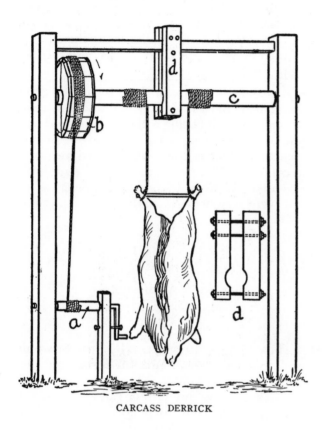

CARCASS DERRICK

Fig. 2.

## Protecting Trees in Winter

In the colder portions of the country it is impossible to raise some of the finer fruits unless the trees are protected during the winter. Even in more temperate localities it is necessary to protect some trees, especially evergreens, during the first few years of their growth. If red cedar boughs can be readily obtained, a sufficient protection can be afforded by tying a number of these among the branches of the tree.

The following plan is especially suited for protecting dwarf trees in gardens. Bring the limbs of the tree together and bind them so as to occupy as little space as possible. Drive four stakes into the ground at proper distances apart and saw the tops off evenly a little higher than the tree. Take a board about 1 foot square and drive a nail down through each corner into the top of the stakes. Put a board around the bottom 15 or 20 inches high, and nail a few strips to the stakes at equal distances apart, the upper one 2 or 3 inches below the cap board. Take long grass or straw and double it over the lower strip, letting the ends hang ouside the bottom board. Put some on the second strip, letting the ends hang outside of the first, similar to a thatched roof, and continue the process to the top. To prevent the wind from displacing the grass, wind a strong cord around, taking an extra turn around each corner stake, or pass two cords through the grass in the same manner that a shoemaker sews with two waxed ends. Bank up with manure around the bottom board and place a few forkfuls inside around the tree. *Fig. 1* shows the tree with the frame ready for the grass, and *fig. 2* illustrates the end of bottom board, strips, and cap, with the manner of placing the grass.

## About Cisterns

Every good home should have a cistern. Indeed, a barn can hardly be considered complete without one. A good cistern is a good thing, and a bad one is not much short of a nuisance. How to build a good cistern is a thing worth knowing, and, having built one, it is a thing to be proud of. All cistern water should be filtered to take from it whatever impurities may have been gathered from the roofs, pipes, etc. How to filter cistern water, or to build cisterns with filters, is here illustrated.

*Fig. 1* represents a style of filter which is not capable of filtering water very fast—making it suitable for buildings where the area of roof is not great and hence for small houses. It is simply a box about 32 inches in height and 2 feet square. The bottom is full of small holes, and this (*5*) is covered with coarse gravel to the depth of 4 or 5 inches; next (*4*) clean sand, say 5 inches; then pounded charcoal (*3*), 10 inches; on this (*2*) another layer of clean sand; and in the top (*1*), clean, coarse gravel. The water passes from the leader into the top of the box, and in passing through the strata of sand and charcoal, is freed from all deleterious matter, and the water is fit for any use. The pump is usually placed upon this box, and the pipe passes through it into the cistern. Such a filter can be attached to almost any cistern already built.

Fig. 2.

Fig. 1.

*Fig. 2* represents a round or square cistern, half of brick or stone and well cemented in the sides and bottom. Across the middle a wall is built of soft bricks to the height of the cistern. These are laid in cement, *but the face of the wall is not cemented.* The philosophy of this filter is this: the water passes from the roof into compartment *A* and is filtered *through the bricks* into compartment *B*, in which the pump is placed. This wall should be 8 inches thick. Great care should be taken that the joints are well closed with cement and that no holes are left for the passage of water except through the bricks, each alternate layer of which should be laid across the wall. Such a wall, if well constructed, is the best and most reliable filter one can imagine.

198

Fig. 3.

*Fig. 3* is a brick filter, easily constructed, and can be readily applied to any cistern now in use. It consists of a sort of box or pen built of brick on the bottom of the cistern, 15 or 20 inches in diameter, and the same in height, and can be built of one or two thicknesses of brick laid in cement, the top arched and the joints well closed. The lower end of the pump pipe enters this box, and as fast as the water is exhausted in the box, it filters it through the bricks. One hundred bricks would make a filter, and almost anyone could build it. It is the acme of cheapness, simplicity, and durability.

We prefer square cistern to round ones because they are in all respects as good and are more readily constructed. If built adjoining a building, the foundation wall could be used for one side of it. If this is a basement or cellar wall, a faucet could be placed in the cistern as *A*, in *fig. 1*. A waste pipe as *B*, in *fig. 1*, should be placed in all cisterns. The end of this should be so arranged with a valve as to close itself, except when water is passing out of it; otherwise mice and insects would get into the cistern and injure the water. Cisterns outside of buildings should be covered with earth, as in *fig. 1*, to prevent their freezing, and the covers should be constructed with a trap door (*A, fig. 3*) so that they can be entered to be cleaned or repaired. If the covering is of plank, it should be well joined, laid in cement upon the walls, and the outside thickly coated with coal tar and sand, and be of durable timber.

Brick filters are not new; the Egyptians used them three thousand years ago. In New Mexico, the water from the muddy sluggish streams are filtered in this manner: the natives dig a hole beside

the stream, several feet below the surface. This is bricked up, and the water that percolates through the brick is clear and limpid.

## Covers for Wells

The water of our wells is often contaminated by dead animals such as mice, moles, toads, etc., falling into it. This may be in a great measure, if not totally, prevented by a good curb set upon a stone or cement base. A more constant source of impurity, though not so disagreeable, is the falling in of leaves and such things, together with the dust and small particles of grass, wood, seeds, and insects. This can only be prevented by a cover, which, if it must be lifted by the hand, gives so much additional trouble to the persons who draw the water that they are apt to fasten it open, and it is almost never closed.

To obviate this trouble sevral plans have been proposed. One of the simplest is herewith illustrated. Applicable to any well from which water is drawn by the bucket, it consists of a light cover made of matched ½-or ¼-inch stuff, fastened to a 4 x 4 crosspiece at the back part of the well curb. This crosspiece has a gudgeon of oak or iron in

A COVERED CURB FOR WELLS.

one end, and the other end is cylindrical and grooved to run in a bearing upon the sill of the well curb and extending through it. (In the illustration, some of the boards of the well curb are removed.)

Outside the curb, and attached by a leather strap or bit of chain to the end of the crosspiece, as shown, is a treadle, which works up and down in a box. One end of this rests upon a pin or cleat in the end of the box or is hinged upon it. When anyone wishes to draw water, he puts one foot on the treadle, and bearing his weight upon it, the cover rises, and he can raise the bucket. Removing his foot, the lid falls of its own accord, provided some contrivance, like a lath nailed between the rear posts of the curb, prevents its passing the center. The cover is made without the slot to receive the rope, only having a notch to "gather" it. With the slot, such a cover is perfectly applicable to wells that are worked with the old-fashioned sweep and pole.

growth. Bolts are not likely to cause any harm. The heads are soon covered up by the new growth, and no trace is left of them.

### Repairing Split Trees

When crotches have been split apart, the branches may often be brought together again and secured with bolts. The following case amply demonstrates the procedure. An overladened apple tree, a foot or more in diameter, the top of which started about four feet from the ground, was broken down by a windstorm. The broken portion included nearly half the tree, and it split away from the main portion and lay flat upon the ground. The split reached the heart of the trunk and extended to the ground.

Ropes were secured to the fallen portion and were then passed around limbs on the standing portion so that the broken part could be pulled up as with so many ropes and pulleys. Several men pulled up the broken half, and a 3/4-inch iron rod was then passed through the body, and the two parts were brought snugly together by a heavy nut. Two rods, 5 or 6 feet long, were passed through the branches higher up and were drawn tight by nuts. The heads of the bolts were large and flat so that they could not be pulled into the wood, and the nuts had large washers underneath them. The split was then thoroughly waxed over and covered with a piece of rubber cloth. The two parts of the tree united, and in two years there was no evidence of a split except the bolts. Bands placed about trees to brace them are always injurious, as they restrict

# FARM
# AND GARDEN WORK FOR

# December

Winter is here! Short days grow shorter, cold ones colder. We seek our pleasures indoors, as a rule, and our labors, as farmers, are chiefly those incident to the season and, wherever performed, have only an indirect reference to the soil. Long evenings invite to reading and study; to the laying out maps of the farm and plans of the labors to be undertaken next summer; of improvements to be set on foot upon the homestead or for benefitting the public. They offer also an invaluable opportunity for looking over the labors of the past year, going over the accounts, taking an inventory of stock and property of all sorts. The farmer has a multitude of subjects to interest himself in, and it is worth a great deal to any young farmer to take up some one specialty and devote himself so thoroughly to it that his knowledge upon it will be far in advance of his neighbors.' For instance, a young man may take up sheep and wool and find in them material for a lifetime of study and experiment, and the more he knows of what other people have done and thought, the more profitable will he be able to make his own knowledge. Almost every department of farming offers similar subjects. Breeding, and feeding for milk, swine, poultry of various kinds, fish culture, and forest tree culture are some very attractive objects of study, and a score might easily be named. There is no surer or pleasanter road to fame and to the real respect and honor of the best men in the country than that by which a man becomes an "authority" on any important subject connected with agriculture.

## HINTS ABOUT FARM WORK

**Buildings** — Protect cellars against the frost by banking up earth against exposed and thin foundation walls. Stop cellar windows, except well-glazed ones, with strawy litter, protected by stakes on the outside to prevent hens scratching it all about. Pumps, cistern, hydrants, and water pipes need similar protection if exposed. Horse manure and litter is better than any other packing we know of to keep frost out of water pipes. It is a good thing to line stables which are against the sides of old buildings with strips of board tacked on so that swamp hay or straw can be stuffed in between them and the weatherboarding. It makes them much warmer and saves fodder in proportion.

**Ventilation** — Close stables may be warm, but without ample provision for ventilation they will be unhealthy. The stock will be found "off their feed" and ailing in various ways. With sufficient ventilation, which is easily secured, warmth and healthfulness are entirely compatible.

**Roots** — Feed sliced, chopped, or mashed, in such pieces that a cow or "young critter" will not choke itself. It is rarely best to feed more than 4 quarts of carrots a day. Their highest effect is observed when fed with other roots, grain, etc. Common turnips are the first roots to be fed, as they soon grow pithy and lose much in value.

202

**Livestock** of all kinds should be looked to daily; they should be fed and watered with the regularity of clockwork. The card, brush, and curry comb will, if frequently used, not only promote health and cleanliness, but effect a great saving of fodder, while at the same time the paradox of sharpened appetites will be observed. A well-cleaned ox, whose skin has its pores thoroughly opened twice a week by the friction of the brush and card, feels well and will eat coarser fodder with a better relish than an uncleaned one, and eat it cleaner, and it will do him more good. All kinds of stock should have salt before them so that their natural craving may be satisfied. Salt and ashes is a good mixture, and a few sods, thrown where animals can work them over, will be mumbled and chewed often with a relish which makes it evident that it is no unnatural appetite, but that they get something which the pastures would supply in summer and which their systems need equally in the winter.

**Cows**—Do not dry off for the mere sake of saving labor. It is injurious to the milking qualities of both the cows and their female offspring. The milk-giving tendency should be encouraged to the utmost if milk is an object with the breeder. Feed well, whether cows are in milk or dry.

**Oxen**, if worked should be kept sharp-shod, and,

**Young Stock** should be maintained constantly growing and not exposed to the weather, if simply for the sake of economy of fodder and in the production of manure. Pine lumber is a great deal cheaper than hay as a means of warming stock, for fodder is little besides fuel to maintain the internal heat in exposed animals.

**Horses**—Always rub down and blanket one that comes in wet or tired. Never expose a horse to drafts of air, or let him stand in the wind, if it can be helped, and if obliged to leave horses in the wind always blanket them. In the stable, pull off the blanket soon after a horse is cooled off. A horse ought to have a good portion of hay daily. High feeding without it gives him a neater barrel, but it is unnatural diet, and of course less healthful. The good grooming and regular care and exercise of city horses, and those fed in the same way, make good in a measure the defects of this diet, while farmers' horses that live on dry hay and corn stalks the winter through, and are only brushed off a little to get the hayseed out of their foretops, Sundays, remain healthy (if they do) on account of their more natural fare.

**Swine**—As a rule, kill family pork when the weather becomes cold enough. It requires so much more feed to make a pound of pork in cold weather than when it is mild that it will not pay to continue the fattening. Market hogs, if they have warm quarters, may be held for a short time if the markets are crowded, but it generally pays better to hold *pork* for a few days rather than live swine, if the weather is cold, so that it will keep well.

**Sheep**—Feed so as to keep them gaining. If fattening, feed pretty freely, being careful that none get too much, and none too little grain. A sheep overfed a few days is apt to get seriously off its feed and decline so that it will hardly recover its former stand all winter. Litter the yards freely.

## HINTS ABOUT HORTICULTURAL WORK

By the almanac, this month closes the year. To the horticulturist there is no such abrupt division of time; each month is linked with that which preceded it and with that which shall follow, and at present he is much more inclined to look forwards than backwards. It is always well to look back a month or two to see if our notes do not suggest something that has been left undone—or forward a month, which will require turning to last January's notes, to find if matters are not indicated there which can be more favorably done now than at any other time. While we would not disregard the lessons of our successes or our failures, we mainly look towards the New Year in our plans for work. Snows and bad weather stop out-of-door labor, and we congratulate ourselves that at this season there is time to read, and think, and discuss.

### Orchard and Nursery

Wherever the condition of the soil will allow, manure, plow, and subsoil, and prepare for planting.

**Heeled-in Trees** should be made all safe for winter. If there is any danger of water settling around the roots, make a ditch to carry it off, and if, in the hurry of heeling-in, the roots were not thoroughly covered, bank them up well with earth. Put no straw or other litter over the limbs to harbor mice.

**Domestic Animals** often do much damage to trees, especially young ones. Good fences and well-closed gates are a preventive against these, as well as those human vandals who think it their right to disregard roads when there is snow on the ground.

**Mice**—Various devices are suggested to keep off these vermin—wrapping the tree with cloth or tarpaper; or surrounding it by a cylinder of tin, sheet iron, or two horseshoe tiles; and putting a mound of earth around the tree about a foot high. If the soil of the orchard is light, clay or stiff loam is sometimes carted in for the purpose. Clear away weeds and litter of all kinds from around the tree, and, if the earth protection is used, trample the snow hard after each fall.

**Rabbits**—Use traps and guns. Sprinkling the trees with blood is said to be effectual, as is the use of tarpaper. Laths bound on with wire are also used.

**Water** should not stand upon the surface; open ditches to let off such accumulations.

**Old Orchards** are better pruned in winter than to be neglected altogether. Old and decaying limbs are to be cut out altogether, as well as those that crowd one another. Others are to be headed back to get a new growth. Where large cuts are made, they should be covered with melted grafting wax.

**Cions,** for root-grafting this winter, or stock-grafting in the spring, may be cut wherever the wood is not frozen. Label carefully after tying in convenient bundles. Sawdust is the best material for packing. Where there are but few, they will keep well in a close tin box or tight glass jar with no packing if kept in a cellar or other cool place.

**Manure** may be applied to the orchard. Good rich compost is the best. Long or littery manure should never be put near small trees. It harbors mice.

**Fruit**—Watch fruit in the cellar, and, as its period of ripening approaches, bring it into a warm room to finish the process. Send off fruit to market before softening begins.

**Root Grafting** may occupy the time when outdoor work cannot be done. It is best to work at but one variety at a time, to avoid mixing.

**What to Plant** may well be considered in time. Get all possible neighborhood experience.

**Labels**—A good stock of these should be made during the winter months—some notched to receive a wire by which to fasten them to trees, and others pointed at one end to enter the earth. Have one side, at least, smooth. Pine will last one season in the ground; if desired for a longer time, use cedar. Smear the place to be written on with paint or linseed oil, and write with a soft pencil.

### Fruit Garden

The care of trees in the fruit garden is the same as mentioned for young trees in the orchard.

**Fruit Trees** must not be allowed to become injured by accumulations of snow.

**Protection** is to be given to all plants requiring it. Raspberries of the tender sorts are to be covered with earth, as are grape vines where protection is needed. Cover the earth around strawberry plants, but do not cover the plants themselves too heavily. Straw, bog hay, or corn stalks are used for this purpose, and, when it can be obtained, "pine straw," or fallen pine leaves, answers.

**Grape Vines**—Finish up the pruning in mild weather. Save such wood as is needed for propagation. See last month's notes on pruning.

### Kitchen Garden

**Crops** that have been harvested should be looked after and made secure, and roots, celery, etc., in pits and trenches must have a covering proportioned to the severity of the weather.

**Parsnips, Horseradish, and Salsify**—A good portion of the crop of these is usually left in the ground to be dug in early spring or during mild spells in the winter. By covering the beds with litter, the freezing-up may be postponed and the season of digging prolonged.

**Spinach, Kale, Leeks,** and other crops left in the ground in Northern localities need a covering of straw, leaves, or some other similar matter.

**Cabbages**—Cover the inserted heads with earth, if not already done. The earth should be about 6 inches deep over the heads, and the edges pointed and smoothed with a spade so as to shed rain.

**Cold Frames** must not on mild days be allowed to become "hot frames." There will be but few days on which the plants will not need air and many on which the sash may be kept off until night.

**Tools**—Many conveniences of the garden may be made during the winter. Arrange for a toolhouse in some convenient place if there is not one already.

**Manure** is the gardener's main care in winter. Every town and village allows valuable fertilizers to go to waste, as does almost every farm. Have an eye to the various factories, breweries, and the like in the neighborhood, and see what their waste products are. It often happens that good fertilizers may be had for the expense of carting.

**Seeds**—If any are not put away, thrash or rub out, label, and put in a safe place. Overhaul old stock, and keep none the vitality or identity of which is doubtful. Those who purchase their seeds should be prepared to order early, as some kinds are always likely to be very scarce.

### Flower Garden and Lawn

There is usually more or less clearing up to be done of the remains of those vines and herbaceous plants which, after a long struggle, have at last yielded to heavy frosts. Take timely care of

**Trellises,** and all supports of a movable character. They should be put under cover and permanent ones repaired and painted if they require it.

**Bulb Beds,** whether new or old, if not already covered, should be protected by coarse manure.

**Protection,** with a covering of earth, will enable many half-hardy roses, wistarias, etc., to winter safely much further north than they would if left exposed upon the trellises.

**Herbaceous Perennials,** such as peonies, phloxes, dicentras, and the like, come out all the better in spring for a forkful of manure as a winter blanket.

**Half-Hardy Shrubs,** deciduous as well as evergreen, do much better with some cedar boughs tied or stuck around them than in the old way of bundling them in straw, and with less trouble.

**Snow** will often break down or bend out of shape evergreens and dense masses of shrubbery. Shake out the snow before it becomes icy.

**Cold Frames,** in which roses, verbenas, and other half-hardy plants are stored for the winter, will need careful management. These plants will endure a low temperature, and even a slight freezing, provided they are perfectly dormant. Endeavor to preserve an uniformly low temperature, by airing by day and covering at night.

**Chrysanthemums** that have been potted for house-blooming should be cut back when they have passed out of flower, and the pots stored in a cellar or shed if it is desirable to preserve the roots for spring propagation. They are easily multiplied.

### Greenhouse and Window Plants

**Heat**, in houses where plants are to bloom, must be at least 60 or 65 degrees during the day and fall to 15 degrees less during the night and remain in health. In houses where plants are merely kept out of the frost, the night temperature may go down to within a few degrees of freezing.

**Bulbs** that were potted and set in a cool, dark place may be brought to the light if they have formed good roots.

**Air** the house whenever it is safe; and air should be given to window plants every pleasant day.

**Water**—Plants suffer more from overwatering than from dryness as a general thing. Each plant has its requirements, and no general rule can be given. A little experience will teach one when a plant needs watering. Give house plants a sprinkling overhead every now and then. This can easily be done by setting the pots in a sink or bathtub. It will remove

**Dust**, which is one of the greatest enemies of window gardening. Plants with large, smooth, and thick leaves, like camellias, ivy, etc., can have the leaves cleaned by means of a damp cloth or sponge. This operation will help remove

**Insects**, which will often get upon house plants in spite of the best care. The green fly, or aphis, is readily disposed of by tobacco smoke, and the red spider will yield to frequent showerings. The last named insect is generally the cause of browned leaves which appear upon plants in dry rooms.

# PROJECTS FOR
# DECEMBER

## How to Make an Iceboat

Even homesteaders require time for leisure and entertainment—and what better way to spend a spare winter hour than to enjoy the pleasures of sailing a homemade iceboat?

Iceboats vary greatly in size, shape, and value, many of them being carved and gilded, costing many hundreds of dollars. The one shown in our illustrations can be made with very little expense by anyone who is at all handy with tools. *Fig. 1* shows the manner in which the frame is made. The materials required for the frame consist of one board (*a*), 12 inches wide and 12 feet long; two boards (*b,b*), 10 feet long by 12 inches wide; and another (*c*), 9 feet long by 12 inches wide and 2 inches thick. Two pieces, 5 by 5 inches and 12 inches long, and 5 by 5 inches and 20 inches long are needed for the legs. The mast must be a well-seasoned pole, 12 feet long and 5 inches in diameter at the lower end and tapered to 3 inches at the top. Spruce or Virginia pine are the best woods for the purpose. The boom and gaff should be of a somewhat lighter material. For the runners, three ordinary ice skates may be fastened to the legs.

The two side boards (*b, b*) are bolted on top of the crosspiece (*a*) about 2 feet from each end, as shown in *fig. 1*, the bottom board (*c*) being under the center of the crosspiece (*a*) and under the stern (*d*). A deck may be made by nailing two or three boards on top of the bottom board and under the side boards. The two 12-inch legs (*e, e*) should be bolted

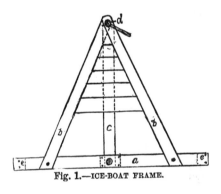

Fig. 1.—ICE-BOAT FRAME.

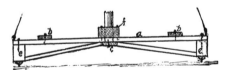

Fig. 2.—CROSS-SECTION OF FRAME.

Fig. 3.—STEERING RUDDER.

at the extreme ends of the crosspiece and braced as shown in *fig. 2.* The third leg, which serves as a rudder, should be rounded off down to half its length from the top and passed through a hole mortised at *d.* A handle is placed in this (as seen in *fig. 3*) to steer by. A block, 12 by 14 inches and 9 inches thick (*fig. 2*), is bolted on top of the crosspiece, and a hole is mortised through both so that the mast, which fits in this hole, rests on the bottom board. It is braced by two ropes or stays from the masthead to eyebolts on the ends of the crosspiece.

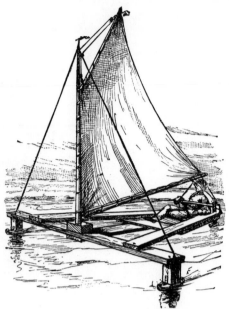

Fig. 5.—SAILING THE ICE-BOAT.

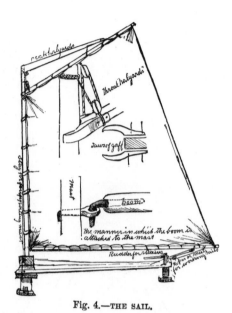

Fig. 4.—THE SAIL.

The sail, seen in *fig. 4,* is made of light drilling or duck. It is 12 feet at the foot, 9 feet at the head, 14 feet at the outer edge or leach, and 8 feet at the inner edge or luff. The head of the sail is laced to the gaff, which is 9 feet 6 inches long, and is joined to the mast by jaws, so as to keep it from swinging away, as shown in *fig. 4.* It is also laced at the foot to the boom (which should be a little longer than the foot of the sail and should be attached to the mast by rings). The sail is hoisted by two ropes called the throat and peak halyards, their ends leading down to the deck, where they are fastened to a couple of cleats, which should be made at each side of the block in which the mast fits. The boom is 4 inches in diameter and tapers to 3 at the outer end, and is fastened to an eyebolt in the mast-hook, which goes in the thick end of it. The gaff is 3 inches in diameter and tapers to 2. *Fig. 5* shows the iceboat completed and the way of sailing it.

## Preparing Homemade Kindling

Take 1 quart of tar and 3 pounds of resin. Melt them and bring to a cooling temperature. Mix with an equal amount of sawdust, with a little charcoal added. Spread out while hot upon a board. When cold, break it up into lumps of the size of a large hickory nut and you will have, at a small expense, enough kindling material for one year. Such kindling will easily ignite from a match and burn with a strong blaze long enough to start any wood that is fit to burn.

## Building a Simple Water Boiler

A device which is superior to the old iron kettle for heating water is shown in this sketch. Take a piece of 2-inch iron pipe 8 feet long and have it securely screwed into the bottom of a stout vinegar barrel. In the other end of the pipe screw a large wooden block.

By arranging the affair as shown in the sketch, water in the barrel will be heated rapidly and can be removed as desired without bothering the fire. Do not make the mistake of putting a metal cap on the

SIMPLE WATER BOILER

end of the pipe, or the steam may sometimes burst the piping before the cap will come off. The wooden block acts as a safety valve and will fly out if pressure is too great.

## Building Cold Frames

In the South cold frames are in use all winter. The principal winter crops grown are lettuce, radishes, beets, cauliflower and occasionally cabbage, while these crops are commonly followed in spring by cucumbers, cantaloupes and, sometimes, Irish potatoes. The frames are easily made. Rough inch lumber (heart of pine is best in the South, and hemlock in the North) and 2 x 4 or 2 x 3-inch scantling are all that is required. For the double frames, strips 3 inches wide and 3/4 or ½-inch thick, long enough to extend across the frame, should be provided for rafters. The back or north side of the single frame should be 12 or 15 inches high, while the front should slope down to 8 inches. In Southern practice, where canvas covers are used, the back should be 2½ feet and all cracks should be well covered with tarpaper, held in place by laths tacked over it.

Good treatment for the posts used in construction is to dip them in kerosene overnight. This will preserve them indefinitely. Drive the posts into the ground 18 inches and let them extend upward to the top of the boards, putting a post at the union of each pair of boards and nailing them to it. All ends and rafters may be made so that they can be quickly removed so that the frames can be plowed and the

ground prepared with a horse or mule. The sides of the double frames are best made 1 foot high, with the ends sloping upward to 2½ feet. Down the center of the frame, a row of 2 x 4-inch posts, 2½ feet above ground, are set 8 feet apart. Over each one of these a rafter is bent and fastened to the sides of the frames.

For cold frames in the North, glass is the only covering to be thought of. By all means, put the frames up facing the south or southeast, and to afford protection against the north and northwest winds—cold the country over—a high wall, a thick hedge, or a piece of thick woodland should be close at the back of them.

The soil in the frames should be thoroughly prepared, rich, and pulverized thoroughly. An abundance of well-rotted stable manure should be used—if thoroughly decomposed, the rate of 75 to 100 tons an acre is not excessive unless the soil is already very rich. Whether glass or canvas is used as a covering, great attention must be given to water and ventilation. The land should be well drained so that no water will stand, or the soil will become waterlogged. That is one side of the water question, but, in addition, the plants should be carefully watered from time to time to provide moisture sufficient for their needs.

If the coverings are kept down too constantly, the growth of the plants will be weak and spindling, and the disease of damping-off will work havoc with them. Careful attention to watering, ventilation, and keeping the surface of the ground stirred are the genuine secrets of controlling this problem. Watch the temperature. Do not let it rise too high and lower it by raising the sash or drawing back the covers. The canvas covers should be drawn back a portion of every day when the temperature is not too low, and at other times the ends may be raised to allow the air to circulate under them. A sharp eye must be kept on the possibility of frost. Sometimes steam heat is provided. Oil stoves may be used, and glass-covered frames should be covered with burlap or straw mats, securely held down either by tying them in place or by weighting them down. Both canvas and the glass covering should be well fastened to prevent their being lifted off by strong winds.

The upper end of the glass sash may be held down with a hook and staple, a hook being placed on the back of the frame at the center of each sash with the staple in the end of the sash. Canvas covers are best held down by nailing them along the center to a board run lengthwise on the center of the rafters, in the case of double coverings, or along the back, in the case of single ones.

## Felling Timber

Large trees of valuable timber are sometimes seriously injured by splitting when they fall simply because those who cut them down do not know how to do it well. The sketch shows a large stump and a tree which was badly damaged in the felling, and another well cut and ready to fall. Almost everyone who has been among the woodchoppers when they have felled large trees of tough timber will recollect having seen the "butt logs" of many trees split, as seen in the sketch. And the long splinters remaining on the stump, which were pulled out of the tree, are very common.

When a large tree stands perpendicularly, brace it on two sides, as represented, with long poles, having the lower ends secured by wide stakes. If the wind does not blow, a large tree may be cut nearly off before it falls. The way is to leave a small strip on each side of the tree, while at the middle it is cut entirely through, as represented. When a tree standing as shown in the figure is ready to fall, remove one of the braces by prying out the lower end with a handspike, and it will come down without any damage. When a tree leans to the north or south, for example, it should always but cut to fall east or west, and always, if possible, at right angles to the way it leans. If cut to fall the way it leans, there is great danger that it will split at the butt.

It is often desirable to have a tree fall in a certain place, though it leans in an opposite direc-
tion. To do this, fasten a chain or strong rope to the body, 10 or 20 feet from the ground, and secure the other end fast to the short end of a long lever. Then fasten another chain to the lever, some 3 or 4 feet from this end, and hitch it to some tree, stump, or post standing near, and in the right direction. Fasten the long end of the lever so as to hold the chain taut and the tree in its place till it is cut almost off. A system of pulleys, or a tackle in which the rope is reeved through double and triple blocks, will serve the purpose of a lever.

When it is desirable to have a large tree fall in a certain direction, let the kerf on the side where it is to fall be cut deeper, and 2 to 6 inches lower than that on the opposite side. If a large tree is cut nearly off on one side, it will usually fall on that side of the stump. For this reason, if a longer and deeper kerf is made on one side of a tree than on the other, and the small one is a few inches higher than the large one, it will be easy to make a large tree fall in the desired direction without the aid of braces or chains.

A tree may sometimes be sawed down quite as advantageously as felled with an ax, if a saw is in good order. To facilitate starting a saw in the right direction, bore a hole horizontally into the tree about two inches deep, and drive in a wooden pin, on which the blade of the saw may rest, until the kerf is sufficiently deep to steady it. Decide where the tree is to be felled, and saw the side in that direction half off first; then saw the opposite side. Two broad and thin iron wedges should be driven after the saw into the kerf to prevent the saw from being pinched so tightly that it cannot be worked nor drawn out. The ears on the end of a saw for felling timber should be secured with bolts, so that, when it is difficult to knock out the wedges from the kerf, one ear may be removed and the saw withdrawn.

## Cutting Ice

Cutting ice is a very simple operation and requires only such tools as any farmer can command. All that are necessary are a common crosscut saw, properly arranged, an ax, and a board on which to draw the blocks out of the water and into the sled or wagon. Ice tongs may be used with advantage, but they may easily be dispensed with. An ordinary crosscut saw of small size may be used by taking off the socket for the handle at one end. In the other socket a handle may be fitted which will be handier to use if it is set in at right angles to the blade of the saw, as in *fig. 2*.

Fig. 1.—BOARD FOR HAULING OUT ICE.

Fig. 2.—SAW.

To start cutting, first make a hole with the ax large enough to start the saw, and cut strips 18 inches wide. These may be cut across into squares with the ax, first cutting a slight channel in the direction in which the ice should break; then with a smart blow the square piece will be loosened. To get it out of the water, take the board (*fig. 1*), which is about 5 feet long, with handles on one end and a cleat fastened on the other. This is slipped under the block of ice, the cleat takes hold of it, and it is drawn out. A pair of light runners of strong hoop may be fixed underneath, and the board will make a sort of hand-sled on which the piece of ice may be drawn up to and into the sled or wagon. Nothing else is necessary to perform this job as well as it can be done with the most costly tools.

## Building a Smokehouse

A good smokehouse should be found upon every farm, large or small, and there are many other families besides those of farmers which would equally be benefitted by one. The object is to be able to expose meats to the action of creosote and the empyrheumatic vapors resulting from the imperfect combustion of wood, etc. The peculiar taste of smoked meat is given by the creosote, which is also the preservative principle, but sundry flavors, agreeable to those who like them, are also imparted by other substances in the smoke.

All that is necessary for a smokehouse is a room—from the size of a barrel to that of a barn—

Fig. 3.—GETTING OUT ICE ON THE FARM.

212

which can be filled with smoke and shut up tight, with conveniences for suspending the articles to be smoked. In common smokehouses the fire is made on a stone slab in the middle of the floor. In others a pit is dug in the ground, say a foot deep, and here the fire is placed. Sometimes a stone slab covers the fire at the height of a common table. This is a good plan for all kinds of smokehouses as it diffuses the rising smoke and prevents the direct heat of the fire affecting the meats hanging immediately above.

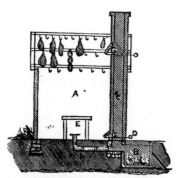

INTERIOR OF SMOKE HOUSE.

Another plan, engraved here, is a little more expensive, but, if properly made, highly approved. The house we show a section of is 8 feet square and built of brick. (If of wood it should be plastered on the inside.) It has a chimney (*B*) with an 8-inch flue; a fireplace (*C*) is on the outside below the level of the floor. From this a flue (*F*) is carried under the chimney into the middle of the floor where it opens under a stone table (*E*). In kindling the fire, a valve is drawn directing the draft up the chimney. The green chips or cobs are thrown on, and the valve is then placed so as to throw the smoke into the house. Both in the upper and lower parts of the chimney there are also openings (*G*) closed by valves regulated from the outside. The door has to be made to shut very close, and all parts of the building must be as tight as possible. The advantage of such a house as this over others is that the smoke is cooled considerably before it is admitted; no ashes rise with the smoke; meats may be kept in it the year round, and not very much smoked either, for the smoking may be occasionally renewed so as to keep the flies away. The table placed in the center will be found a great convenience in any smokehouse.

## Hints on Hog Slaughtering, or, How to Use "Everything but the Oink"

Slaughtering may be most conveniently done as soon as the weather is so cold that meat will keep well. Give the hogs no breakfast. Have an abundance of boiling water ready—say two-thirds of a barrel to a barrel for one or two hogs, according to size—a large half-hogshead tub half full for a 180 to 250 pound hog, and add about two or three pailfuls of *boiling* water for each additional hog to keep up the temperature, taking out an equal quantity, if necessary. *The water ought not to be boiling hot when the pig is scalded.* If it is too hot, the skin will be partially cooked and the hairs will stick fast. It is best to try it by dipping an ear or the nose first. It is usual to add about one-twelfth part of cold water. Scald as soon as the hog has done bleeding and is dead, and remove the bristles at once. Never let a hog lie after scraping, but put in the gambrel and hang him up. If left to lie, the blood will settle in the flesh and skin where it is subjected to pressure. If there are several hogs to kill, there should be hands enough to stick and scald some while others are being scraped and dressed, otherwise much more hot water will be required or the animals will cool too much. The sooner the insides are taken out the better, for the easier it will be to remove the fat from the entrails. This is readily done, when one gets the knack, with a sharp knife held still while the entrail is drawn across it.

MANNER OF KILLING A HOG.

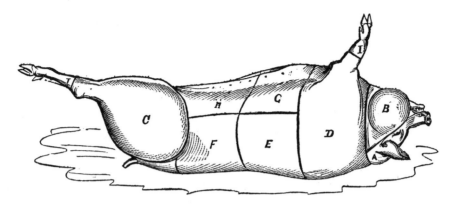

Fig. 1.—OUTSIDE OF CARCASS OF HOG—SHOWING THE CUTS.

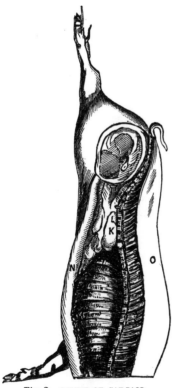

Fig. 2.—INSIDE OF CARCASS.

When the hog is hung up, make a clean straight cut from the vent to the breast bone, cutting through the "Aitch" or pelvis bone (L, fig. 2) between the hams, first, and then, passing two fingers of the left hand into the cavity of the abdomen, draw the belly out. Hold the knife with the right hand between these fingers, and as it cuts, follow down with the left, drawing the walls of the abdomen out so as not to cut the entrails. Then splitting the breast bone (M), cut through to the sticking place, and put in a brace to hold the sides apart. In cutting the breast

bone, be very careful not to let the knife touch the stomach and defile everything with its contents. Now grasp the intestine at the vent and cut it clear. Holding the entrails in the left hand, let their weight aid the right hand in tearing them free from their attachments. At the skirt, or diaphragm, the stomach being removed with them, it will be necessary to use the knife to sever the connection. Then, lowering them down, cut off the gullet at the throat and lay them on a table to be cleared from the fat while warm. The liver may now be disengaged, by working if off from the attachments next to the kidneys, and then it is removed with the heart and lights (lungs), cutting off the windpipe at the throat. Finally wash out and wash off the carcass with cold water and let it hang to cool. Clean the intestines while they are still warm.

When the carcass is perfectly cold, it is ready for cutting up and may be kept for many days in cold weather. When a hog is to be cut up, first lay it upon its back. Cut off the head as shown in *fig. 1*. Then split the carcass, cutting straight through the backbone from the tail to the neck with a cleaver and knife. It is best to saw the bone sometimes, especially if frozen. The leaf fat and kidney fat with the kidneys (K), seen at *fig. 2*, are now taken out, using the knife only to loosen them from the skirt (P) and tearing them off towards the hams. Then take off the hams. Cut from the tail, and saw the small "aitch" bone at the loin. Then cut rounding to the flank so that they will need little trimming. Next take off the shoulders cutting straight to the end of the spines; this leaves a good portion of lean meat on the ribs. Loosen the tenderloin at the rear and tear it out. Then cut off the flank (H) and brisket (G) in one piece, and cut in two if desirable. The thick clear back fat (O) is now cut off from the rib-piece (E) and loin (F) which, left in one piece, are as needed for use fresh, or cut into two or more

pieces at once. The cheeks (*B*) are removed from the pate (*A*) by a cut passing from the mouth close under the eye (*see fig. 1*), and the jaw is cracked in the middle. Thus the cheeks are held together and are conveniently hung up. They are cured like hams and shoulders. Headcheese is made of the pate and trimmings. The feet (*I, I,*) are cut off at the hocks and knees, as shown in *fig. 1,* and soused.

## Fences for Soil Likely to Heave

The main point in such a fence is either to set the posts and place a pin through them near the bottom so that the frosts may not throw them out, or to so attach the boards that the posts may be redriven without splitting them or removing the rails from

the post. The latter is, perhaps, the best plan and may be accomplished in several ways, the most desirable of which is shown in *figs. 1 and 2.*

The post (*h*) is driven in the usual manner, when a strip of board (*g*) is fastened to it by three or four spikes, depending upon the height of the fence. A space just sufficient to insert the ends of the boards (*a, c, fig. 2*) is left between the post and outside strip, the ends of the boards resting upon the spikes. The advantages of such a fence are many. It looks neat and any portion is easily removed, making a passage to and from the field. A new post is easily put in when required, and any may be redriven when heaved by the frost.

Where iron is cheap, a rod about 3/8-inch in diameter is cut in lengths of about 7½ inches. One end is sharpened, while the opposite end, for 3 inches, is bent at right angles. After the boards are placed in position, the hooks should be driven in so that they will firmly grasp the boards and hold them in place. The general appearance of the finished fence is shown in *fig. 3* and is one adapted to almost any locality.

Another plan is to attach the boards (or even rails) to the posts by wires and notching in the post so the wire will not slip down; or placing the wire through ½-inch holes bored in the post at proper intervals. This method allows the posts to be re-driven without loosening the boards or rails.

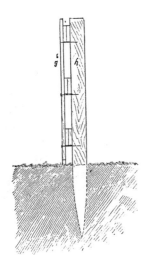

Fig. 1.—END VIEW OF FENCE.

### A Snowplow

A properly constructed snowplow is worth several times its cost. After every storm which covers up the roads, if a good snowplow is drawn around and the roads and paths opened, the snow is packed down and becomes consolidated. It does not then melt away rapidly, and sleds will not cut down to the ground.

Fig. 2.—SIDE VIEW OF FENCE.

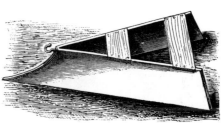

A SNOW-PLOW.

Fig. 3.—FENCE WITH IRON HOOKS.

To make such a plow as is illustrated here, take two planks 8 or 10 feet long. Bevel the end of each plank and bring it to a point so that when put together they will form something like a double-mold board plow. Let the planks slope outwards from the upper part so that the sled will be wider by a few inches at the bottom than on the top. It will not then ride on the snow, but will push it sideways and throw it off. A floor may be laid on the plow on which the boys, who will always be on hand to assist, may ride, and this necessary job of clearing away snow will become one of the regular winter sports. The hook by which the plow is drawn must be fixed at the top of the nose, or it will be lifted up when in motion.

TWO CONVENIENT WAGON JACKS.

### Two Jacks

A jack, simple in construction and easily made, is shown at the right in the illustration. The upright post can be attached to the lever by a piece of leather tacked over the top by an iron hinge or by a mortise and bolt. The axle can be held in place and prevented from slipping by wooden pegs in the lower part of the lever.

A strong jack is shown at the left in the drawing. The lever moves in a slot or mortise in the top of the post and also on the end of the post which goes under the axle. When the axle is elevated, the pin in the end of the lever should be directly above the one in the post, which will prevent its falling back. The lever under the axle should be 3-inches square, and of hardwood; the handle end should be 1-inch thick, running from 1¼-inches wide at the small end to 5 inches at the upper end. Pegs in the lower end will keep the axle from sliding down after it has been properly raised.

### Painting Tin Roofs

Remove all rosin and other loose substances from seams and see that the roof is clean. Paint immediately after laying is finished; do not allow the tin to rust. Since the base plate is coated with tin to prevent rust, you should paint the finished goods to prevent oxidation of the coating. Use only the best red or brown oxide of iron, mixed with pure raw linseed oil, or half-raw and half boiled. Use litharge only as a drier. Litharge makes paint adhere hard to the coating so that when thoroughly dry it cannot be scraped off. Don't use any turpentine or patent driers.

Apply all paint with hand brushes and rub in well. This is very important. Don't put paint on thick. One coat that covers well and is thoroughly rubbed in is better than three put on thick. Let the roof stand two weeks to a month before applying a second coat. Six months or so after applying the second coat, put on a third coat. After this you do not have to paint the roof more than once every two or three years. Too much paint injures a tin roof. Keep the paint well stirred up; put on thin and rub it in well. By following these directions you will have a roof that will last many years.

# Index

Ageratums, propagating, 158
Annuals, 32, 65, 100, 118, 173, 192
Aphids, 80, 98, 132, 192, 206
Apples, 119, 132, 147, 159-60, 170
Ashes, saving, 37
Asparagus, 49, 54, 64, 81, 99, 117, 133, 172, 191; salting, 64

Barbed wire, 54-55
Barley, 61, 129
Barn plans, 35-37, 122-23
Barnyard, constructing a, 184
Beans: bush, 64, 99, 117, 133; field, 97, 147; lima, 81, 99, 152; poles for, 31, 81, 93; snap, 54, 81, 152
Bedding plants, 65, 173
Beehives, 103-4
Beeswax, extracting, 127
Beets, 49, 54, 64, 79, 81, 88, 99, 117, 148, 172, 188, 209; thinnings as salad, 99; see also Sugar beets
Birds, 79
Blackberries, 31, 48, 63, 98, 116, 133, 151, 190
Black-eyed Susan. See Ox-eye daisy
Black knot, 116, 132
Blanching vegetables, 134, 152
Blueberries, 133, 143-44
Borders, garden, 65
Borers, 80, 98
Bridges, building, 121-22
Brine, preparing, 103
Broccoli, 81
Buckwheat, 113, 115, 129, 149
Budding, 98, 116, 119-20, 132, 150
Building maintenance, 13, 45, 61, 95, 169-70, 201
Bulbs, 49, 118, 152, 172-73, 178-81, 192, 205; forcing, 49, 118, 152, 172-73, 178-81, 192, 205
Bulls, 77
Butter, making, 96, 102-3, 168, 190

Cabbage, 46, 48, 49, 54, 59, 63, 64, 81, 98, 99, 113, 114-5, 117, 152, 172, 174-75, 191, 204, 209; as green fodder, 97; cutters, 162, 174-75
Callus, plant, 158
Calves, 44-45, 60, 77, 164, 168
Camellias, 49, 83, 118, 192
Cannas, 172
Carrots, 45, 49, 59, 62, 64, 79, 81, 88, 96, 99, 130, 134, 148, 180, 201
Cattle, 14, 28, 59, 115, 138, 149, 150, 167, 168, 190
Cauliflower, 46, 64, 81, 117, 152, 172, 209
Celery, 63, 64, 82, 99, 117, 134, 152, 172, 191
Cheesemaking, 110-11
Cherries, 47, 98, 116, 132
Chickens, 14, 29, 60
Chives, 64
Chrysanthemums, 135, 152, 172, 192, 205
Churning, 89-90, 102
Cider making, 177-78, 190
Cions, preparing, 15, 19, 30, 31, 50, 51, 79, 190, 203
Cisterns, 125, 197-98
Clearing land, 14-15, 45-46, 158-59
Cleft grafting, 50-51
Climbers, 65, 192
Clotheslines, elevated, 93
Clover, 46, 79, 96, 105, 113
Cocks. See Haystacks
Cold frames, 16-17, 18, 31, 32, 48, 191, 204, 205, 209
Coloring whitewash, 69
Colts: breaking and training, 123-25; weaning, 131
Compasses, garden, 75
Composting, 61, 131, 152, 162, 172, 188; see also Manures
Concrete buildings, constructing, 185
Constipation in animals, cures for, 45
Cooking feed. See Steaming

Cooking with a lamp, 23
Coolers: food, 140; water, 143
Corn: field, 78, 79, 97, 114, 147, 148, 169, 188; husking rack for, 184-85; seed, 148, 162; sweet, 49, 54, 82, 96, 99, 117, 134, 152
Corncribs, building, 104-5
Cow barns. *See* Barn plans
Cows, 14, 28, 44, 60, 77, 95, 102, 115, 131, 168, 190, 202; milking, 25, 77, 102, 164; preventing, from kicking, 162-64
Cress, 49, 64, 81, 82
Crocuses, 152, 172
Crop rotation, 20
Crown grafting, 51-52
Cucumbers, 46, 49, 54, 59, 64, 82, 100, 134, 152, 209
Curculio, 80, 98
Curds, 110-111
Curing cheese, 111
Currants, 48, 81, 98, 116, 145, 191
Cuttings, propagating plants from, 40-41, 49, 62, 135, 153, 156-58, 173; blackberries, 190-91; currants, 48, 63, 145, 191; gooseberry, 48, 191; grape, 31, 48, 191; quinces, 191; raspberries, 190-91
Cutworms, 99

Dahlias, 65, 118, 135, 152, 173, 192
Damping off, cure for, 56, 98
Dams, stone and earth, 54
Ditching, 131
Dog power, utilizing, 24-25, 89-90
Double cropping, 59
Drags. *See* Sleds
Draining land, 14, 30, 61, 113, 116, 131, 134-38, 169, 176-77, 184, 203
Drill marker, 75
Drought, 113, 129, 133
Drying fruit, 125-26, 150
Ducks, 60-61

Earth closets, building, 87-88
Edgings, lawn, 65, 135
Eggplant, 46, 48, 64, 82, 100, 117, 134
Endive, 100, 117, 134, 152
Evaporating pans for maple sugar, 34-35
Evergreens: broad-leaved, 83, 118; raising, 56-57

Fairs, agricultural, 129, 150
Feed cutter, homemade, 185
Fences, 14, 30, 46, 56, 165, 188, 214-15; picket, 56; running, 56; straight board, 56; strip, 56
Fertilizers. *See* Manures
Figs, 63
Filters, 125, 197-98
Fire alarm, homemade, 23
Fire blight, 132

Firewood, 14, 27; splitting, 52-53
Fish, breeding, 175-76
Flax, cultivating, 69-73
Flower gardens, 17-18, 32, 49, 65, 100-1, 118, 135, 152, 172-73, 192, 204-5
Fodder. *See* Cabbage; Clover; Corn, field; Hay; Millet; Orchard grass; Redtop; Sorghum; Timothy
Foliage plants, 118
Food Cooler, 140
Forage crops, 113
Forcing plants, 31, 32, 65, 173
Forsythias, propagating, 158
Fruit drying houses, 125-26
Fruit gardens, 16, 31, 47-48, 63, 80-81, 98, 116-17, 132-33, 151, 171, 190-91, 204
Fuschias, 100, 135; propagating, 158

Gapes, prevention of, 60
Garden plans, 53-54
Garlic, 64
Geraniums, propagating, 158
Girdling, repairing damage from, 30, 47
Gladioluses, 135, 172, 178, 192
Glassware, mending, 24
Goat power, utilizing, 90
Gooseberries, 48, 63, 191
Grading barnyards, 184
Grafting, 30, 47, 50-52, 62, 79, 98, 203; *see also* Root grafting
Grafting clay, 50
Grafting wax, making, 19, 50
Grains. *See under individual varieties*
Grapes and vines, 31, 63, 80, 90-92, 98, 117, 133, 151, 191, 204
Grasses, 46, 59, 79, 105, 131, 148; *see also* Hay
Green fly. *See* Aphids
Greenhouses, 18, 32, 49, 65, 83, 101, 118, 135, 153, 173, 192, 206; plans for building, 141-43
Grooming stock, 45

Hanging baskets, 153, 192
Harrows and harrowing, 28, 46, 88-89
Harvesting, 129, 167, 187; *see also under individual crops*
Hay and haymaking, 20, 95, 96, 105-6, 113, 168
Haystacks, making, 105-7, 114
Herbaceous plants, 65, 160, 205
Herbs, 63, 64, 82, 117
Hoeing, 88, 97, 113, 114, 129, 130, 181
Horseradish, 31, 64, 81, 172, 191, 204
Horses, 13-14, 29, 59-60, 77, 95, 149, 168, 189-90, 202; breaking and training, 123-25; breeding, 108-9
Hotbeds, 16, 20-21, 31, 46, 53, 65; building, 48

House plants. *See* Window plants
Huckleberries. *See* Blueberries
Hyacinths, 100, 118, 152, 172, 181

Iceboats, constructing, 207-8
Ice: cutting, 211; freezing, in blocks, 22-23
Icehouses, 15, 27-28, 193-94
Insects, controlling, 15, 18, 21, 31, 49, 63, 65, 79, 80, 81, 82, 98, 103, 116, 117, 132, 134, 135, 173, 192, 206
Irrigation, 116
Ivy, 83, 183

Jacks, constructing, 217

Kale, 152, 204
Kindling, homemade, 208
Kitchen gardens, 16-17, 31, 48-49, 63-65, 81-82, 98-100, 117, 133-35, 152, 171-72, 191, 204
Knots, tying, 122
Kohlrabi, 81, 82

Lambs. *See* Sheep
Lamp for cooking, 23
Land, clearing, 14-15, 45-46, 113
Land measurer, 136
Lantanas, propagating, 158
Lawns, 17-18, 32, 49, 65, 117-18, 135, 172
Layering, 81
Laying out a garden, 53-54
Leach, building a, 37-38
Leaf mould, 160
Leaves as mulch and manure, 160-62, 173
Leeks, 49, 64, 82, 204
Lettuce, 46, 49, 64, 81, 82, 100, 172, 209
Levers, making, 92
Lilies, 135, 172, 178, 192
Lime, making homemade, 66
Liquid manure. *See* Manure
Livestock, maintaining, 13-15, 28-29, 44-45, 59-61, 77-78, 95-96, 115, 131, 138, 149-50, 167-68, 189-90, 201-3
Lye, making, 37-38

Mangels, 62, 79, 187
Manures and manuring, 14, 17, 20, 28, 31, 45, 61, 65, 78, 79, 96, 115, 131, 151, 152, 154, 168, 188-89, 191, 203-4
Maple sugar, making, 33-35
Marker, garden, 63, 75
Measuring land, 136
Melons, 46, 49, 54, 82, 100, 117, 134, 152, 209
Mice, damage from, 15, 30, 203
Mildew, 98
Milking stools, 25

Millers, 103
Millet, 96
Moles, trapping, 74
Moonseed, 65
Mulches and mulching, 63, 80, 98, 116, 133, 173, 188, 204, 205
Mushrooms, cultivating, 86

Night soil, 14
Nodes, plant, 156, 158

Oats, 46, 62, 78, 129
Oil cake, defined, 69
Okra, 49
Onions, 49, 54, 59, 82, 88, 100, 117, 134, 152
Orchard grass, 105
Orchards, 15-16, 30-31, 47, 62-63, 79-80, 97-98, 115, 116, 132, 150-51, 170-71, 190, 203-4
Owls, catching, 55
Oxen, 28, 59, 77, 95, 202
Ox-eye daisy, 96
Oyster plant. *See* Salsify

Packing fruit, 132, 150, 170
Painting: buildings, 188; tin roofs, 217
Papering a room, 38-39
Parsley, 64, 82
Parsnips, 31, 49, 54, 62, 64, 79, 100, 148, 187, 191, 204
Pastures, maintaining, 79, 96, 114, 120-21, 130, 148, 158-59
Paving: barnyards, 184; wells, 154-56
Peaches, 116, 119, 132
Pears, 80, 119, 132, 150, 151, 190
Peas, 46, 49, 59, 61-62, 64, 82, 100, 117
Peonies, 172, 205
Peppergrass. *See* Cress
Peppers, 46, 48, 64, 82, 98, 100
Perennials, 49, 118, 152, 172, 205
Petunias, propagating, 158
Picking fruit, 132, 150, 159-60, 170
Pig catcher, making a, 121
Pigs, 14, 45, 60, 96, 115, 131, 148, 149, 168, 189, 203; butchering, 213-15
Plank: for drains, 176-77; for sowing, 75
Planting. *See under individual variety of vegetable, shrub, etc.*
Planting, best time for, 42
Plows and plowing, 28, 43, 137-38, 165, 168
Plums, 47, 62, 119, 132
Plunging plants, 83, 100
Poles, bean and pea, 31, 81, 93
Pomace, 178
Posts: making, 165; preserving, 209; removing, 40

222

Potatoes, 31, 46, 49, 54, 59, 62, 64, 79, 82, 114, 147, 168-69, 209; digging, 181-82, 188; dropping, 86-87; seed, 148
Potting plants, 32, 65
Propagation. *See* Budding, Cuttings, Grafting, Layering, Root grafting
Pruning: currants, 16; grape vines, 16, 47-48, 91-92, 191; shrubs, 32; trees, 32, 47, 97-98, 116, 151, 203
Pump, dog-power, 24-25
Pumpkins, 168

Quassia water, 80, 98
Quinces, 132, 151, 191

Rabbits: damage from, 15, 21-22, 30, 203; hunting, 21-22
Radishes, 46, 49, 54, 64, 81, 82, 100, 134, 152, 209
Raspberries, 31, 48, 63, 116, 133, 151, 190, 204
Red spiders, 132, 192, 206
Redtop, 105
Reel, garden, 81
Rennet, 110
Reservoirs. *See* Dams
Rhubarb, 49, 53, 64, 82, 100, 191; forcing, 31; propagating, 172
Ripening fruit, 190, 204
Roads, repairing, 30, 188
Root crops. *See under individual vegetables*
Root cuttings, 190-91
Root grafting, 15, 19-20, 62, 203, 204
Root pits and cellars, 168, 172, 191, 204
Rope: splicing, 144-45; straw, 106
Roses, 65, 101, 118, 135; propagating, 158
Roup, cure for, 60
Rowboats, building, 138-40
Rutabagas, 59, 96, 100, 113, 114, 129, 135, 152, 187
Rye, 46, 148, 169

Salsify, 31, 49, 64, 81, 100, 124

Salsify, 31, 49, 64, 81, 100, 204
Salting livestock, 14, 29, 60, 102, 115, 202
Saucer propagation. *See* Cuttings
Sauerkraut, 174-75
Saw, starting a, 210
Scions. *See* Cions
Scissors, sharpening, 38
Scours, cures for, 45, 60
Seedbeds, 63, 80, 98
Seedlings, protecting, 190
Seeds, 16, 32, 65; evergreen, 56-57; saving, 117, 131, 134, 135, 148, 150-51, 162, 204; sowing, evenly, 85-86; testing vitality of, 16
Shallots, 152

Sheds, straw, 136-37
Sheep, 14, 29, 45, 60, 77-78, 107, 131, 149, 167, 189, 203; shearing, 78, 107
Sheep power, utilizing, 89-90
Shrubs, 32, 49, 173, 192, 205
Singling. *See* Thinning
Sizing, recipe for, 38
Slaughterhouse, building a, 195-96
Sleds, homemade, 40, 109-10
Slugs, 98
Smokehouses: permanent, 211-12; temporary, 23-24
Smut, preventing, 61, 148
Snowplows, constructing, 215
Snow, protection from, 13, 18, 205
Soapmaking, 37-38, 67
Sods, planting on, 46, 48-49, 81
Sod walls, building, 84-85
Soiling crops. *See* Corn, field; Oats; Rye
Soil: potting, 101; preparation of, 48, 70, 191
Solar wax extractor, 127
Sorghum, 149, 169
Sorting fruit, 132
Sowing device, 85
Spinach, 49, 64, 81, 82, 100, 134, 152, 172, 191, 204
Splitting bench, making a, 52-53
Squash, 46, 54, 82, 100, 117, 134, 172
Stakes, 18
Staking stock, 89
Steaming feed for stock, 138, 167, 170
Stock, preparing for grafting, 19-20, 190
Stone walls, building, 79
Strawberries, 31, 48, 54, 63, 81, 98, 116, 151, 160; forcing, 133
Straw mats, making, 16, 31
Straw rope, making, 106
Straw sheds, 136-37
Sugar beets, 62, 187
Swamps, 131
Sweet potatoes, 49, 54, 64, 82, 100, 117, 134, 152, 172
Swelled-head, cause of, 60
Swiss chard, 64

Tent caterpillars, 15, 79, 80
Thatching roofs, 194-95
Thaws, 15
Thinning, 81, 88, 98, 116, 117, 129, 130, 132, 148, 152, 160
Timothy, 105
Tobacco, 79, 113; curing and hanging, 127; fumigating with, 49, 65, 192, 207
Tobacco water, 80, 98
Tomatoes, 46, 48, 54, 64-65, 82, 98, 117, 134-35, 152
Tools, garden, 17, 80-81, 88-89, 204

Tool sleds, 110
Trees: care of, 30, 80, 97, 117, 133, 151, 196-97, 199, 203; dwarf, 31, 133; felling, 210-11; heeling-in, 47, 203; moving, 93; planting, 30, 47, 49, 62, 79, 150, 190, 192; transplanting, 104, 173
Trellises, 18, 205
Troughs, 24
Trout, breeding, 175-76
Tuberoses, 65
Tulips, 100, 118, 152, 172, 181
Turkeys, 60, 182-84
Turning out plants, 83, 100
Turnips, 49, 59, 65, 81, 113, 129, 135, 148, 152, 168, 201

Vegetable gardens. *See* Kitchen gardens
Verbenas, propagating, 158
Vinegar, 132, 150, 178, 190
Violets, 152
Virginia creeper, 65

Washing machine, unique, 24

Washing utensils, 102, 111
Water boiler, homemade, 208-9
Watering: livestock, 73; plants, 18, 65, 135, 206
Water pipes, protecting, 201
Water pump, dog-power, 24-25
Water troughs, 24
Waxed cloth. *See* Grafting wax
Waxwork, 65
Weeds and weeding, 79, 81, 88, 97, 100, 101, 114, 116, 117, 130, 132, 133, 148, 151, 152, 169, 170
Weigelas, propagating, 158
Wells: covers for, 198-99; digging, 154-56
Wet ground, plowing, 165
Wheat, 61, 113, 129, 148, 169
Whiffletrees, 89
Whitewashing, 67-69
Windmills, constructing, 87
Window plants, 18, 32, 49, 65, 83, 101, 172, 192, 206
Winter cherry, 152
Winter protection, 172, 192, 196-97, 201, 204, 205; *see also* Mulch
Working stock. *See* Horses and Oxen